European
multiculturalism
revisited

European
multiculturalism
revisited

EDITED BY ALESSANDRO SILJ

Zed Books

LONDON | NEW YORK

European Multiculturalism Revisited was first published in 2010 by
Zed Books Ltd, 7 Cynthia Street, London N1 9JF, UK
and Room 400, 175 Fifth Avenue, New York, NY 10010, USA

www.zedbooks.co.uk

Editorial copyright © Ethnobarometer 2010
Copyright in this collection © Zed Books 2010

The right of Alessandro Silj to be identified as the editor
of this work has been asserted by him in accordance with
the Copyright, Designs and Patents Act, 1988

FSC
www.fsc.org
MIX
Paper from
responsible sources
FSC® C013604

Designed and typeset Monotype Ehrhardt
by illuminati, Grosmont
Index by John Barker
Cover designed by Transmission
Printed and bound in Great Britain
by CPI Antony Rowe, Chippenham and Eastbourne

Distributed in the USA exclusively by Palgrave Macmillan, a division of
St Martin's Press, llc, 175 Fifth Avenue, New York, NY 10010, USA

A catalogue record for this book is available from the British Library
Library of Congress Cataloging in Publication Data available

ISBN 978 1 84813 561 1 hb
ISBN 978 1 84813 560 4 pb
ISBN 978 1 84813 566 6 eb

Contents

Acknowledgements

I wish to thank the Compagnia di San Paolo, our main sponsor when we started working on multiculturalism in Europe, and the Freudenberg Stiftung, who hosted the first meeting of the research team in Weinheim. Above all, I am grateful to all the members of the team who co-authored this book, which is not simply a reader. The project was discussed with the authors before Ethnobarometer decided to proceed with it, the methodology and preliminary papers were discussed in Weinheim, we met again in Turin after the first drafts were completed, and subsequently all chapters were revised to update them. I wish to thank Tariq Modood and Anne Phillips who participated as discussants in the Turin meeting, contributing ideas and suggestions, and to Christophe Bertossi, who wrote the Conclusion. Finally, thanks also to Jonathan Chaloff, whose knowledge and experience on migration and integration issues was a most valuable resource when editing this book.

Introduction

Alessandro Silj

Ethnobarometer's research on multiculturalism in Europe, whose findings are presented in this volume, began in 2007, following fieldwork on European Muslim communities after 9/11. Popular opposition to immigration had been growing for some time and integration processes, which in the past had not been nearly as successful as liberal public opinion had hoped, were in serious trouble. The very meaning of the term 'integration' was being questioned by a growing number of people, and what some called multiculturalism and others different names was becoming a negative value rather than one of the founding principles of Western democracies. This trend was not new but was beginning to have an impact on both local and national policies and practice.

Multiculturalism has been, from the very early days, a very ambiguous and therefore inevitably controversial concept. Originally the term 'multiculturalism' was put forward by those who were (politically and ideologically) against the concept and policies of assimilation – that is, the French approach to integration. Integration, on the other hand, is a rather loose concept that stands in between the other two and is common to both. In its more general meaning it assumes that the immigrant fully participates in the socio-economic life of the host country, and the term is being used without specific reference to the institutional and cultural parameters that shape such participation. It can mean different things depending on the context. We have assimilation when the immigrant renounces his or her claim to a distinct national, ethnic, cultural or religious identity and blends into the identity of the host country. We have multiculturalism when diversity is recognized and perceived as being positive and desirable, and the Other is not perceived as a threat to the identity, values and culture of the host society.

The ambiguity of the concept of multiculturalism is clear from the many alternative words with which it has been called by scholars and politicians. In addition to 'integration', 'assimilation' and 'multi-culturalism', some have used 'incorporation', and others 'pluralism' and even 'plural monoculturalism' (Amartya Sen), or 'pluriculturalism', 'interculturalism', 'communitarianism' (co-existence of communities within the same political space), and still others such apparently intricate concepts as 'disintegrated multiculturalism' and 'integrated multiculturalism' (Michel Vieworka, in discussing the USA, on one hand and the cases of Canada, Australia and Sweden, on the other). Some have spoken of 'assimilation without participation' (related to Switzerland). Finally, multiculturalism has been described as a fraudulent alternative to equal opportunity (John Rex).

However, our aim is not to engage in the theoretical and ter-minological debate on this issue. We have opted for an empirical approach, using case studies to review and analyse the main 'models' of multicultural societies that Europe has experienced from the end of World War II until the present day. Multiculturalism has never been immune to criticism or opposition, but it hit the media headlines and climbed the agendas of governments (indeed, in some countries, became an electoral issue) – after 9/11 and the bombings in Madrid and London, in the Netherlands after the assassination of Van Gogh, and in Denmark following the *Jyllands-Posten* cartoon affair. These events influenced public opinion in most European countries, including France, where in the meantime doubts about the country's assimilation approach had grown stronger, and where riots in the *banlieues* signalled serious social problems.

Our research, conducted by local scholars, covered six countries: Great Britain, the Netherlands, France, Germany, Denmark and

Italy (the Italian model being the lack of a model). Each case study consisted of a historical account of how in that country the model developed (underlying principles, policies) and was implemented in practice, followed by an analysis of the factors that have led to the claim that the model has failed. The question asked was, did the model actually fail, and if it failed was this because of intrinsic weaknesses, or rather because of external and contingent circumstances, and if so does this justify the claim – that is, are the British and other models really bad? The research team met in Germany in December 2006 to discuss the first outline and methodology of the country reports, then again in Italy in 2007 to discuss preliminary drafts. Some of the reports were updated in 2008.

European responses to multiculturalism

The most important and controversial issues that 'multiculturalism' has raised in European societies are cultural rights, legal pluralism and integration in state schools, among others. However none of these issues alone could have caused such wide and dramatic waves of public concern about the future of our societies. In each country, the research analysed the factors that might offer clues to aid our understanding of the roots and nature of that concern.

Thus Maleiha Malik, after observing that there has always been cultural, linguistic, ethnic and religious diversity in Britain, remarks that post-war immigration has resulted in new challenges to the accommodation of minorities on the basis of their racial, cultural and religious differences. The British response to this migration has taken the form of policies of tolerance and non-discrimination, supplemented by strategies of multicultural accommodation, especially in areas such as education. The two factors to be considered, Malik writes, are the increasing importance of global context and the shift by minorities towards a more confident 'politics of recognition'. Official accommodation of this diversity within the definition of the nation has depended on different forces: the social and political power of the group that is seeking accommodation; the relationship between the domestic and the international context; and access to socio-economic wealth.

In France, according to Valérie Amiraux, the archetypical republican model of integration, where citizens are considered to be equal political actors independent of specificities (cultural, ethnic, religious), has been directly challenged during the last two decades by a series of public controversies (on the legitimacy of wearing the headscarf in state schools; on the justification for including ethnic data in public statistics) and social crises (e.g. urban riots in November 2005) that made its limits clearer to French and international public opinion. Multiculturalism never became a proper policy in the French context (although specific measures have been introduced in social policies, in particular, so far as territorial segregation and social housing are concerned); thus there has been no institutional recognition of differences and of the pluralism of identities in French society. The gap between principle and practice has been growing. If the notion of 'integration' was the dominant reference for public policymaking until the end of the 1980s, the concept is nowadays highly contested by many actors, in particular by the main targets of integration policies. Principles, official narratives and practices – institutional, daily and individual – in many ways contradict each other.

In Germany, Stephan Lanz points out, although in the early days the debate took over basic concepts from earlier discourses that had developed, for example in Canada and Australia, the model of multiculturalism cannot be understood properly without taking into account the context and history of German immigration policies, which have been ambiguous both in public discourses and in national as well as regional politics. The case of the city state of (West) Berlin is a particularly interesting and telling example. On the one hand, Berlin was the first West German state to pursue its own multicultural integration policy; on the other hand, the city has for decades been used as the main reference point, both by advocates and by opponents of multiculturalism in Germany. The contemporary formation of discourses on multiculturalism in Germany shows the existence of these two main positions. On the one hand, the political focus narrows down to the assumed cultural fundamentalism of Muslim immigrants who are constructed as radical 'others' and are increasingly excluded from an imagined community of the 'self'. On the other hand, a positive reference to cultural plurality and hybridity has evolved. Minorities, particularly in Berlin, are valued as a relevant social resource for the future. In some instances, minorities are even represented as an economic and social avant-garde that facilitates the shift towards a neoliberal society. At the same time, the pedagogical socio-multiculturalism which had characterized a great deal of the integration policy of the municipal authorities since the 1980s seems to have become obsolete.

In Italy, immigration is a recent phenomenon. Whilst this can explain the absence or weakness of policies, it hardly explains why even the legislative process concerning migration has been advanced without a model or a reference This is due to the fact that governments in Italy are often short-lived – the principles motivating laws on immigration can change when a new government comes in. Lack of experience and contact with the real world, or simply the absence of pragmatism and willingness to take risks, are other factors. It is also true, Allievi points out, that Italy has difficulty in acknowledging religious plurality. On the other hand, the Catholic Church has an important influence in matters concerning foreign immigrants, just as it has had during the period of internal migration. Given the key role played by Catholic organizations in helping migrants at all levels, and the importance of the Catholic vote for both centre–left and centre–right coalitions, Catholic opinion has in part mitigated, in practice, the effects of the differences in the legislative agenda. Today Italy, like other European countries, is going through a phase of reactive identities and cultural conflicts, which is producing, Allievi argues, unlike in other European countries, a diffused *anti-multiculturalism in spite of the absence of multiculturalism*. Becoming plural, he points out, is not a neutral process. The presence of ever-increasing numbers of immigrants is not merely a quantitative fact with different consequences for the many social and cultural dynamics: changes in the quantitative levels of the many different indicators (economic, social, cultural, political, religious) completely alter the scenario. Overall, the indicators that are currently changing as a result of the presence of immigrant populations in Europe are producing and creating new problems, new processes of interrelation, new conflicts, and new solutions. In a word, they are producing *qualitative* changes – that is, nothing less than a type of society quite different from the one conceived according to the founding principles of the nation-state. Italy has not yet found a blueprint establish a system of interrelations among cultures and religions. To what extent the new law on security, approved by the Italian parliament in 3 July 2009 under pressure from the Lega Nord (and in the face of strong criticism from Catholic clergy and militants), which has made undocumented immigration a crime, will change the present situation it is too early to say. But it will inevitably make life for immigrants and for the many individuals and NGOs who assist them much more difficult and painful.

In Denmark, where public voices often deny the existence of multiculturalism, geographical smallness is used as an argument for characterizing Denmark as a monocultural country. Smallness is associated with cultural and historical homogeneity, and the economic success realized in the post-war development with a specific form of universalistic welfare state. Tina Gudrun Jensen argues that, according to typologies of multiculturalism, the country falls somewhere in between multiculturalism and assimilation. It takes a colour-blind, tolerant liberal position as regards the question of equality; equality being a notion – equal rights and participation in Danish democracy – that strongly characterizes the discourse on immigrants and integration. Yet this discourse tends to neglect the question of cultural differences, and thus the actual premises for participation in this democracy. While there is rhetoric on cultural diversity as something beneficial to Danish society, this is somehow in tension with another rhetoric on fundamental Danish values. The construction of the Danish model hence reflects a tension between multiculturalism as an ideal and assimilation as a necessity, illustrating antagonisms between cultural diversity and the need for a common identity – the notions of 'sameness' and 'agreement' conflicting with the notion of difference. The model is challenged when difference becomes reality. An illustration of this is the *Jyllands-Posten* cartoon affair, which is interpreted as a potential implosion of the assimilatory and encompassing model. The cartoon affair and its aftermath in an old nation-state such as Denmark reflects the frictions that accompany the process of integrating Muslims into European society, but it can also be seen as part of the process of Europe's long history of integrating new social projects. While this process is not an easy one in Danish society, it does not rule out new understandings and negotiations between diversity and national identity.

The Netherlands, until the end of the 1990s, was regarded as one of the most advanced democracies in Europe: multi-ethnic, libertarian, open to and tolerant towards other cultures. It is today a country that practises zero tolerance, with one of the strictest immigration policies in Europe and an uncompromising assimilationist policy. However, Thijl Sunier claims that the image of the Netherlands as a once almost unique case of multiculturalism, and the idea that the country is today torn by violence and has set itself adrift, are both myths. He argues that the Netherlands' encounter with Muslim violence is not exceptional, let alone unique, compared to other countries in Europe and the United States, and that the level of religiously inspired violence in the country is modest. Yet he recognizes that there is indeed a very strong sentiment of anti-multiculturalism among politicians and opinion leaders, and that the question that needs to be addressed is what caused such a shift in public and political attitude. Sunier believes that there has been much greater continuity in Dutch integration policies than the present debate seems to suggest. If this is so, then one should ask, if it is the case that the policies have not essentially changed, what other factors intervened to cause such a shift in public opinion? Sunier answers that the aim of Dutch policies has always been to achieve equality and full participation in the three fields that form the basis of integration: housing, labour and education. This required social engineering with a strong pedagogical underpinning, based on the idea that immigrants would gradually assimilate and be absorbed by Dutch society. In the 1980s and the early 1990s there was a widely held belief that this process of assimilation would evolve automatically and naturally, when immigrants would integrate socially and economically and realize that Dutch society is *morally* superior to theirs – in France assimilation is good for the Republic, in the Netherlands it is good for the immigrant. This is what can be called 'assimilation by conviction': the assumption being that immigrants must be made socio-economically equal, but that their cultures are not equal. Through a successful integration programme that enhances economic equality, immigrants will 'in the end' understand that it is in their best interests to subscribe to the Dutch moral community. It differs from the French 'republican' philosophy that cultural and religious differences are irrelevant to the building of nationhood and citizenship, but it also differs from any multiculturalist creed that considers cultures as essentially equal. The real issue then as Dutch people see it is, according to Sunier's analysis, the erosion of their own culture and certainly not a re-evaluation of cultural differences. Today the general assumption is that cultural diversity tears a country apart and that social equality cannot be accomplished without strict and coercive assimilationist policies. The adage is: 'if they are not convinced themselves, we have to force them' – in other words, a shift from 'assimilation by conviction' to 'assimilation by coercion'. Although 9/11 has intensified certain political trends, it did not turn the tide from a multiculturalist to an anti-multiculturalist discourse, and there is much more continuity in Dutch integration policies over the last two decades than is often assumed. Such reasoning draws a very thin line between policies and attitudes, and doesn't make it clear that the attitude of policymakers has also changed. Sunier says that the shift is only 'apparent'. His analysis is certainly intellectually stimulating, and somewhat intriguing, but the fact is that today The Netherlands is a dramatically different country from the one we used to know.

This Introduction was drafted before we had seen Christophe Bertossi's Conclusion. The essence of the conclusions we reached, focusing on integration, are the same, although Bertossi's analysis attaches more importance to the issue of European citizenship (he notes that in the six country reports references to a new European model of citizenship are strikingly few), and his theoretical framework is much more developed. He agrees with the authors of the country reports that a 'European multicultural model' does not exist. Furthermore, he stresses that in every country the supposed national models are contradicted by policy and social practices, and argues that what in reality we are talking about is 'modelling practices'. Yet, he writes, while it is a fact that models do not exist, they cannot be dismissed; actors in the various national contexts take them very seriously, however contradictory they may be. A 'model', Bertossi remarks, is more often justified *ex-post* rather than *ex-ante*. Unfortunately, he concludes, today the politics of integration in Europe involves the re-politicization of ethnicity, race and immigration, which leads to the reframing of traditional discourses on integration and identity. Consequently a new crisis may well follow, as backlash against the crisis of multiculturalism, in the form of a homogeneous, essentially nationalistic conception of the nature of European societies.

The crisis of multiculturalism

In comparing these various situations, one can see that while the crisis of multiculturalism hit most European countries – not only the six we studied but presumably all those where the population includes a significant percentage of non-European immigrants – national context, along with the political and cultural discourses that accompany the crisis, include, in each country, problems and concerns specifically related to the history and the culture of that country.

Nonetheless, I believe that the main factors that caused the crisis of multiculturalism, without which it would have been much less serious and dramatic, or might never have occurred, are common to almost all countries. They emerged, explicitly or implicitly, from the discussions at our two meetings. First is the growing number of immigrants who have entered Europe in recent years. Second is economic recession. These two factors are obviously linked, especially so in the last two or three years: the fear of losing or not finding a job and the unwillingness to share with immigrants, in particular recent immigrants, the ever-shrinking financial resources for health and social services, are factors that must not be underestimated. Last but not least is the growing presence and visibility of the Muslim population.

The presence of Islam in Europe is not a recent phenomenon. In fact it was the Rushdie affair that made Europeans first aware, in 1988–89, that Islam could become a problem, not only on account of religion but, in particular, because its set of values had very little in common and often contrasted with their own. Then came 9/11, the Madrid and London bombings, the van Gogh assassination, and other events that made Islam not only just an 'Other', but a threat of the kind that countries normally meet only in wars, feeding Islamophobia and playing into the hands of nationalist, populist, and often racist and right-wing movements. The main victim of this climate so far is Turkey, whose accession to the EU has been postponed indefinitely.

Finally, when looking at the consequences of the crisis, one common feature that clearly emerges from our comparative study is that assimilation is now the main thrust of immigration policies in most if not all countries, a policy that is likely to further delay integration processes and make them much more impervious.

1

Progressive multiculturalism: the British experience

Maleiha Malik

It is precisely because the 'multiculturalism' debate touches on issues that are of profound importance to all British citizens, and not only a small group of minorities, that it is often so heated and politically charged. The public debate about multiculturalism acts as a form of 'symptomatic politics'.[1] As well as raising issues about minority integration, it frequently masks anxieties and confusion about the public identity of all British citizens. Within this form of 'symptomatic politics' controversy over historical events such as slavery takes on a particular significance because acts of 'national remembrance' are not solely about the past; they are also a vital public discourse in the present that allows individuals to form their identity as public citizens in the here and now. This chapter sets out an overview of the British model of multiculturalism. In the first section I set out some of the distinctive features of the 'multiculturalism' as compared with other models for integrating minorities. In the second section I set out a historical overview of the British response to the challenge of integrating minorities. I then move on to an evaluation of British multiculturalism: why is it perceived to have failed; has it failed or succeeded; what risks does it pose; what are its weaknesses?

Multiculturalism as a model for minority integration

What are British values? What are the norms into which minorities are being asked to integrate? These issues are often neglected in an analysis of multiculturalism in favour of a focus on the beliefs and conduct of minorities. This issue is often a hidden assumption in debates about minority integration but it becomes more prominent where multiculturalism is proposed as a model for integration. In addition, a number of other criteria are relevant to issues of minority integration. One broad categorization is the contrast between separation, assimilation and integration. More specifically, other 'markers' of integration include, inter alia: social and economic mobility, geographical dispersal, social assimilation and cultural distinctiveness. Racism in the form of anti-Semitism against British Jews and anti-Catholic discrimination is relevant to understanding the treatment of British minorities before the twentieth century.

Different models of integration give weight to different aspects of these criteria. For example, models of integration that assume that assimilation is an appropriate goal will problematize cultural distinctiveness, unlike more pluralist models that seek some accommodation of cultural difference. However, there are dangers in describing the debate in terms of a clash of models, such as 'British multiculturalism' versus 'French integration'. Such a reductionist analysis underestimates the complexity of terms such as 'multiculturalism', which have, as set out below, a variety of different meanings. This stark contrast also distorts the way in which a model that has been labelled 'British multiculturalism' includes many of the same components as other models which seek 'integration' as a more explicit goal.

Multiculturalism: descriptive versus normative

Popular myths about multiculturalism make it more difficult to delineate a precise definition for this form of minority protection. There are a number of ways in which the term can be used. Multiculturalism is used in the British context in two ways. First, at a descriptive level, it is used to describe the factual changes that have occurred in Britain which have resulted in a more marked racial, ethnic and cultural diversity. Second, at a normative level, it is used as a term to describe a state response to this increasing diversity which advocates policies of 'recognition' and 'accommodation of difference'.

At a descriptive level 'multiculturalism' refers to the increasing cultural diversity of modern liberal democracies. 'Culture' is a term that can include a wide range of attitudes, beliefs and practices. Sometimes the terms 'diversity' and 'multiculturalism' are used to include differences based on gender or sexuality, or differences that are a fundamental 'lifestyle' challenge to the predominant values that govern public life, such as the anti-globalization or environmental movements. This is diversity that is based on different beliefs about lifestyle and values. Bhikhu Parekh sets out a detailed distinction between 'wide' definitions of cultural diversity, which include 'perspectival diversity' such as challenges to the public structure by feminists or gays and lesbians, and 'narrow' definitions, which limit the use of the term 'multiculturalism' to a 'communal diversity' focusing on factors such as race, ethnicity, religion and language, and groups organized as distinct cultural communities. This chapter focuses on 'multiculturalism' in its more narrow sense (Parekh, 2006: 3–4). Here, the word 'culture' serves to capture a number of important distinct sources of diversity. First, it includes the traditional sources of 'difference' that are associated with marking out a social group as a distinct minority within a larger political community: for example, colour, race and ethnicity, religion and language. These social groups can be recognized as communities that are distinct from the prevailing culture of the nation-state.

There have always been recognizable and distinct cultural communities in Britain; that is, social groups that can be distinguished by reference to criteria such as race and ethnicity, region, religion or language. Prominent and well-established social groups that fall into this category includes Jews, the Roma and also the Celts. Concepts such as 'cultural pluralism' and 'multiculturalism' are now being deployed to describe such a wide range of phenomena that they are at risk of losing their intellectual power. Nevertheless, these terms convey the important social changes that have taken place in the European liberal democracies in the last fifty years. At a descriptive level 'cultural pluralism' or 'multiculturalism' usefully describes the increasing diversity of culture, race and religion of citizens in liberal democracies.[2] Some, although not all, of this diversity is the result of increased migration into European liberal democracies of people from non-Western cultures. This type of diversity is also encouraged by political liberalism and is an inevitable by-product of modern liberal democracies. John Rawls, for example, writes:

> A modern democratic society is characterized not simply by a pluralism of comprehensive religious, philosophical, and moral doctrines but by a pluralism of incompatible yet reasonable compre- hensive doctrines. No one of these doctrines is affirmed by citizens generally. Nor should one expect that in the foreseeable future one of them, or some other reasonable doctrine will ever be affirmed by all, or nearly all, citizens.

He is willing to label a doctrine 'reasonable' where it does not reject the essentials of a democratic regime, but states that

> Of course a society may also contain unreasonable and irrational, and even mad, comprehensive doctrines. In their case the problem is to contain them so that they do not undermine the unity and justice of society. (Rawls, 1993: xvi)

In this normative sense, multiculturalism is one policy response to the presence of increasingly diverse social groups and 'minori- ties' within a political community. At a normative level, therefore, 'cultural pluralism' or 'multiculturalism' are terms suggesting that the correct legal and political response to the increasing cul- tural diversity of European citizens is to adopt polices of public accommodation.

Once the distinction between 'descriptive' and 'normative' multi- culturalism is emphasized it becomes clear that multiculturalism is not the only state response to the challenge of increasing cultural diversity. It can be understood as one of three normative policy responses to – that is, models of integration of – increasing diversity: (1) assimila- tion; (2) liberal toleration and the principle of non-discrimination; and (3) liberal pluralism that encourages the 'accommodation of difference' (which can also be called multiculturalism). Minority integration can be said to cluster around these three models: (i) conservative nationalism and assimilation; (ii) traditional liberal tolerance; and (iii) plural liberalism and models of multiculturalism.

Assimilation, the first model, requires that these groups should, wherever possible, give up those characteristics that distinguish them from the mainstream national culture. In some cases, this assimilation could be 'forced', where a religious minority is prevented from manifesting the religion in practice or there is a legal requirement to give up speaking a national language in public life.

The principle of 'liberal toleration', the second model, allows individuals to manifest their particular difference in the private sphere but organizes public life according to individual civil and political rights. These individual rights (e.g. freedom of religion, freedom of speech) provide a framework within which individuals can manifest some of their 'differences' in the public sphere. However, 'liberal toleration' treats the public sphere as a neutral space and relegates issues of personal identity to the private sphere. Citizens are free to manifest their private identity in the private sphere, either individually or in association with others, without state interference. However, this form of 'liberal toleration' remains focused on individuals and treats culture and community as factors that have an 'instrumental value' to individuals.[3] Therefore models of minority protection based on 'liberal toleration', which safeguard individual civil and political rights, seldom provide specific 'state support' to ensure that minorities have the resources they need to continue and flourish (Kymlicka, 1989). This strategy of 'liberal toleration' has been supplemented by strategies of 'non-discrimination' for minorities in key areas such as employment and education. The focus on non-discrimination ensures that, as well as allowing minorities the right to manifest their 'different' private identities in the private sphere, they are not also penalized in key areas such as the workplace and education. A move towards a strategy of non-discrimination is significant because it shifts issues concerning private identity and the 'difference' of minorities from the private into the public sphere. Moreover, policies of non-discrimination will increasingly impact on majorities in key areas such as the workplace and education. Therefore policies of non-discrimination will increasingly become issues about the appropriate allocation of power and resources between majorities and minorities.

'Liberal pluralism', the third model, may include some features of the other two responses but it also goes further than simply tolerating and not discriminating against minorities in one key respect: it argues that some of the most pressing 'differences' and distinct needs of minorities can and should be positively accommodated within the public sphere. This additional requirement of 'accommodation of difference' generates models of multiculturalism.

Traditional models of citizenship based on 'conservative nationalism' define the terms of belonging to a political community according to a range of criteria, such as race, common memories, a dominant culture, language or a majority religion. These criteria favour a definition of national identity and citizenship that is based on history or immutable characteristics, rather than treating it as a matter of choice or negotiation. The descriptive reality of multiculturalism – the increasing cultural diversity in many European liberal democracies, including Britain – means that there are now increasingly large numbers of citizens who will not be able to meet these historical and immutable criteria. The risk in states that are liberal democracies and are also increasing culturally diverse is that the inflexible use of historical and immutable criteria will exclude or coercively assimilate increasingly large numbers of citizens. In liberal democracies, the presence of these citizens who cannot participate in historical or majority definitions of race, religion or language is a permanent barrier to forging a national identity, or definition of citizenship, along the lines advocated by conservative nationalists.

The liberal alternative to conservative nationalism tends to define citizens as members of a political community based on rational, liberal values. Citizenship is constructed through an unmediated relationship between the citizen and the state based on the state's guarantee to respect key constitutional rights (e.g. civil and political rights or promises of socio-economic welfare). The culture of minorities is safeguarded through their freedom to be involved in voluntary private activities and associations. Traditional liberal responses to minorities have taken the form of 'toleration': that is, a minority group is permitted a set of individual rights (e.g. the right to free speech or freedom of religion) but is required to operate in a neutral public sphere which often does not accommodate their cultural needs. This approach of liberal tolerance has been supplemented by a second strategy of non-discrimination against minorities in key public areas such as employment, education and housing. However, neither liberal toleration nor non-discrimination is able to respond to the demands by minorities that some aspects of their private identity should be recognized or accommodated in the public sphere. It is out of this theoretical and practical 'politics of difference' that multiculturalism has emerged as an alternative to both conservative nationalism and assimilative liberal tolerance.

Multiculturalism:
hard versus progressive

'Hard multiculturalism' can be distinguished from its 'progressive' variants in a number of ways. 'Progressive multiculturalism' can be presented as a requirement rather than a negation of liberal pluralism: it is based on a belief in the incommensurability of values rather than scepticism about the possibility of human values. Liberal political theory and practice have been criticized by a number of writers as being inhospitable to cultural diversity.[4] It is also argued that traditional liberal definitions of the nation-state and political community have adopted a reductionist and uncritical assumption that there is only one way (rather than many) to organize private and social life.[5] Some writers argue that this bias in favour of 'uniformity' helps define modern liberal constitutionalism and renders it inhospitable to claims of cultural accommodation (Tully, 1995: esp. chs 1–3). 'Liberal pluralism' goes further than toleration and non-discrimination and favours the public accommodation of minorities in the public sphere (Raz, 1994: ch. 8).[6] The inclusion of the term 'pluralism' draws on the traditional liberal concern, in the work of writers such as J.S. Mill, with ensuring that there is freedom for different points of view and diversity of lifestyles to flourish in the public sphere of liberal democracies. The arguments in favour of multiculturalism vary considerably, but in their most powerful formulation they also introduce the idea that public recognition of the core features of a person's private identity is important to their sense of self-worth and autonomy (Taylor, 1992). The misrecognition of a person's private identity in the public sphere, and especially by the state or its agencies, can cause harm to that person's autonomy. This analysis builds on some of the foundations of feminist critique to develop a form of 'identity politics' or the 'politics of recognition'.⁷ In addition, this distinct form of politics challenges the traditional dichotomy between public and private spheres and seeks the public accommodation of 'difference'.

Once we move from the claims of individuals to those of groups we can notice that there has been a significant change in the form and content of the political claims made by minority groups in recent times. Many no longer ask for the 'same' rights as the majority. Some of the most compelling demands of minorities now take the form of calls for the accommodation of 'difference' in the public sphere. The 'politics of recognition' provides a significant challenge to the liberal settlement by pointing out that the failure to recognize distortion or misrecognition of a person's private identity in the public sphere is one of the faces of oppression confronted by minorities. Iris Marion Young argues that this oppression 'involves the universalization of a dominant group's experience and culture, and its establishment as the norm', as well as

> the paradox of experiencing oneself as invisible at the same time that one is marked out as different. The invisibility comes about when dominant groups fail to recognize the perspective embodied in their cultural expressions as a perspective. These dominant cultural expressions often have little place for the experience of other groups, at most only mentioning or referring to them in stereotyped or marginalized ways. (Young, 1990: ch. 2)

The shift from liberal toleration and non-discrimination to policies of cultural accommodation – and multiculturalism as the appropriate model for the integration of cultural minorities – presents a very distinct challenge to the modern liberal state. Claims for accommodation by social groups vary greatly: the categories range from race, culture and religion through to gender and sexual orientation and disability. It is worth noticing that as the analysis of minority rights moves from 'tolerance' to 'cultural pluralism', the nature of the debate shifts focus from claims by individuals to claims by social and political groups. Liberal theory is more comfortable dealing with the individual action of a one-off extremist individual. This may be easier to tolerate because he or she can be seen to be a solitary figure. Once we move from the solitary figure to an organized group there is a subtle shift in the analysis. A social or political group raises distinct and difficult issues because they are seen to be a viable challenge to social and political power (Walzer, 1997: 8–9). Moreover, collective action is a more difficult conceptual category for liberal politics, although recent work by theorists has provided a more complex structure within which to analyse groups.[8] The shift towards multiculturalism also raises the risk of fragmentation of the political and legal authority of the state. Modern nation-states are founded on the principle that a political community should have territorial integrity and that state power should extend to all those within this boundary. This vision brings together issues of physical geography, political community and monopoly over the use of legitimate power and force. There is, as James Tully notes, a very powerful incentive towards uniformity and homogeneity in relation to constitutional principle and political identity: the assumption is that the appropriate constitutional settlement is one which applies a single set of principles and which has a clear and unambiguous definition of citizenship. Within this model, diversity and hybridity at the level of constitutional principles, public identity and definitions of citizenship are problematized (Tully, 1995: esp. chs 1–3; Parekh, 2006: 182–3).

Another powerful idea that informs the modern state and definitions of citizenship is the principle of equality: that the state and its institutions should treat all citizens in the same way irrespective of differences of race, religion or culture. The concept of the rule of law – and the idea of a single source of political and legal authority in one sovereign territory – encourages this definition of equality as universalism. Yet, at the same time, as noted previously, the politics of recognition means that equality has also come to include a sense of 'recognition of difference': that part of what it means to treat all people with equal respect and concern is to recognize and accommodate aspects of their private identity in the public sphere (Taylor, 1992). There is, therefore, a tension in contemporary discussions of 'equality for citizens' between these two visions of equal citizenship: the first vision of 'equality as neutrality' tends towards universal principles, neutrality and homogeneity; and the second vision of 'equality as accommodating difference' tends towards diversity and the accommodation of difference in the public sphere. However, as Charles Taylor notes, the second use of the term 'equality' has become increasingly powerful in our times. Combined with the factual reality of a diversity of cultures in most liberal democracies, this new 'politics of recognition' creates a new set of challenges for liberal forms of minority protection. Liberal pluralism and multiculturalism are one response to these new challenges. In the work of writers such as Charles Taylor this can be seen to be a substantial commitment to pluralism. This can be compared to the conclusions of writers such as John Gray, who offers pluralism as a modus vivendi for peaceful coexistence between incompatible ways of living. However, despite these differences, it is significant that both writers advocate similar policies of liberal tolerance and pluralism as the appropriate response to the contemporary challenge of cultural diversity.[9] A preference for liberal pluralism also ensures that political theory responds and adjusts itself to the reality of the political claims made by individuals themselves. Minorities are no longer willing for their differences to be a matter of 'tolerance' in the private realm: they now demand political rights, accommodation and recognition in the public sphere. Theories about minority protection and integration also need to connect with, and respond to, the reality of minority claims in practice (Malik, 2000).

Progressive multiculturalism as a model for minority integration

'Progressive multiculturalism' as a form of liberal pluralism is similar to other models of minority integration. Progressive multiculturalism is also based on a concern with the 'accommodation of difference' as a requirement of the core values of liberal politics. Therefore, progressive multiculturalism replicates the liberal concern with ensuring a minimum guarantee of tolerance for minorities in the private sphere through the safeguarding of individual rights; and it also includes the right to non-discrimination, which ensures that minorities have access to key public goods such as employment or education. The focus on 'respect' and 'participation' for all citizens ensures that progressive multiculturalism remains a model of integration: for example, its goals include securing autonomy and non-discrimination for all citizens, and the increased participation of minorities along with majorities in mainstream economic, political and social institutions. One recent example of progressive multiculturalism is the work of Tariq Modood. For Modood, the key feature of his model of 'political multiculturalism' is that:

> it begins with a concept of negative difference and seeks the goal of positive difference and the means to achieve it, which crucially involve the appreciation of the fact of multiplicity and groupness, the building of group pride amongst those marked by negative difference, and political engagement with the sources of negativity and racism. This suggests that neither separation nor assimilation but an accomodative form of integration which would allow group-based racialized, ethnic, cultural and religious identities and practices to be recognized and supported in the public space, rather than require them to be privatized. This is justified by an extended concept of equality, not just equal dignity but also equal respect. While the focus is not on anything so narrow as normally understood by culture, and multicultural equality cannot be achieved without other forms of equality, such as those relating to socio-economic opportunities, *its distinctive feature is about the inclusion into and the making of a shared public space in terms of equality of respect as well as equal dignity*. (Modood, 2007: 61–2)

Progressive multiculturalism's distinctive characteristic is that, as well as focusing on the traditional markers of integration (e.g. social and economic mobility or racism), it adjusts itself to these markers in the context of the contemporary reality of increased cultural diversity and the 'politics of recognition'. Modood's multiculturalism is based on a recognition of the reality of distinct groups as a valid category for a theory of justice or minority integration. For Modood, this focus on group difference is not based on an essentialist commitment to groups as a cultural reality. Rather, he argues, group differences remain important in contexts other than the classic definition of the nation-state and citizenship. There are other important sources of group differences such as the co-presence of individuals who have ways of thinking, acting and organizing across many social and institutional contexts that are not contained or limited by the nation-state. These co-presences often have historical roots arising out of relationships of domination–subordination arising from colonial empires. However, whereas previously these groups were relegated to being 'over there', they are now part of the political community within Western cities and are seeking full membership as citizens of the nation-state (Modood, 2007: 39).

One consequence of moving away from an essentialist definition of 'cultural groups' towards a focus on 'group difference' as a matter of social and political reality is that Modood is able to scrutinise and address the way in which groups are formed and transformed through complex processes. This allows him to make a number of adjustments which ensure that his model does not collapse either into communalism or into crude forms of 'hard multiculturalism' that are frequently based on essentialist definitions of cultural difference. More specifically, there are, inter alia, a number of significant advantages to this method. First, it allows Modood to relate his definition of multiculturalism to other key markers of minority integration (such as racism and political–social–economic inequality):

> Multiculturalism is not, therefore, about cultural rights instead of political equality or economic opportunities; it is a politics which recognizes post-immigration groups exist in western societies in ways that both they and others, formally and informally, negatively and positively are aware that these group–differentiating dimensions are central to their social constitution. (Modood, 2007: 40)

Second, Modood is able to make sense of the importance of representation and recognition of groups in the public sphere as a critical matter for models of minority integration:

> To speak of 'difference' rather than 'culture' as the sociological starting point is to recognize that the difference in question is not just constituted from the 'inside', from the side of minority culture, but also from the outside, from the representations and treatment of the minorities in question. (Modood, 2007: 39)

Third, a particularly attractive feature of Modood's method is that it allows our theories about minority integration to align themselves to practical reality, to the claims that minorities themselves feel are important in their daily lives:

> So, rather than derive a concept of multicultural politics from a concept of culture, it is better to build it up from the specific claims, explicitly and explicit, of the post-war extra-European/non-white immigration and settlement and their struggles and the policy responses around them to achieve some form of acceptance and equal membership. (Modood, 2007: 40)

Other 'progressive' accounts of multiculturalism place less emphasis on 'groupness' in favour of a traditional liberal concern with individual autonomy. Although these accounts continue to regard the individual as the main focus for analysis, they recognize the importance of the collective context within which choice operates, and within which autonomy is realized; they are still able to generate a principle of public accommodation of some group differences by the prioritizing of individual freedom and well-being (Raz, 1994: ch. 8). These different foundations for multiculturalism generate considerable variety in terms of defininition and of the optimal relationship between individuals, groups and the state. Yet, all these accounts display similar characteristics: an emphasis on the importance of social, cultural and political context to individual choice and autonomy; the value of groups' membership as either an intrinsic or an instrumental good to allow human flourishing; and the need for liberal theories of justice to move away from strict individualism to recognizing the importance of groups. The model of multiculturalism has a number of distinctive features that ensure that it is 'progressive'. For example, the claims for accommodation by groups are introduced and debated in the public sphere as part of showing them equal respect. However, this public debate is also conducted within a procedure of discourse ethics, with the aim of ensuring compatibility with universal values such as freedom and equality, and protecting individuals' right to self-ascribe their group membership and right to exit (Benhabib, 2002; Malik, 2007b). This model is progressive also because it relates the independent values of recognition to the need to address social and economic inequality. Progressive multiculturalism's predominant concern is with the individual subject: its goal is to ensure that individuals are able to constitute themselves as autonomous subjects; to increase their capacity to exercise choice and responsibility; and to communicate these choices with others through full participation in the public sphere in their political communities.

This 'progressive' multiculturalism has a number of advantages, which are summarized in the following sections. More generally, progressive multiculturalism provides resources to defend multiculturalism against a number of recurring critiques: for example, that it causes harm to women; that it sacrifices 'redistribution' in favour of 'recognition'; that it is a distraction from the fight against racism; that it is a threat to 'secularism'. In addition to answering this critique, a model of multiculturalism also needs to be engaged at two different levels of analysis: participation in the domestic debates about definitions of citizenship in an increasingly diverse 'national' political community; and the ability to offer an explanation for contemporary individual and group politics that cannot be contained within traditional territorial boundaries and definitions of the nation-state.

Multicultural vulnerability

Progressive multiculturalism recognizes the risks that are inherent in the recognition of cultures in the public sphere. The 'multiculturalism versus feminism' debate has highlighted the way in which the accommodation of cultural difference – especially differences that arise from traditional cultures and religions – can pose a risk for women. This 'multicultural vulnerability' means that some groups of citizens, such as women, are asked to bear a disproportionate burden of the costs of multiculturalism.[10] Faced with a conflict between calls for the public accommodation of minority cultures and the rights of vulnerable groups within minorities such as women, it is possible for progressive multiculturalism (which is justified by liberal concerns with individual autonomy) to give weight to the interests of individual women.

Redistribution and recognition

Progressive multiculturalism, as well as giving priority to the importance of public recognition, also seeks to gives greater weight to socio-economic redistribution than hard versions of multiculturalism. A recurring critique of multiculturalism is that it has led to a shift in focus away from redistribution towards recognition, which has a detrimental effect on minorities and the goal of integration. Progressive multiculturalism recognizes that not only social and economic goods but also cultural goods are relevant to any theory of justice. This approach avoids the assumption that there is a reductive choice between 'redistribution' and 'recognition' which does not sufficiently integrate both redistribution and recognition into one theoretical framework. Fraser argues that, beyond one-dimensional concepts of justice, there is the possibility of adopting what Nancy Fraser has called 'two-dimensional justice': encompassing both elements within a broader normative framework which requires 'parity of participation' (Fraser and Honneth, 2003: esp. ch. 1). It is worth noting, however, that this potential for the convergence of 'redistribution' and 'recognition' at a theoretical level does not automatically translate into a unified practice of multiculturalism as a form of minority integration that incorporates both features: that is, recognition in the form of *'inclusion into and the making of a shared public space in terms of equality of respect as well as equal dignity'* (Modood, 2007: 61–2); and redistribution of social, economic and political power to socially excluded groups. This may be one feature where there can be a productive struggle to ensure that there is a unified theory of *integrated* multiculturalism which encourages convergence between the goals of 'redistribution' and 'recognition' (Wierviorka, 1998: 889).

Cultural racism

Progressive multiculturalism remains concerned with issues of racism and discrimination as barriers to the goals of equality and minority integration. However, in this area it adjusts itself to the new challenges that face minority integration. Traditional models of anti-racist politics need to respond to changes caused by increasing cultural diversity and also the emerging 'politics of recognition'. Race as a 'biological' construct is now widely accepted as an inappropriate paradigm for discussions of racism as a 'social' problem. Although difference based on 'colour' or visible ethnic difference remains a crucial way in which individuals and social groups become racialized, there is an increasing recognition that racism also includes other factors. This new wider form of racism is concerned with visible markers of biological difference such as colour, but it also concerns itself with cultural racism. Étienne Balibar develops this concept through an analogy with anti-Semitism and concludes that cultural racism also concerns itself with 'signs of a deep psychology, as signs of a spiritual inheritance rather than a biological heredity'. Balibar also writes that this wider definition is more appropriate to capturing the range of harm caused by 'racism in the era of "decolonization" which is based on the movement of peoples from the former colonies into Western Europe'.[11] This wider definition of racism is particularly important in the context of Britain because of the significance of postcolonial immigration after World War II. Moreover this is a more appropriate analysis given that contemporary British debate about the 'integration' of minorities is not limited to issues of colour but is also dominated by the 'problem' of integrating non-European cultures into a European civilization.

Secularism

The move away from biological racism to cultural racism also forces models of minority integration to face the overlap between race, culture and religion. Progressive multiculturalism avoids a dogmatic and inflexible approach to the accommodation of religion in the public sphere. Claims by religious groups, for the public accommodation of their private religious identity, cause special difficulties because they challenge the secular liberal settlement. These claims for distinct 'religious accommodation' challenge the most fundamental beliefs of secular liberals, for whom the public–private dichotomy is almost an article of faith. Traditional liberals will vigorously defend an individual's right to religion in the private sphere whilst at the same time vigilantly guarding the public sphere as a neutral, religion-free zone. This will be a particular challenge for minority religious groups for a number of reasons: non-Christian religions are unlikely to have developed sophisticated responses to European secularism in a way that has been achieved by majority or well-established religious minorities; and, moreover, the public sphere will often be structured in a way that favours religious minorities, so that those who are seeking the accommodation of religious needs will often be newer religious minorities. The headscarf cases throughout Europe are an illustration of the growing importance of this issue to minority integration. Within this context, issues of minority integration will increasingly need to address questions about the appropriate balance between the values of secularism and equality in a liberal democracy. Progressive multiculturalism recognizes that in some cases the accommodation of minority religious claims in the public sphere may be justified as a requirement of liberal politics, and as an aspect of securing autonomy for individuals. Tariq Modood offers a detailed exposition of a 'moderate secularism' that recognizes the normative significance of religion to individuals but that involves no further theological or ethical endorsement or evaluation. Modood argues for an approach which (a) extends a politics of difference to include appropriate religious identities and organizations; (b) reconceptualizes secularism from a dogmatic version of *laïcité* (with strict neutrality in the public sphere) to a more moderate evolutionary version that has the resources to accommodate the most pressing needs of religious minorities; and (c) ensures that this adjustment/negotiation is carried out through an incremental process – a case-by-case and institution-by-institution process that focuses on pragmatic public accommodation (Modood, 2007: 78–9).

Progressive multiculturalism and political community

One significant advantage of the incremental process of accommodation advocated by Modood is that it generates a definition of citizenship that links membership of a political community with a 'sense of belonging' to public political and legal institutions. Progressive multiculturalism recognizes the increasing importance of 'recognition' and takes seriously the need for all citizen's to feel a sense of belonging to a political community. However, traditional liberal theory does not provide a useful paradigm for addressing issues of 'national belonging'. The traditional liberal approach constitutes the British public as members of a political community based on rational, liberal values. Citizenship identifies an unmediated relationship between individual and state; any involvement by citizens with voluntary, private or civil organizations must be voluntary and consensual. Contemporary approaches to the protection of minorities have supplemented toleration with a second strategy guaranteeing an individual the right to non-discrimination. Although most versions of this right permit a limited measure of discrimination in the private sphere, non-discrimination ensures that minorities have access to politics, the economy and key sectors such as public services and education. This clearly affects the way in which the majority will conduct not only their private but also some of their public affairs.

One alternative to a traditional liberal definition of political community is 'conservative nationalism', which remains a popular mechanism for defining national identity. This strategy defines the terms of belonging to a political community according to criteria such as race, common memories, a dominant culture or a majority religion. In this context national identity becomes something that is given historically rather than as a matter of choice or negotiation. In most Western democracies, the presence of large numbers of racially and culturally diverse groups is a permanent barrier to forging a shared national identity along the lines advocated by conservative nationalists. The fear in contemporary plural states is that the inflexible use of these criteria will necessarily exclude, or coercively assimilate, large numbers of citizens. Conservative nationalism, with its insistence that national identity can be formed around criteria such as a common language, colour, race or religion, is necessarily coercive of large numbers of citizens in modern plural democracies. The traditional liberal cultural contract (which relegates issues of private identity to the private sphere) is also an unsuitable basis for responding to recent demands by minorities for recognition in both the private and the public sphere. Theorists have increasingly questioned the adequacy of traditional liberalism's focus on universal individual rights as a sufficient guarantee of minority protection. Under conditions of ethnic or cultural diversity it is argued that concentrating exclusively on tolerance and an individual right to non-discrimination may operate as a form of 'benign neglect' of minority groups, and that multi-culturalism can provide a solution.

Modood's concept of multicultural citizenship and the incremental process of public accommodation that he develops generate a way of defining national belonging that avoids the pitfalls of exclusionary conservative nationalism and benign neglect of liberal tolerance. The sense of belonging to public institutions that will be an outcome of this incremental process can perform a number of key functions: for example, generating a way of defining membership of a political com-munity that is compatible with liberal values; that is not coercive;[12] and that includes all the citizens in a diverse community.

The priority given to public institutions as the focus for develop-ing a 'sense of belonging' to a political community has a number of advantages. There are certain types of institution that perform a critical function as a locus for private identity. Public institutions allow individuals to participate in shared social practices, and they are a source for creating the common meanings that are a basis for community. The argument that certain political, legal and civic institutions are constituted by, and draw on, common meanings develops the idea of community in a much stronger form. It sug-gests that there are certain institutions that rely on and sustain intersubjective meanings. These meanings can be understood by all participants and therefore contribute to the formation of a common language and vocabulary. Public institutions are not, and should not be, viewed as neutral agents. Rather, they have a wide range of functions, which influence private identity as well as political and civil society. This in turn challenges the strict separation of the private and public spheres. It also raises questions about national identification.

The importance of institutional identification becomes even more significant when we consider that identifying with the fate of a political community is also the only viable way of forming a national identity that can include minority groups (Mason, 1999). This line of argument makes it especially urgent for all minorities to take part in participatory democratic politics. Progressive multiculturalism seeks to ensure that not only majorities but also minorities are included in definitions of citizenship within liberal democracies, and therefore are full and equal participants.

Participatory democracy (defined as institutional and national identification) is important for the majority as well as the minority. However, it takes on special significance in the context of minority integration. Most obviously, minority groups whose members and viewpoints are not represented within major political and legal institutions will find it difficult to identify with them. Some forms of multiculturalism give priority to mechanisms of belonging which draw on the many sources of private identity (both individual and group) such as race, ethnicity or sexuality. Where there is a conflict between the established public or national identity and these various sources of private identity, the latter should always be given preference. This form of multiculturalism can compensate for the obvious defects of the liberal 'cultural contract' which relegates issues of personal identity to the private sphere. It also avoids the exclusionary consequences of 'conservative nationalism' that defines national identity according to historically given criteria. However, seeking a solution in such an uncompromising version of multiculturalism is not free of difficulties. If participatory politics requires national identification by the minority, then this is equally true for the majority. An 'exclusive' version of multiculturalism which ignores the needs of the majority also fails to meet the criteria for an inclusive form of participatory politics.

All of these approaches ignore the possibility that a common public sphere can emerge which is neither neutral between cultures nor a perfect mirror for personal identity. Developing 'a sense of belonging' which remains attentive to both the majority and the minority, and generating a common public culture within which different groups coexist, requires compromise and adjustment by the parties. For the minority, this means that their private identity cannot automatically be reflected in the public sphere without some limited assimilation to the shared values that are the agreed basis for a common public life. For the majority, this renegotiation carries with it the inevitable costs of attempts to transform the public sphere and institutions, from exclusively reflecting the dominant culture towards a common culture which also seeks to accommodate some of the most urgent needs of minorities.

Institutional identification is therefore of critical importance as an aspect of a minority integration. Citizens are more likely to identify with the decisions of representative institutions, and so they are an ideal forum for policies which go beyond the toleration of minorities – for example, non-discrimination policies which impact on the majority and multiculturalism. However, affirming the potential contribution of representative institutions to minority protection generally, and multiculturalism in particular, is not synonymous with displacing the well-earned and pivotal role of judicially protected individual rights for minorities. It is rather a much-needed antidote to the cherished assumption that a judicial remedy should be the sole focus of attention. Minority groups should lobby representatives so that policymakers take their interests, and the interests of other stakeholders, into account before formulating policies.

This is not to say that representative institutions are a panacea. Minorities such as Muslims face obvious difficulties in advancing their interests through political processes in the absence of real political power and adequate representation of their interests. Simplistic appeals to political equality leave all the most intractable difficulties unanswered in this context. 'Each citizen shall count for one' fails to account for individuals who are a permanent minority and whose concerns are not adequately represented within the political process. However, this speaks to the need for reform rather than abandonment of the role of representative institutions altogether, and for a focus on transforming elected assemblies at all levels.

Institutional identification is more likely where substantive issues concerning the common good are discussed. This in turn makes a unique contribution towards developing common meanings and a sense of community. In the context of complex plural states, the only viable and inclusive way of defining national identification is to ensure that all citizens can identify with key political and legal institutions. It is essential that minority issues are raised in forums and at the point where people engage with the full range of political alternatives and the full spectrum of policy concerns (Malik, 2000). The likelihood that not only a minority but also the majority will treat representative institutions as structures of identification becomes critically important for minority protection and is especially important in areas of significant and controversial social reform of the public sphere. This public debate will often include controversy about the meaning of past historical events, such as the debate about slavery. Such reform is also likely to include, inter alia, the reallocation of political, social and economic power from one group to another, such as those involved in aligning recognition and redistribution. Most importantly it will also have to provide political solutions to deep multicultural conflicts that require one group to make important concessions (often arising from the risks of multicultural vulnerability) on key aspects of their principles or identity.

Post-colonialism, globalization and non-territorial politics

A shift towards a wider definition of 'cultural racism' encourages a link between domestic concerns about integrating minorities and wider historical and international issues. This connection was dramatically illustrated by Toyin Agbetu's disruption of the commemoration of the abolition of slavery: that is, his claim for equality for Africans in the present was linked to an objection to the official version of British colonial history (Agbetu, 2007). In such cases, the claim for recognition by a 'British' minority will raise wider questions about the relationship between a nation-state and its colonial past. More dramatically, the claims of the 7 July bombers that their acts were motivated by British foreign policy illustrates that there are also present connections between the integration of minorities and the international actions of the nation-state. These forms of politics challenge the dichotomy between the domestic and the international. They also illustrate the increasing significance of forms of politics that are not bound by territorial limits of the nation-state, and that challenge the centrality of state power (Connolly, 1991: ch. 7).

Traditional liberal political theory is not silent on the issue of the place of 'native' and colonial peoples in definitions of the political community. As Bhikhu Parekh notes, classical liberal theorists such as Locke and Mill had no difficulty in justifying English colonialism: they categorized members of different non-European cultures as 'backward'. These writers saw no reason to respect the integrity of these cultures or to see them as including a valid way of life or value. It followed, therefore, that there were no serious obstacles to dismantling these cultures, denying them territorial integrity and making them subject to an external European 'civilizing' mission (Parekh, 2006: 38–49). James Tully has also noted the relationship between colonialism and traditional liberal constitutionalism. Tully argues that many of the assumptions that underlie modern constitutionalism, and particularly its bias against non-European cultures, were formed during the age of European imperialism, which makes them inhospitable for claims of cultural accommodation. Tully proposes alternative constitutional frameworks and conventions that open up a dialogic process between all citizens, which, he argues, is a form of constitutionalism that can accommodate cultural diversity in liberal democracies (Tully, 1995: esp. chs 1–3). The focus on the history of empire and colonialism is critical in the British context for a number of reasons. It provides the context in which large-scale migration into Britain after 1945 introduced minorities who – unlike national minorities or Jewish and Irish migrants in the nineteenth century – were obviously 'colonial subjects' who were transformed into 'British citizens'. Moreover, as I argue below, the connection between multiculturalism and an 'international' context that transcends territorial boundaries is also crucial because it allows us to connect anxieties about the 'war on terror' with the 'British model of multiculturalism'.

British multiculturalism

In setting out a historical overview of how the British approach to minority integration has developed, and evaluating multiculturalism as a normative model, it is tempting to develop an analysis that neatly tracks a linear movement between different phases. Such a method would allow us to argue that there is a seamless move from assimilation through to traditional liberal tolerance and finally contemporary models of multiculturalism. This method of tracking the phases in the British model would, however, be reductionist and distortive. It would cause us to miss significant sources of complexity:

for example, that different historical periods have included a complex mix of state responses towards minorities; and that public rhetoric about the preferred state model is not always a good guide to the model that is practised.

An early multicultural state

It is often assumed that the British experience of cultural diversity is a new phenomenon. However, as discussed below, Britain has always been diverse in terms of ethnicity, language, religion and culture. Professor Bernard Crick noted this well-established British 'history' of multiculturalism in his report on *The New and the Old: The Report of the Life in the United Kingdom Advisory Group* when he concluded: 'Who are we British? For a long time the UK has been a multicultural state composed of England, Northern Ireland, Scotland and Wales, and also a multicultural society ... made up of a diverse range of cultures and identities' (Crick, 2003: 10). Recognition of the inherent diversity of the category 'British' is important for contemporary discussions and evaluation of the British multicultural model, which is often distorted by either taking a historical perspective or the adoption of post-World War II migration as the main focus for analysis.

The formation of a unitary state of 'Britain' was a complex process. Great Britain includes, inter alia, the union of a number of distinct geographical, cultural and political entities: England, Scotland and Wales. The unification of Wales with England ensured that English law, the Anglican Church and the English language were given precedence in Wales. The Act of Union which created Great Britain linked the physical geography of Scotland to England and Wales and formed one political community. This political community ensured rule by a single Protestant ruler, with one legislature and one established Church.

Yet the simplified picture of 'Great Britain' as a homogenous and seamless whole masks a more complex reality. Physical and political unity did not eliminate diversity. Moreover, the essence of what it means to be British is not straightforward. Matthew Arnold, for example, notes the way in which three 'essences' account for what it means to be British: 'the Germanic genius, the Celtic genius, the

Norman genius' (Arnold, 1883: 87). The presence of 'Celts' challenges the idea that Britain was a racially and culturally homogenous
society before more recent immigration. The recognition of Celts as a
national minority also highlights the fact that there have always been
'indigenous' British minorities with specific political claims such as
language rights (Welsh) and devolution (Scots). This historical context
is significant because it stresses the importance of exploring the
continuities between the principles that underlie the rights of national
minorities and the more contemporary demands for equality by recent
migrants (racial, cultural and religious groups). Nor is the distinct
presence of the 'Celts' merely a matter of historical significance, as
confirmed by the increasing political success of the Scottish National
Party (SNP) in contemporary British politics.

The union with Ireland has always been, and remains, a politically contentious issue. The experience of Catholics and Irish communities in Britain raises a number of issues that are analogous to
contemporary debates about minority integration. For example, the
experience and resistance of Irish Catholics in Northern Ireland to
the category 'British' raises issues about the difficulty of integrating
minorities who have experienced colonialism by a nation-state into
a political community as equal citizens. Moreover, the example of
Northern Ireland also illustrates the way this can lead to a vicious
circle: resistance and in some cases political violence against the state
by a minority; a state response in the form of anti-terror legislation;
and ultimately the creation of the minority as a 'suspect community'.
This vicious circle further hinders the process of minority integration
(Hillyard, 1993).

There were also religious and ethnic minorities in Britain from
the earliest times. Great Britain has always been a mixed racial and
religious population. Contrary to perceptions that non-Christian
religious minorities are newcomers, Jews have had a presence in
Britain since the eleventh century[13] and there is evidence of Muslim
settlement in Britain under the Tudors and Stewarts (in the fifteenth
and sixteenth centuries) (Mattar, 1998). Jews expelled from Britain
in 1290 and then later readmitted by Cromwell in 1656. Jews faced
legal obstacles through such indirect devices as the need to swear a
Christian oath to hold public office (Fredman, 2002: 37). There have

also been Roma populations in Britain from as early as the sixteenth century (Okley, 1983). The Roma faced repressive legislation aimed at expelling them and making their lifestyle more difficult. In the case of the Roma this trend has continued into the contemporary period leading to 'an explicitly assimilationist policy, using the criminal law to repress the nomadic tradition of gypsies' (Fredman, 2002: 39).

There have been black and minority ethnic communities in Britain from the earliest time periods, which includes the importation of African slaves and servants from the sixteenth century onwards. There were earlier experiences of minorities in Britain who were distinguishable in terms of their colour, many of whom were settled as a result of the slave trade or through their inclusion in the merchant shipping industry. The slave trade is an interesting example of the way in which Britain's colonial history impacted on the principle of race discrimination in the domestic sphere. The courts had sought to distinguish between the legitimacy of slavery in the colonies and the principle of the freedom of the individual in relation to slavery in Britain: 'The courts resolved the difficulty by treating slavery as a relationship created under local colonial law, and enforcing that relationship as a matter of colonial rather than domestic English law' (Lester and Bindman, 1972: 29). This is an interesting example of a theme that recurs throughout discussions of the relationship between race and law in the contemporary period: the need to maintain a strict separation between the international/global context and the domestic or issues that are relevant to racism. The abolitionist movement challenged this dichotomy. The subsequent legislation to abolish slavery in the colonies can be seen as an early example of the universalizing of the principle that race discrimination was a moral wrong (Lester and Bindman, 1972: ch. 1). Yet subsequent developments suggested that race remained an important factor in the treatment of minorities in the domestic context. Slavery provided Britain with contact with non-white others, whilst the abolitionist movement provided an example of how political action could challenge injustice or racism.

Despite the early history of migration and diversity, British immigrant populations were small compared with the total population. However, the large-scale Irish and Jewish immigration to Britain in the nineteenth century, and inward migration from the former colonies in the twentieth century, were more substantive. The state and popular response to Jewish migration into Britain before World War II is particularly significant for a number of reasons. First, the initial immigration controls were a direct response to Jewish immigration into Britain from Eastern Europe in the late nineteenth and early twentieth centuries (Gainer, 1972; Sherman, 1973: 259; Kushner, 1994). Second, the form of British anti-Semitism during this period provides a useful comparator to the way in which other non-Christian religious minorities such as Muslims are racialized by British society.[14]

As the preceding analysis confirms, there were minorities (ethnic, cultural, religious and linguistic) in Britain before the mid-twentieth century. However, it was not until immigration from the former colonies in the 1950s that significant numbers of migrant groups became clearly distinguishable on the grounds of their colour. This period provides the immediate context for the introduction of contemporary race relations legislation. However, earlier examples of migration remain important because they reveal some of the recurring themes in British state responses to minorities.

Irish immigration to Britain

Irish and Jews in Britain were not distinguishable in terms of their skin colour. However, both groups were racialized as 'culturally' different. To this extent the racialization process by which these groups were constructed as the 'other' can be expressed as 'cultural racism' rather than 'colour racism'. There was a long-standing tradition of Irish migration to Britain dating back to the eighteenth and early nineteenth centuries. The cause of the migration during this time can be traced to the increasing British demands for labour caused by rapid economic expansion (Miles, 1982: 120–50). The outbreak of the potato famine of 1845, and the resulting starvation, intensified this pre-existing pattern of migration, leading to a large increase in the number of Irish immigrants in Britain. The main settlements of the Irish communities were in London and Lancashire, with smaller communities in the West Midlands and Yorkshire. In Scotland, the main settlements of the Irish community were in the west, especially near Glasgow. This pattern led to distinct communities that could be identified on the basis of cultural and religious differences (Solomos, 2003: 38–40). What is significant about this substantial immigration into Britain was that it was not accompanied by either calls for, or a state response to, regulation. Part of the explanation may be that via a number of legal and political settlements there was already a connection between the Irish and the British state. The Act of Union of 1800 had incorporated Ireland into the UK, which meant that the people of Ireland were already granted status as British subjects. This link was loosened with the establishment of the Irish Republic in 1922 and after Ireland left the Commonwealth in 1947. However, despite these changes the Irish remained free to enter, settle, work and vote in Britain (Solomos, 2003: 38). Although there were no popular demands to regulate Irish immigration, there was a hostile response to the Irish by some sections of the British public. There were also well-established anti-Irish stereotypes in British culture: the Irish were racialized as inferior by reference to 'biological difference' and because of their Catholicism. There were also acts of violence towards Irish immigrants. Significantly, middle-class Victorian attitudes included the belief that there was a wide racial and cultural gap between the English and the Irish. This early construction of the 'essence' of English values, and its difference from 'Irish' values, is significant in considering later responses to immigration by Jews and other minorities (Solomos, 2003: 36–40).

Jewish immigration to Britain

The historical lessons of the political and legal responses to Jewish immigration are especially important for an understanding of racism. As Didi Herman has noted, this precedent is critical in understanding the way in which processes of racialization of minorities are transferred rather than extinguished. Herman writes:

> given Jews were amongst the earliest 'raced' peoples in England, there is a debt that all contemporary racialization processes owe to these earlier ones that has remained largely unexplored, and that

is not adequately accounted for in work that roots 'race' or 'strangers' or 'alterity and difference' in imperial and colonial projects. (Herman, 2006)

The migration of large numbers of Irish people to Britain did not give rise to calls for immigration controls and legal regulation. In sharp contrast to this fact, the arrival of large numbers of Jewish immigrants who were fleeing persecution in Eastern Europe in the late Victorian and early Edwardian period led to a very different political response, producing the assertion of the idea of 'England for the English' by a wide spectrum of the British public, conservatives and trade unionists (Lebzelter, 1982: 90). According to one commentator on political anti-Semitism, the presence of Jews in the 1880s and 1890s became associated with domestic issues such as unemployment and poverty, and foreign policy issues such as anti-colonial struggles (Lebzelter, 1982: 120). Despite the small numbers of Jews compared to Irish migrants, there were calls for the state to restrict Jewish immigration. The perception of social problems associated with Jewish immigration in the East End of London led to trade-union support for immigration control (resolutions were passed by the Trade Union Congress in 1892, 1894 and 1895) (Garrard, 1971: 71, 174). Jews, concentrated in the worst sectors of 'sweated' labour, were accused of undercutting local labour conditions (Fredman, 2002: 37). There was political agitation in the East End on the part of the British Brothers League to end Jewish immigration, as well as support in Parliament for state regulation of immigration (Gainer, 1972). With the election of a Conservative government in 1895 the political stage was set for the introduction of legislation in the form of the Aliens Act, 1905. Subsequently, more detailed legislation in the form of the Aliens Restriction Act 1914 was passed. This legislation gave the government wide-ranging powers to control immigration through the use of prerogative powers via Orders in Council. These powers were justified as required by national security in times of war. The legislation allowed the government to decide who could enter and be deported as well as allowing restrictions on where they lived and travelled. After World War I this legislation was not fully repealed but rather was subject to new and amended legislation. The Aliens Order 1920 allowed immigration officials to refuse entry to an alien who was considered unable to support him- or herself, and granted wider powers to deal with those aliens who evaded immigration control. It was within this paradigm that Britain responded to the plight of the growing numbers of Jewish refugees who fled Nazi Germany in the 1930s. The government justified its restrictive approach to the entry of refugees from fascism by asserting that Britain's large population and high unemployment made it an unsuitable host country (Sherman, 1973: 259). Commentators have attributed the failure to act decisively to help Jewish refugees during this period to widespread anti-Semitism in British society (Kushner, 1994). It is also worth noting that anti-Semitism continues to be a phenomenon in Britain and in the EU context.[15]

A knowledge of the response to Jewish immigration is particularly important in understanding contemporary attitudes towards race relations law and policy. The fact of increasing Jewish immigration, with the resulting political resistance, introduced race into politics. It also ushered in what was to become an ongoing and symbiotic relationship between calls for immigration and race relations. Irish and Jewish immigration focused on cultural and religious differences. The British state's and the popular response to the mid-1950s immigration of large numbers of Afro-Caribbean and Asian workers from the former colonies built on these historical attitudes, and also introduced a new set of challenges. These new immigrants were not white. The models of assimilation that could be applied to Irish and Jewish migrants were not appropriate to take into account differences based on colour. These new immigrants were clearly distinguishable from the majority population because of their colour which could be used as the basis for ongoing differences in treatment.

Commonwealth citizens

During the 1950s, immigration of ethnic minorities was that of British Commonwealth citizens. As stated earlier, there was a well-established link between these 'new' migrants and the UK. They were workers (and their descendants) in India, Africa and the Caribbean – territories that had been colonized by the British. These historic links gave these individuals a right to entry to the UK by virtue of common membership of the British commonwealth. The post-war British economy's need for labour provided the demand which attracted them to Britain. Earlier patterns of Jewish immigration had led to a political reaction in the form of calls for immigration controls. This pattern of a link between immigration and race relations was repeated in the 1950s as a response to immigration from the commonwealth. The principles that underlie the early state response to post-World War II immigration laid the foundations for subsequent race relations policy.

What remained more obscure within this analysis was the process through which these individuals who were formerly 'over there' as colonial subjects were suddenly transformed into British citizens who were 'over here'. One explanation for the failure to conduct a public discussion about these issues was that there was an emerging cross-party consensus on the issue of minority integration. Not only the Labour Party but also the Conservatives concluded that there was a need to 'take politics out of race'. The fear of public disorder in cities during the late 1960s, and the expulsion of Enoch Powell from the Conservative Party, ensured that, despite some differences about the appropriate strategy, both political parties were agreed on the need for the peaceful integration of the new citizens into British society. Perhaps one consequence of this depoliticizing of race issues is the lack of a public discourse about the new migrants from the former colonies that goes beyond the language of 'managing race relations and preventing public disorder': a discourse that allows a public discussion about the responsibility of the nation for its colonial past; and about why these migrants are connected with Britain.

The political, social and economic context

During the 1960s there was an increasing recognition of the dis-advantaged social and economic position of the new migrants. Roy Jenkins's speech in 1966 illustrates some of the themes. Commenting on the justified expectations of second- and third-generation immigrants, he said: 'if we allow their expectations to be disappointed we shall both be wasting scarce skills and talents, and building up vast troubles for ourselves in the future. In the next decade this, to my mind, will become the real core of the problem' (Lester and Bindman, 1972: 84).

Linked to the issue of immigration was the political context of race in the 1960s and, especially, the rise of Powellism. In 1968 Enoch Powell made his famous 'Rivers of Blood' speech in which he set out his prediction that the new wave of immigration would be the cause of serious social unrest in Britain. Powell was, not surprisingly, opposed to the extension of race relations legislation via the Race Relations Act 1968. Significantly, the rise of 'Powellism' provided an incentive to tackle the problems of race relations within the mainstream. One response to Powellism was to 'take race out of politics' by accepting that (a) there was a need to tackle immigration and (b) there should be a stable and orderly integration of migrants. This is in sharp contrast to the treatment of race in the US context, where the Civil Rights Act was introduced after a wide-ranging political struggle that involved alliances between African Americans and other American citizens. Unlike the British focus on 'taking race out of politics', the US civil rights movement was the outcome of a deep-rooted social and political movement.

It is not surprising that employers were opposed to the legal regulation of race discrimination in employment, as envisaged by the Race Relations Act 1968. More surprising is the clear objection of the trade union movement to this legislation. This resistance can be explained, in part, by a suspicion of legal regulation of collective bargaining and a preference for voluntarism. Both sides of industry gradually moved to accept that there might be some role for legislation in this area. Political support for an extension of legislation to employment and housing was also provided by changes on the left. The Labour Party working party on race relations reported to the Annual Conference in 1967 and unanimously voted to extend the 1965 Race Relations Act to the main areas of racial discrimination such as employment and housing. This reflected the increasing interest and research on race issues on the left (Sooben, 1990).

This grassroots support for race relations legislation within the Labour Party was accompanied by effective political leadership. Significantly, Roy Jenkins had made some strong statements in support of a principled approach to race relations and the need for equality of opportunity. Lester and Bindman summarize this contribution in the following terms:

> the brief period in which Roy Jenkins was Home Secretary was of decisive importance. Unlike many of his political contemporaries, he was sensitive to the pressing international imperatives of the second half of this century, which have made equality of opportunity a requirement for a civilized modern society. Jenkins's personal qualities of skilful and determined leadership have often been stressed by commentators on these events; but what mattered was his awareness of the need to achieve racial equality. What was crucial was Roy Jenkins's perception, as a liberal, reforming Home Secretary, that in the moral and political climate of the twentieth century, no civilized society could permit the growth of racial injustice. (Lester and Bindman, 1972: 149)

Race and immigration

Legislative action on immigration and race relations followed on from these debates in the 1950s and 1960s. What is particularly striking about the legislative activity around issues of race is that it is accompanied by legislative action on immigration. The three key statutes on race discrimination were the Race Relations Act 1965, the Race Relations Act 1968 and the Race Relations Act 1976. At each stage the political and legal debate about the legal regulation of race relations was accompanied by a debate and legislation on immigration to control the entry of people (mainly aimed at those from the former colonies/the commonwealth) into Britain: the Commonwealth Immigration Act 1962, the Commonwealth Immigration Act 1968, and the Immigration Act 1971. Together this legislation reversed the previous definition of British subjects as including those who were colonial subjects in the former colonies. This legislation was justified as necessary to achieve good race relations.

The connection between the regulation of migration and issues of race has been mentioned in the context of Jewish immigration. The connection of immigration to race relations continued and became more intense in the context of post-war migration from the former Commonwealth. The government's White Paper on *Immigration from the Commonwealth* in 1965 gave official recognition to the need for controlled immigration policy on the one hand and the problems of the integration and community cohesion issues of migrants already lawfully resident in Britain.[16] Immigration also played a critical role in the period just before the introduction of the Race Relations Act 1968. In 1967 an increasing number of UK citizens of Asian origin were leaving Kenya as a result of Kenyan 'Africanization' programmes. The Commonwealth Immigrants Bill 1968 was introduced, which restricted the right to UK citizenship. The Kenyan Asian 'crisis' and the resulting immigration legislation which severely restricted the citizenship rights of mainly ethnic minority British nationals was at the forefront of discussions just as the Race Relations Act 1968 was being prepared as a bill for discussion.

Understanding the link between race relations and immigration remains important because of contemporary discussions about asylum. The White Paper on *Racial Discrimination* that preceded the Race Relations Act 1976 recognized that immigration was a key issue in good race relations. One example of this link is the speech made by Roy Hattersley in a debate on immigration in March 1976 where, after recalling his earlier opposition to the immigration control, he said

> the Labour Party of that time should have supported it ... I now believe that there are social as well as economic arguments [for limiting Commonwealth immigration], and I believe that unrestricted immigration can only produce additional problems, additional suffering and additional hardship unless some kind of limitation is imposed and continued. (Lester and Bindman, 1972: 120)

Despite the intimate connection between race and immigration in the lead-up to the Race Relations Act 1976 there was an increasing awareness amongst activists and progressives that race was an independent sphere of policy: that is, racial equality (like gender equality) was part of a 'principled' response of a modern liberal state rather than an aspect of immigration controls (Bleich, 2003: 91). Nevertheless, debates about immigration continued to be a strong factor in the context of race relations law reform. The argument was that the fewer the number of immigrants the easier the task of integration. These debates in the 1960s were also taking place against a backdrop of the civil rights movement in the USA and an awareness that social problems relating to immigration could give rise to 'racial tension' and violence on the American model (Solomos, 1989). The US experience also influenced a number of progressive campaigners such as Geoffrey Bindman and Anthony Lester, as well as Roy Jenkins, who provided political leadership on race issues throughout the 1960s and early 1970s. These 'progressives' represented certain sections of policymaking and increasing numbers of campaigners within all the parties. However the Labour Party, and especially Roy Jenkins, continued to be concerned with race relations as an important liberal principle that should guide policy in this area.

Race and the emerging anti-discrimination law

The main legislation that emerged from these discussions was the Race Relations Act 1976, which became the focus for minority integration. The Act was modelled on a version of equality based on treating 'like with like', which arose out of the US Civil Rights Movement's challenging of racial segregation and call for the elimination of difference. Therefore this model was predominantly focused on ideas of assimilation and liberal tolerance rather than the accommodation of group difference that we associate with progressive multiculturalism. However, the Race Relations Acts of 1965 and 1968 were significant because they paved the way for this model of anti-discrimination law in important respects. They set up special bodies (e.g. the Race Relations Board under the 1965 Act and the Community Relations Board under the 1968 Act) to deal with the problems faced by immigrants (mainly concerned with housing and social welfare). They also had the function of educating the general public about the wider issues of 'race relations', which can be seen as part of a general strategy to avoid the confrontation between racial groups that characterized the US experience with the Civil Rights Movement. These developments are significant because they mark the start of the use of specialized administrative bodies rather than government departments to deal with race relations.

A historical study of the period that immediately preceded the Race Relations Act 1976 remains important for understanding the legislation. It is worth identifying a number of recurring themes that had an influence on the 1976 Act, although it is also worth emphasizing the impossibility of concluding whether these factors were a significant cause. Rather than seeking to identify cause and effect with precision, this section sets out the background and some of the recurring themes that influenced the Race Relations Act 1976. Some of these aspects can be identified as a causal factor (e.g. the increasing evidence of actual discrimination against minorities, such as the PEP Report) whilst other aspects are relevant as an important influence on the form and context of the legislation (e.g. the comparison with US legislation in the late 1960s).

The move away from criminal law regulation between the 1965 and 1968 Race Relations Acts, which eventually culminated in the preference for a civil law paradigm for the Act of 1976, is significant. The 1965 Act had placed great emphasis on race discrimination in the public sphere, where it could become a catalyst for more serious public order problems. Hence, priority was given to the introduction of a criminal offence of incitement to racial hatred, which continued throughout the reforms of race relations legislation and which is now included in British public order legislation.[17] Sir Frank Soskice emphasized this point in the second reading of the RRA 1965 when he stated that the Bill was 'concerned with public order. Overt acts of discrimination in public places, intensely wounding to the feelings of those against whom these acts are practised, perhaps in the presence of many onlookers, breed the ill will which, as the accumulative result of several such actions over a period, may disturb the peace' (Lester and Bindman, 1972: 114). This was a classic enunciation of the use of the criminal law to preserve the peace and justified the legal regulation of race discrimination as part of this overall strategy.

The period between 1965 and 1968 saw developments that complicated this initial justification for race relations legislation. Was there, as a matter of empirical fact, discrimination against these new migrants that justified legal regulation? During this period it increasingly became clear that the answer to this question was clearly 'yes'. First, increasing research confirmed high levels of discrimination in areas such as employment, housing and education. The most comprehensive treatment of the extent of actual discrimination in

Britain in the period preceding the 1976 Act was carried out in the report of an independent research organization called Political and Economic Planning (PEP), which published its report in 1967 (see Daniel, 1968).

The PEP Report was based on interviews with white and non-white immigrants and these were compared with a series of 'situation tests' carried out in six towns. In these tests a number of people of different races applied for the same positions in employment, housing and commercial services. The different individuals were: a black West Indian applicant; a white immigrant of Hungarian origin; and a white Englishman. In each test the three applicants claimed equivalent occupational qualifications or housing requirements. The PEP Report confirmed that 'the groups who were most physically distinct in colour and racial features from English experienced the greatest discrimination … The Report illustrated how the processes of racial discrimination tended to push or keep immigrants in poorer housing and lower status jobs, reinforcing the stereotypes and preventing integration' (Lester and Bindman, 1972: 83). Moreover, the Report confirmed the fact that racial discrimination would, if left unregulated, be a growing rather than a stable problem. If discrimination was linked to colour then the passage of time and the transformation of certain migrant communities into an indigenous population would not solve the problems associated with racial discrimination. The PEP Report also suggested that one of the causes of discrimination was the perception that others (e.g. white customers) would react badly to employees of other racial groups. Thus, part of the analysis suggested that people practised discrimination against their own better judgement or wishes.

This analysis represented a shift from the main paradigm for the Race Relations Act 1965 which had focused on issues of racism in the public sphere as a threat to public order and emphasized a criminal law remedy for incitement to racial hatred. In the words of Bindman and Lester, the argument in the 1965–68 period increasingly acknowledged that one of the causes of discrimination was prejudice by proxy rather than personal bigotry. Criminal law regulation of the most pernicious forms of racism in public, for example by criminalizing incitement to racial hatred, would not eliminate this source of race discrimination. This issue, of the ongoing problem of discrimination that would face second- and third-generation immigrants, became increasingly important in the pre-1976 period, as reflected in the White Paper that preceded the Race Relations Act 1976.

The US Civil Rights Movement and Britain's anti-discrimination law

Throughout the 1960s the political conflict and violence accompanying the Civil Rights Movement was the backdrop for a discussion of race and immigration in Britain. Moreover, US models of anti-discrimination law had a more direct influence on the form and content of British anti-discrimination law. The US experience had a number of very specific influences on the Race Relations Act 1976. Roy Jenkins's visit to the USA in 1974, as well as the influence of US law on policy advisers such as Geoffrey Bindman and Anthony Lester, had a critical influence on the legal framework of the 1976 Act. First, the development of a more extensive definition of discrimination as including 'indirect' discrimination, as developed by the US Supreme Court in *Griggs* v. *Duke Power Co.*, was explicitly imported from the USA. Second, this shift away from formal equality towards a more sophisticated understanding of equality and discrimination paved the way for overcoming initial resistance towards endorsement of the earliest examples of positive action in British anti-discrimination law (Sooben, 1990: 38–9). Roy Jenkins summed up his new attitude on positive action measures in the Sex Discrimination Act in the following terms: 'I believe that we should not be so blindly loyal to the principle of formal equality as to ignore the actual and practical inequalities between the sexes, still less to prohibit positive action to help men and women to compete on genuinely equal terms and to overcome an undesirable historical link.'[18] The choice of the civil model rather than the criminal law paradigm by the Street Committee was based on the Ives Quinn Act, first introduced in New York in 1945, which had introduced the idea of a special administrative machinery to deal with problems of discrimination. The subsequent prevalence of the idea of anti-discrimination commissions in the form of the Race Relations Board and subsequently the Equal Opportunities Commission and the Commission for Racial Equality were also modelled on US-type administrative bodies.

What is less clear from discussions during this period is an appreciation of the limits of the comparison with the USA and the importing of anti-discrimination law concepts from another jurisdiction. There were, and are, important disanalogies between the US experience and the British situation. For example, in the USA a long history of slavery and racial segregation, as well as a political context that made the demand for inclusion and an end to segregation the main focus, ensured the symmetrical nature of the Civil Rights Act 1964: that is, non-discrimination was defined in a symmetrical way; both blacks and whites, men and women, could rely on the legislation in exactly the same terms. There was no recognition that anti-discrimination law can play a role in allowing minorities to advance their goals whilst at the same time recognizing important differences (whether of different economic positions or different cultural claims) between them.

The White Paper on Racial Discrimination

There are a number of predominant themes in the White Paper on *Racial Discrimination* that need to be explored as the essential background to the introduction of the Race Relations Act 1976, and to an understanding of British anti-discrimination law in this area.[19] It is worth examining the precise language of the White Paper, which reveals the state of mind and intentions of politicians and policymakers and their ambitions for the 1976 Act. First, within the first few paragraphs of the document the relationship between domestic race relations legislation and immigration is given priority (para. 3). The document goes on to highlight the importance of understanding that there was a need for a long-term strategy to deal with the 'inter-locking problems of immigration, cultural difference, racial disadvantage and discrimination' (para. 22) and that 'legislation is the essential pre-condition for an effective policy to combat the problems experienced by the coloured minority groups and to promote equality of opportunity and treatment. It is a necessary precondition for dealing with explicit discriminatory actions or accumulated disadvantages' (para. 23). Despite giving priority to legal regulation, the

White Paper also acknowledges the importance of non-legal responses to the problem of racial discrimination:

> Legislation is capable of dealing not only with discriminatory acts but with patterns of discrimination, particularly with patterns which, because of the effects of past discrimination, may not any longer involve explicit acts of discrimination. Legislation, however, is not, and can never be, a sufficient condition for effective progress towards equality of opportunity. A wide range of administrative and voluntary measures are needed to give practical effect to the objectives of the law. (para. 25)

The use of legislation to regulate discrimination was intended to be supplemented by policies that were intended to include supply-side investment to overcome the problem of racial disadvantage:

> The Government recognizes that what is here proposed for a further attack on discrimination will need to be supplemented by a more comprehensive strategy for dealing with the related and at least equally important problem of disadvantage. Such a strategy has major public expenditure implications, including a reassessment of priorities within existing programmes. (para. 6)

The ambitions of the White Paper to use both legal regulation and investment to deal with racial discrimination and wider disadvantage were, however, thwarted by the economic and political conditions which immediately followed the introduction of the 1976 Act and which set serious financial constraints on the ability of central and local government to undertake a wide-ranging investment programme to supplement the 1976 legislation (Sooben, 1990: 56).

The emergence of multiculturalism

There are ways in which earlier British policies towards minorities were 'multicultural'. For example, there had been exceptions granted to Jews to allow them to work on Sundays as compensation for the fact that they could not work on the Sabbath; and they were in some instances allowed to adjudicate private disputes through recourse to religious law and religious courts. Moreover, the model of race relations, along with the Race Relations Act that was developed and advocated by politicians such as Roy Jenkins, was explicitly justified as favouring integration rather than assimilation. The Race Relations Act 1976 was very much a symmetrical model of anti-discrimination law that had little space for the accommodation of difference. As stated, the US experience has had a significant influence on contemporary British anti-discrimination law. In the area of race discrimination, the use of the British model as a paradigm in the Race Equality Directive has ensured that this influence now extends to EU member states. The general approach of that model yields a number of features that are reflected in the law: a focus on symmetrical protection for both majorities and minorities; the importance of comparison in establishing discrimination; the choice of a civil law model that uses private law to promote a goal associated with human rights and constitutional rights; and the use of individual remedies supplemented by administrative support to enforce these rights. Nevertheless, the 1976 Act included provisions that allowed positive action for ethnic minorities in areas such as training.

One predominant context within which the term 'multiculturalism' emerged, and was applied, was in the context of the education of children from ethnic minorities. As Modood and May (2001) illustrate, the debates and policies concerning the need for multiculturalism in education emerged in the 1970s and 1980s. These were given partial institutional support by the findings of the Swann Report, *Education for All*, in 1985, which advocated a modest form of multiculturalism.

It is also noteworthy that the issue of public order and immigration are a constant theme not only in the run-up to the introduction of the 1976 Act but also in the subsequent race relations legislation. As we saw in the chapter in positive action, the other substantial race discrimination statute in Britain was also introduced in response to an event: the introduction of the Race Relations Amendment Act 2000 was a response to the murder of a black teenager, Stephen Lawrence. The McPherson Inquiry, which subsequently implicated the police and their procedures in the failure to prosecute for this murder, provided the impetus for regulating institutional racism in Britain. The most recent positioning of the government response to the issue of racial equality uses the paradigm of 'community cohesion' that has developed out of the analysis of the riots in northern British cities in spring and early summer 2001 (Home Office, 2001). This suggests a reactive approach to race relations legislation as a response to public order and outside influences rather than a more principled approach that treats issues of racial equality as an important part of the framework of rights for individuals in a liberal democracy. However, as stated earlier, it is also possible to trace other aspects of the 2000 Act. Although the immediate political context for its introduction was the murder of Stephen Lawrence, it is also possible to read this as a significant development for the accommodation of multiculturalism within the British model of minority integration. The introduction of a general and specific duty on all public authorities to promote racial equality and good race relations can be seen as a legal means to ensure the public accommodation of racial minorities, similar to the requirements of multiculturalism as defined by writers such as Modood (see the first section of this chapter). Moreover, the duties of consultation and monitoring that are included in the legal structure of the 2000 Act can be seen to be part of the public recognition of minorities. Public-sector duties to promote equality on the grounds of gender and disability have now been introduced by the Equality Act 2006. The significant gap that remains involves religion and sexual orientation, but this will be filled by the Equality Act 2010. The coverage for religion is significant in the British context because the anomaly of the *Mandla* v. *Dowell Lee*, definition which protects ethnic religious minorities (such as Jews and Sikhs) but leaves unprotected non-ethnic religious minorities (such as Rastafarians and Muslims), means that there is an unequal public accommodation of the needs of minorities.

The Equality Act 2006 continues this focus on social exclusion and includes powers for the newly formed Equality and Human Rights Commission (EHRC) to promote good relations between different groups, which are an echo of the recurring argument that the treatment of ethnic minorities requires the managing of good 'race relations' between groups rather than a focus on individual rights of citizens. However, the ECHR also links the issue of race relations with those of human rights and socio-economic factors such as social exclusion. There is, therefore, an opportunity for the EHRC to develop a more cohesive and principled approach. The EHRC will bring together the existing Commission for Racial Equality, the Equal Opportunities Commission and the Disability Rights Commission into a single equalities body. This reform should assist in the aim of tackling social exclusion and multiple discrimination in a more coherent and effective way. The EHRC has a number of important powers that go beyond the traditional regulatory format of anti-discrimination law. These include the powers of investigation and support for individual litigation, which are vested in the single commissions such as the Equal Opportunities Commission and the Commission for Racial Equality (see Equality Act 2006, ss. 20–32). Significantly, these powers also contain, inter alia: the power to issue an unlawful act notice (s. 20); the power to demand the production of an action plan within a time limit, which is backed up by the ability of the EHRC to go to the County Court to demand compliance (s. 22); the power to apply to court for an injunction to prevent an unlawful act (s. 24); and an important role in the enforcement of the public duties to promote equality (ss. 31–32). In addition to dealing with discrimination on grounds such as sex, race and sexual orientation, the EHRC also has a role in providing legal assistance (s. 28); and the power to intervene in judicial review proceedings in relevant cases that fall within its area of jurisdiction (s. 30). The other novel feature of the EHRC is that it brings together the different strands of anti-discrimination law in Britain into one body; that is, it has a mandate to deal with the civil, some criminal and the human–rights aspects of equality legislation and policy. For example, as well as its pivotal role as the enforcement agency for anti-discrimination law, it has a function in promoting a better understanding of human rights (s. 9) and also a function to promote good relations between different groups and prevent hatred and prejudice between groups (s. 10). The next stage in the development of British anti-discrimination law will be to relate the institutional framework to the new Equality Act 2010.[20] In Britain, the EHRC creates a greater convergence between the various administrative bodies which tackle discrimination, and it should ensure the harmonization of the different forms of law (civil, criminal and human rights) that provide the source of British anti-discrimination law into one enforcement agency. It also has a role to play in developing a more proactive (preventative) rather than reactive (deterrent) strategy for addressing the causes of discrimination and disadvantage. This should enable a more unified approach, using legal and non-legal means, to address the increasingly complex and multiple causes of discrimination, inequality and social exclusion. It is still not clear how the EHRC will respond to the debates about multiculturalism despite some recent statements by the newly appointed chair, who has voiced concerns (since the 7 July bombings) about the dangers of self-segregation.[21] These have been challenged by leading academics who conclude that British minorities are not self-segregating on any of the significant indicators (Simpson, 2004: 679).

Post-7 July: the movement away from multiculturalism

There has, as stated in the first section, always been a critique of multiculturalism. This critique, however, has been aimed predominantly at 'hard' versions of multiculturalism, which almost none of the advocates of the concept in this book advocates. It often focuses on the argument that multiculturalism is, inter alia, a relativist doctrine that decrees that no culture is inferior or superior to another; it is anti-West and the Enlightenment; it requires the one-way imposition of the culture of minorities on the majority. Finally, critics of multiculturalism argue that it supports barbaric and oppressive practices that oppress women and gays.[22] These myths and criticisms are in fact a reaction to a model that very few advocates of multiculturalism support, involving the imposition of minority cultural values. Such 'hard' multiculturalism is far removed from the models of plural accommodation which are advocated by most sophisticated advocates (Modood, 2007). Progressive multiculturalism, unlike 'hard versions', is able to answer these charges.

These myths about 'British multiculturalism' need to be distinguished from 'progressive multiculturalism' as a normative model for the integration of minorities. Such popular myths also need to be carefully distinguished from an assessment of 'British multiculturalism' in practice. Distinguishing myths from reality has been made more difficult since the 7 July 2005 London bombings. The post-7 July critique of British multiculturalism – and claims that it is a failed model – have taken a different form. Since the 7 July bombs the rhetoric of migrants becoming segregated and weakening the political community has been a recurring feature of the contemporary critique of British multiculturalism. In the popular debate, the British model of 'multiculturalism' was one of the main 'causes' for British-born young men of Pakistani Muslim origin carrying out suicide attacks in the heart of London. Significantly, this critique of multiculturalism came not only from the right but also from the progressive left.[23] This crude reductionism was encouraged by politicians and those responsible for race relations, who, despite academic evidence to the contrary, insisted that Britain was 'sleepwalking to segregation' (Phillips, 2005). After the 7 July bombings, it was argued that the Muslim community needed to do more to 'integrate' into Britain, and a new body there was launched to encourage 'integration'.[24] Also issues such as full facial veiling (the niqab) were becoming a focus for the construction of visible Muslim women as 'separate' (Parris, 2005). These recurring fears about segregation and separation reached a climax during the period October–December 2006, when there was widespread criticism by leading ministers of state, journalists and public figures of the practice of full facial veiling by a small number of Muslim women.[25] In many cases, this critique of a different religious practice by a small minority of British women was justified as a defence of 'secularism' and 'Enlightenment values' in ways similar to the French 'headscarf debate'.[26]

These popular rhetorical assessments of multiculturalism causing segregation and separation are not backed up by leading academic researchers in the field, who often reach the opposite conclusion after sustained research and analysis. A recent report into the issue by Dr Ludi Simpson of the University of Manchester confirmed the trend towards integration. It also confirmed the importance of poverty, access to housing and education, rather than geography, as key contributors to social exclusion:

> The researchers compared data from the 1991 and 2001 censuses, and analysed the change in different ethnic groups in 8,850 electoral

wards in England and Wales. It found that the number of mixed
neighbourhoods or wards – where at least 10 per cent are from an
ethnic minority – increased from 964 to 1,070 in the decade, and
predicts that by 2010 the number will rise to 1,300. The author
of the study, Ludi Simpson, said: 'The common myth is that the
growth of the ethnic minority population is due to immigration.
That's not true – it is more due to the growth of [ethnic minority]
people born in Britain.

Simpson said: 'Segregation does not cause social exclusion.' There
were 118 neighbourhoods where all non-white groups together were
greater than half, and he found there was no ward where white people
were less than 10 per cent of the population. 'The idea of no-go areas
or apartheid does not stand up', he said. Simpson said his study suggests factors such as poverty have to be taken into account more than
racial tension. In short, where people live is not as big a factor as some
people are claiming. 'The research shows that geography is not the
issue', Simpson said. 'Social conditions on the ground such as poverty
and equal access to housing and the jobs markets for all groups are
more important factors' (Simpson in Dodd, 2005; see also Simpson,
2004: 679).

It is also sometimes argued that multiculturalism has been the
'cause' of the radicalization of Muslims at the level of 'values', which
was considered a factor in the bombings of 7 July. This was the argument in a report by the think-tank Policy Exchange entitled *Living
Apart Together*, which concluded that young British people were
increasingly becoming radicalized, developing values different from
the rest of British society, and laid part of the blame for this alleged
separation on policies of multiculturalism. However, these conclusions were challenged by leading academic researchers in the field
of radicalization, Dr Marie Breen Smyth and Dr Joeren Gunning,
who argued that Policy Exchange's report was an 'abuse of research'.
They concluded that

A closer scrutiny, however, suggests the report cannot be regarded
as a reliable guide to formulating policy. Its findings are at odds with
much other research, which would not be a problem if the writers engaged with the body of scholarship in this field. But without
such an engagement, their validity remains dubious. This is further

undermined by dealing collectively with 'Muslim attitudes' without any recognition of diversity among British Muslims. This is not only unhelpful analytically, but also runs the risk of replicating stereotypes. The report implies that multiculturalism is responsible for exacerbating differences between Muslims and the rest of the population without any evidence to justify these claims. Reports such as *Living Apart Together* in fact contribute to problems of 'living together' by constructing a homogeneous category of British Muslims on the basis of certain alleged differences between 'them' and other Britons. (Breen Smyth and Gunning, 2007)

The net effect of this representation of Muslims as segregated in terms of geography and values from the rest of British society, combined with anti-terror law and policy aimed at Muslims, is to reinforce the idea that British Muslims are 'different'. The most recent and comprehensive empirical study confirms that Muslims are the social group at the greatest risk of prejudice, discrimination and hatred.[27] This suggests that British Muslims are likely to be constructed as a 'suspect community' through similar social processes and in ways that are reminiscent of the treatment of Irish Catholics when there was a risk of political violence by the IRA (Hillyard, 1993). One of the most significant challenges that is faced by the British model of minority integration is whether it has the resources to intervene in this process that is bringing together cultural racism, social-economic exclusion and the discourse about terrorism to construct British Muslims in opposition to, and sometimes as a threat to, the British nation.

Despite the conclusion of leading security and intelligence agencies that foreign policy has been an important factor in the radicalization of some British Muslims, the government has been unwilling to debate this link publicly. One consequence of this refusal has been to exaggerate the possible role of 'cultural and religious difference' as a cause of the 7 July bombings. One further consequence is that what are essentially religious differences between British Muslims and other Britons (such as the wearing of the niqab) have been converted into entrenched ideological differences – a clash of civilizations – that are beyond political debate and negotiation (Modood, 2007: 128). This is the exact opposite of the model of modest secularism, and the negotiated accommodation of group difference, that is required by progressive multiculturalism. The current public debate in Britain is

poised between those critics of multiculturalism who place the blame
for events such as 7 July on the shoulders of British multiculturalism
and those who advocate policies of multiculturalism and pluralism
as an essential response to the new challenges posed by Muslims
in Britain. Although leading politicians and public figures are now
leading the field as critics of multiculturalism and reviving the debate
about 'Britishness' as a bulwark against security risks, it is significant
that two of the leading thinkers in this field have unequivocally
suggested that the appropriate state response to the new security
risks from extremism is more not less multiculturalism and its liberal
pluralist variants. Modood concludes that:

> Ideological and violent extremism is indeed undermining the condi-
> tions and hopes for multiculturalism but, contrary to the multi-
> culturalism blamers, this extremism has nothing to do with the
> promotion of multiculturalism but is coming into the domestic arena
> from the international. The government having created extremism
> through its foreign policies, by blaming multiculturalism and the
> Muslims community for the crisis, is losing one sure resource that is
> necessary for a long-term victory over domestic terrorism: namely,
> the full active 'on-side co-operation' of the Muslim communities.
> (Modood, 2007: 139)

On the issue of replacing diversity with a more homogenous public
culture John Gray also concludes:

> The attempt to create a liberal monoculture, which many commen-
> tators have urged, founders on the fact of diversity. The fantasy of
> a morally cohesive society has inspired some of the worst types of
> repression. It is ironic that a panicky reaction against the idea of
> multiculturalism should have engendered a liberal variant of this
> dream. The reality is that we cannot hope to share many of our
> fundamental values. But we can still rub along together, if we can
> relearn the habit of tolerance. (Gray, 2007)

Conclusion

Any evaluation of the British model of multiculturalism after the
London bombings of 7 July 2005 has to contend with the myths
that now dominate the public sphere. It is impossible to confirm the

'start date' or delineate with precision the exact phases of British multiculturalism. Nevertheless, it is possible to observe that there has always been cultural, linguistic, ethnic and religious diversity in Britain. The official public accommodation of this diversity within the definition of the nation has depended on different forces: the social and political power of the group that is seeking accommodation; the relationship between the domestic and the international context; access to socio-economic wealth.

Cambridge historian Quentin Skinner recently summarized this relationship between history, power and exclusion by concluding:

> It stems from the fact that all communities tell stories about them-
> selves, about the distinctive nature of their formation and achieve-
> ments. These stories can have a powerful role in constituting our
> identities, and so in defining and sustaining our common life. But
> they are also subject to endless manipulation, for it will always be
> in the interests of the powerful – rulers and opinion-formers alike
> – that certain stories should be remembered, and in certain ways,
> and that other stories should be forgotten. That being so, it is I
> think part of the moral importance of historical study that historians
> should be ready to engage with these stories and take a critical stance
> towards them. The role, you might say, is that of bearing witness,
> ensuring that the stories which define and sustain us are as little as
> possible imposed upon us in such a way that particular groups or
> ideals are misleadingly praised, or misleadingly blamed, or unjustly
> omitted from the record altogether. (Skinner, 2005)

Debates about the appropriate place of cultural minorities in Britain, therefore, are best understood as part of an ongoing process whereby not only minorities but also majorities are integrated into national life. Debates about 'multiculturalism' are at the heart of more profound national questions about what it means to be 'British'.

Notes

1. See, for example, Joan W. Scott's use of the phrase 'symptomatic politics' in relation to the French headscarves controversy (Scott, 2005: 106).
2. For an overview of these demographic and social changes in the context of Islam and Muslims see Fetzer and Soper, 2005: ch. 1. For Britain, see Choudhry, 2005. For France, see Laurence and Vaisse, 2006. For an overview

of the French approach to these social changes see Amiraux and Simon, 2006: 191–215.

3. For a critique of definitions of liberal 'instrumental' definitions of community see Sandel, 1982: ch. 4.

4. For a critique of traditional liberal responses to cultural diversity, see Kymlicka, 1989. For different perspectives and critiques of Kymlicka see the essays in Kymlicka, 1995b. For a discussion about an alternative formulation of liberal politics that is more hospitable to 'cultural diversity' see Kymlicka, 1995a.

5. See Bhikhu Parekh's discussion (2006: 38–49) of John Locke's and J.S. Mill's treatment of cultural diversity, especially in relation to colonial peoples. Parekh calls this the 'moral monism' of the classical liberal tradition.

6. John Rawls (1993) categorizes the issue in terms of concepts of the 'good' and calls it 'reasonable pluralism'.

7. For a detailed discussion of these issues see the debate between different types of feminist theorists in Nicholson, 1995; Irigaray, 1993; Butler and Scott, 1992.

8. See, for example, Raz, 1988, who includes community within his account of what constitutes an autonomous life.

9. For a discussion of the differences between Charles Taylor and John Gray, and a summary of their responses to cultural diversity, see Curtis, 2007.

10. For a detailed discussion of 'multiculturalism vulnerability' see Shachar, 2001.

11. For a general discussion of cultural racism and see Modood, 2005a: ch. 1; the Balibar quotation is on pp. 27–8.

12. See Raz's discussion of reconciling autonomy and authority in a liberal state. Raz, 1994: ch. 15.

13. For an overview see Poulter, 1998: 3–4.

14. See the summary of the common features of anti-Semitism and anti-Muslim prejudice in Malik, 2007a.

15. See Runnymede Trust, 1997; and EUMC, 2003, which was the largest ever study of anti-Semitism in Europe.

16. *Immigration from the Commonwealth*, White Paper, Cmnd 2739, August 1965, London: HMSO.

17. Public Order Act ,1986.

18. *Hansard*, vol. 889, col. 514, cited in Sooben, 1990: 39.

19. *Racial Discrimination*, White Paper, Cmnd 6234, 1975, London: HMSO.

20. The Equality Act 2010 received Royal Assent in April 2010, and is due to be in force from autumn 2010.

21. Trevor Phillips questions, in the context of a speech concerned with 'a society ... becoming more divided by race and religion', an '"anything goes" multiculturalism ... which leads to deeper division and inequality.... In recent years we've focused far too much on the "multi" and not enough on the common culture' (Phillips 2005, cited in Modood 2005b).

22. For a critique of 'hard multiculturalism' and 'cultural relativism' see West, 2006.

23. See Tariq Modood's summary of the post-7 July critique of British multi-culturalism (Modood, 2005b).
24. Ruth Kelly launched a Commission on Integration and Social Cohesion on 24 August 2006 (see www.communities.gov.uk/speeches/corporate/commission-integration-cohesion).
25. For a discussion of these issues, see the letter of the Right Honourable Jack Straw MP, which raised the issue of full facial veils (Straw, 2006). For media commentary in favour of Jack Straw, see Alibhai Brown, 2006; against Jack Straw, see Bunting, 2006. For a discussion of the international context in which the British facial veil incident arose, see Malik, 2006.
26. See Joan Smith's lecture to the Fawcett Society's Veil Debate on December 2006, at http://fawcettsociety.org.uk/documents/Joan%20Smith%20presentation.pdf.
27. See, for example, the results of the latest survey on prejudice against social groups in contemporary Britain. The survey confirms that the highest levels of prejudice are against (a) Muslims and (b) gays and lesbians (Abrams and Houston, 2006).

References

Abrams, Dominic, and Diane M. Houston (2006) *'Equality, Diversity and Preju-dice in Britain', Report for the Cabinet Office Equalities Review 2006*, Centre for the Study of Group Processes, Canterbury: University of Kent.
Agbetu, T. (2007) 'My protest Was Born of Anger, Not Madness', *Guardian*, 3 April.
Amiraux, Valérie, and Patrick Simon (2006) '"There Are Not Minorities Here": Cultures of Scholarship and Public Debate on Immigrants and Integration in France', *International Journal of Comparative Sociology* 47(3–4): 191–215.
Arnold, Matthew (1883) *On the Study of Celtic Literature and on Translating Homer*, New York: MacMillan.
Benhabib, Seyla (2002) *The Claims of Culture: Equality and Diversity in the Global Era*, Princeton NJ: Princeton University Press.
Bleich, Erik (2003) *Race Politics in Britain and France*, Cambridge: Cambridge University Press.
Breen Smyth, Marie, and Jeroen Gunning (2007) 'The Abuse of Research', *Guardian*, 13 February.
Brown, Yasmin Alibhai (2006) 'It's Not Illiberal for Liberal Societies to Disap-prove of the Veil', *Time Europe Magazine*, 16 October.
Bunting, Madeleine (2006) 'Jack Straw Has Unleashed a Storm of Prejudice and Intensified Division', *Guardian*, 9 October.
Butler, Judith and Joan W. Scott (eds) (1992) *Feminists Theorise the Political*, Routledge: London.
Choudhry, T. (ed.) (2005) *Muslims in the UK: Policies for Engaged Citizens*, New York: Open Society Institute.
Connolly, William (1991) *Identity/Difference: Democratic Negotiations of Political Paradox*, Minneapolis: University of Minnesota Press.

Crick, Bernard (2003) *The New and the Old: The Report of the 'Life in the United Kingdom' Advisory Group*, London: Home Office.

Curtis, William M. (2007) 'Liberals v Pluralists: Charles Taylor v John Gray', *Contemporary Political Theory* 6: 86–107.

Daniel, W.W. (1968) *Racial Discrimination in England*, London: Penguin.

Dodd, Vikram (2005) 'Racial Integration Increasing, Study Shows', *Guardian*, 15 November.

EUMC (2003) *Manifestations of Antisemitism in the EU 2002–2003*, EUMC: Vienna.

Fetzer, Joel S., and J. Christopher Soper (2005) *Muslims and State in Britain, France and Germany*, Cambridge: Cambridge University Press.

Fraser, Nancy, and Axel Honneth (2003) *Redistribution or Recognition: A Political-Philosophical Exchange*, London: Verso.

Fredman, Sandra (2002) *Discrimination Law*, Oxford: Clarendon Press.

Gainer, B. (1972) *The Alien Invasion: The Origins of the Aliens Act 1905*, London: Heinemann.

Garrard, J.A. (1971) *The English and Immigration 1880–1910*, Oxford: Oxford University Press.

Gilroy, Paul (2004) *After Empire: Melancholia or Convivial Culture?*, London: Routledge.

Gray, John (2007) 'Islam Rejects the Liberal Consensus: The Best We Can Hope For Is Tolerance', *Spectator*, 17 February.

Herman, Didi (2006) '"An Unfortunate Coincidence": Jews and Jewishness in 20th Century English Judicial Discourse', *Journal of Law and Society* 33(2): 277–30.

Hillyard, Paddy (1993) *Suspect Communities: People's Experiences of the Prevention of Terrorism Acts in Britain*, Pluto Press: London,

Home Office (2001) *Community Cohesion: A Report of the Independent Review Team Chaired by Ted Cantle*, London: Home Office.

Irigaray, Luce (1993) *An Ethics of Sexual Difference*, London: Continuum.

Kushner, T. (1994) *The Holocaust and the Liberal Imagination: A Social and Cultural History*, Oxford: Blackwell.

Kymlicka, Will (1989) *Liberalism, Community and Culture*, Oxford: Oxford University Press.

Kymlicka, Will (1995a) *Multicultural Citizenship*, Oxford: Oxford University Press.

Kymlicka, Will (1995b) *The Rights of Minority Cultures*, Oxford: Oxford University Press.

Laurence, Jonathan, and Justin Vaisse (2006) *Integrating Islam: Political and Religious Challenges in Contemporary France*, Washington DC: Brookings Institution Press.

Lebzelter, G. (1982) *Political Anti-Semitism in England*, Basingstoke: Macmillan.

Lester, Anthony, and Geoffrey Bindman (1972) *Race and Law*, London: Longman.

Malik, Maleiha (2000) 'Minorities and Human Rights', in T. Campbell et al. (eds), *Sceptical Approaches to Human Rights*, Oxford: Oxford University Press.

Malik, Maleiha (2006) 'This Veil Fixation Is Doing Muslim Women No Favours', *Guardian*, 19 October.

Malik, Maleiha (2007a) 'Muslims Are Now Getting the Same Treatment that Jews Had One Hundred Years Ago: Both Minorities Abused as an Alien Security Threat', *Guardian*, 2 February.

Malik, Maleiha (2007b) 'Engaging with Extremists?', *International Studies*, August.

Mason, Andrew (1999) 'Political Community', *Ethics* 109: 261.

Mattar, N. (1998) *Islam in Britain*, Cambridge: Cambridge University Press.

Miles, R. (1982) *Racism and Migrant Labour*, London: Routledge.

Modood, Tariq (2005a) *Multicultural Politics: Racism, Ethnicity and Muslims in Britain*, Edinburgh: Edinburgh University Press.

Modood, Tariq (2005b) 'Remaking Multiculturalism after 7/7', *openDemocracy*, 28 September, www.opendemocracy.net/conflict-terrorism/multiculturalism_2879.jsp.

Modood, Tariq (2007) *Multiculturalism*, Cambridge: Polity Press.

Modood, Tariq, and Stephen May (2001) 'Multiculturalism and Education in Britain: An Internally Contested Debate', *International Journal of Educational Research* 35: 305–17.

Nicholson, Linda (ed.) (1995) *Feminist Contentions: A Philosophical Exchange*, Routledge: London.

Oakley, J. (1983) *The Traveller-Gypsies*, Cambridge: Cambridge University Press.

Parekh, Bhikhu (2006) *Rethinking Multiculturalism: Cultural Diversity and Political Theory*, London: Palgrave Macmillan.

Parris, Matthew (2005) 'Never Mind What the Woman Thinks, Wearing a Veil is Offensive to Me', *The Times*, 27 August.

Phillips, Trevor (2005) 'After 7/7: Sleepwalking to Segregation', speech delivered at the Manchester Council for Community Relations, 22 September.

Poulter, Sebastian (1998) *Ethnicity, Law and Human Rights: The English Experience*, Oxford: Clarendon Press.

Rawls, John (1993) *Political Liberalism*, New York: Columbia University Press .

Raz, Joseph (1988) *The Morality of Freedom*, Oxford: Clarendon Press.

Raz, Joseph (1994) *Ethics in the Public Domain: Essays in the Morality of Law and Politics* Oxford: Clarendon Press.

Runnymede Trust (1997) *A Very Light Sleeper – The Persistence and Dangers of Antisemitism*, London: Runnymede Trust.

Sandel, Michael (1982) *Liberalism and the Limits of Justice*, Cambridge: Cambridge University Press.

Scott, Joan W. (2005) 'Symptomatic Politics: The Banning of Islamic Headscarves in French Public Schools', *French Politics, Culture and Society* 23(3), Winter: 106.

Sherman, A. (1973) *Island Refuge: Britain and Refugees from the Third Reich*, London: Paul Elek.

Shachar, Ayelet (2001) *Multicultural Jurisdictions: Cultural Differences and Women's Rights*, Cambridge: Cambridge University Press.

Simpson, Ludi (2004) 'Statistics of Racial Segregation: Measures, Evidence and Policy', *Urban Studies* 41(3): 661–81.

Skinner, Quentin (2005) 'The Place of History in Public Life', *History and Policy*, Policy Paper 35, November, www.historyandpolicy.org/archive/policy-paper-35.html.

Solomos, John (1989) *From Equal Opportunity to Anti-Racism: Racial Inequality and the Limits of Reform*, Policy Paper in Ethnic Relations no. 17, Centre for Research in Ethnic Relations, Warwick: University of Warwick.

Solomos, John (2003) *Race and Racism in Britain*, Basingstoke: Palgrave Macmillan.

Sooben, Phillip N. (1990) *The Origins of the Race Relations Act*, Centre for Research in Ethnic Relations, Research Paper no. 12, Warwick.

Straw, Jack (2006) 'I Felt Uneasy Talking to Someone I Could Not See', *Guardian*, 6 October, www.guardian.co.uk/commentisfree/story/0,,1889081,00.html (accessed 20 October 2006).

Taylor, Charles (1992) *Multiculturalism and the Politics of Recognition*, Princeton, NJ: Princeton University Press.

Tully, James (1995) *Strange Multiplicity: Constitutionalism in an Age of Diversity*, Cambridge: Cambridge University Press.

Walzer, Michael (1997) *On Toleration*, London: Yale University Press.

West, Patrick (2006) 'The Poverty of Multiculturalism', London: Institute for the Study of Civil Society.

Wierviorka, Michel (1998) 'Is Multiculturalism the Solution', *Ethnic and Racial Studies* 21(5): 882.

Young, Iris Marion (1990) *Justice and the Politics of Difference*, Princeton NJ: Princeton University Press.

2

Crisis and new challenges?
French republicanism
featuring multiculturalism

Valérie Amiraux

Français encore un effort si vous voulez être républicains!

(Marquis de Sade, 1796)

A rationalist universalism, rooted in the philosophy of the
eighteenth century enlightenment, now looks more and more
like a form of European ethnocentrism, and thus like a form of
domination rather than liberation. (Jennings, 2000: 579)

The dominant representation the French have of the historical trajectory of republicanism as a pillar of national identity and core of the
political ethos of the nation can best be summed up as exceptionalism.
Exceptionalism underlies what led revolutionary France to become 'an
indivisible, secular, democratic and social Republic. It shall ensure the
equality of all citizens before the law, without distinction of origin,
race or religion. It shall respect all beliefs. It shall be organized on a
decentralized basis', as stated in Article 1 of the 1958 Constitution. It
is also to be found in the four elements, inherited from the French
Revolution, that structure the republican project: the unmediated
relationship between the citizen and the state (equality through
belonging to a national political community); secular public education;
the belief in France's international mission; and a strong activist
state (Cole et al., 2008: 2). These elements actively contribute to the
conviction that how France produces the conditions of equality among

different citizens is exceptional. This chapter proposes to elaborate on the main elements of this representation of French exceptionalism in dealing with diversity (section one) and to discuss the contemporary challenges embodied in recent episodes or public discussions that have opened up new avenues for thinking about the republican ability to govern ethnic and cultural pluralism (section two).

I share with Walzer the idea of contemporary France as a paradox rather than an exception, a 'complicated case' in the matter of politics of difference, as it is a country of migration that does not think of itself as a pluralistic society (Walzer, 1997). The current context can probably best be defined by underlining the evidence of, first, the growing gap between historical narratives and practices, and second, the conflict between political principles and pragmatic implementation. For the sake of brevity, while society is entangled in concrete and pragmatic problems, the elites (political, intellectual, administrative) still promote an abstract promise of universalism and equality. This abstraction does not mesh with the expectations of a plural and complex citizenry whose social reality constantly challenges this universal aim and illustrates 'the French impossibility to do what we pretend to do: knowing abstract individuals' (Baubérot, 2003: 28, author's translation).

This volume, providing a European perspective on multiculturalism, adds another level of difficulty to the one already present in the fantasy of exceptionalism: it introduces a term that remains, from the point of view of the philosophy of equality, alien to the French politics of integration and difference, just as ethnicity and minority long were (Amiraux and Simon, 2006). Multiculturalism never became a proper policy in the French context. This claim has to be nuanced, as I will try to do in the second part of the chapter, through examination of specific initiatives where, for example, ethnicity was introduced into social policies through proxies. What is meant here is that it never became an actual policy leading to the institutional recognition of differences and the pluralism of identities in French society. Jennings (2000: 589) puts it nicely by saying that multiculturalism is un-French, because it places culture before politics and groups before individuals. However, discussing multiculturalism in the French context, as I do in this chapter, means discussing the link between access to, and practice of, citizenship and the claim for expression of differences.

Citizenship hereby refers both to a political project and to institutional and individual practices, the gap growing between the historical legacy of republican ideology, its principles as the main horizon for political action, and the daily interaction between citizens. The meaning of the politics of difference in the French conception refers to a never-ending polemical discussion about the fundamental denial of public recognition of racial, ethnic and religious distinctions in the public space. The current situation very much bears the direct legacy of the Third Republic project, when the school system or other institutions such as the army were charged with fostering social cohesion by offering individuals equal access to national culture. The role of these institutions failed to adapt to new societies. Evoking recent history, Weil speaks of the constant French oscillation between refusing and accepting cultural differences to describe the constant tension between central and occasionally contradictory principles such as equality or neutrality, and of the difficulty in putting these principles into practice (Weil, 2005). Is the French Republic compatible with multiculturalism? What does 'politics of difference' mean when applied to the French context? These questions structure my discussion of multiculturalism.

Globally, since the French Revolution, the republican narrative has become the dominant and exclusive paradigm framing the migrant's path to integration and citizenship. Beyond stereotypes and schematic representations that equate France with a united Republic whose citizens are abstract and 'culturally neutral', the last decade has seen many opportunities to discuss the adequacy of the French 'philosophy of integration' (Favell, 1998) for contemporary social demands. The comparative reading of what is happening in different contexts, such as provided by this edited volume, seems valid as a means to achieve a better understanding of the singular situation in national contexts. The current situation may be summarized as follows. While in Britain the debate is open regarding the definition of Britishness and the reshaping of multiculturalism as a political and legal project, in France public discussion is whether the republican model has failed or still has a chance of surviving such episodes as the 2004 headscarf controversy, the November 2005 urban riots, the public debate over the collection of ethnic data in autumn 2007. The colonial legacy within the integration policy is another aspect that has, since 2000, been more actively cited as a symptom of the Republic's limited capacity to embrace its own diversity.

Rather than define the present moment as a crisis of the republican model, I would suggest that France is experiencing the reality principle, watching its own idealistic representation undergo field testing. Universalism and colour blindness are the two main features under discussion. Some authors have spoken of 'dramatic changes' taking place around the politics of difference in the French context (Lépinard, 2008: 92). And, notably, one of the major influences on the French way of addressing ethnic diversity and inequality came from the implementation of the European Commission's legal and political anti-discrimination framework (Geddes and Guiraudon 2006; Fassin, 2002). The new set of European norms has affected legal instruments, the political vocabulary and citizens' expectations. The emergence of the notion of 'discrimination', 'affirmative action' and 'ethnicity' is probably the best illustration of the beginning of a possible retreat from this 'exclusive focus on principles'.

I open with a historical assessment of the trajectory of a political project (republicanism) and focus on its articulation with the policies aimed at incorporating migrants (integration, assimilation), which later included anti-discrimination provisions. The second part of the chapter is based on illustrative accounts of the way the 'republican heritage' has been recently challenged in ways that question the limits of the French approach to ethnic and cultural difference.[1]

The historical path to colour-, race- and culture-blind France

Here I provide a historical overview of French republicanism and examine its relation to contemporary challenges affecting its civic and political capacity to deal with diversity in French society. Republicanism is less a doctrine than a cluster of socio-political attitudes, beliefs and values (Hazareesingh, 1994: 99). 'One can hardly understand the forms of the relations to otherness and policies towards foreigners living in France without taking into account French Jacobinism, with its links to a conception of the nation whose origins date back to the Middle Ages, and the fact that the rationalist universalism of the Revolutionaries has strengthened' (Schnapper, 1999: 18, author's translation). French understanding of equality as both culture blind, and colour blind is mostly based on the idea that justice can only be achieved by considering individuals abstracted from what differentiates them from each other; that the separation between public and private is the key to protecting individual rights. The historical dimension of the republican myth had to a large extent gone undiscussed until the recent surge of post-colonial debate. I suggest in this first section that, though deeply challenged by changing societal expectations, the Republic is still 'a regulative ideal of significance in French politics' (Jenkins, 2000: 576).

Exceptionalism as an effect of comparison

In the European Union context, France is still perceived as the archetypal republican model where citizens are considered to be equal political actors independent of any specificities (cultural, ethnic, religious). Equality and freedom are equated with the idea of emancipated citizens who are unaffiliated to any forms of collective-coercive authority or belonging. The core of French republicanism lies in this equation of freedom with non-domination of the individual. This can be traced back to the French Revolution. The French Revolution first defined French citizenship as an institution simultaneously promoting social justice and indifferent towards any type of distinction. The idea of an equality among citizens that remains not only indifferent but to some extent hostile to cultural and racial aspects of identity is thus rooted in the historicization of Enlightment philosophical ideals, revolutionary projects and intra-European conflict. Weil connects the concepts of popular democracy, civic equality and sovereignty with the stabilization of a French conception of citizenship (Weil, 2002; Kriegel, 1998). For instance, the project of categorization of the population by ethnic origin does not fit with the global perspective on national integration that is grounded in the voluntary participation of free men as defined in the Declaration of the Rights of Man and of the Citizen of 1789. Integration within the emerging nation was from the start based on an individual project of equality disconnected from any claim for recognition of rights justified by any kind of distinction.[2] What would later be called a 'privatization of cultural identities' – which extends far beyond secularization[3] – is sustained in the name of a universal and liberal neutrality embodied in the central state. The French historical trajectory is not so far from liberal theory pleading for a political sphere of universalism (the realm of the citizen) free of non-public particularistic identities that attach to individuals through membership of certain groups or communities (Rawls, 1985). A modern and rational citizen is therefore an individual emancipated from his/her primary ties, from his/her emotions and affects in response to contingent cultural specificities. She/he is freely willing to be part of the nation and be a Frenchman/Frenchwoman.[4] Based on individual willingness to participate and commit to the promotion of republican principles, the institutional design of citizenship as the way to keep state and society together mixes rational motives with an emotional link to politics.

This French formula is the exact opposite of the Anglo-Saxon tradition of recognition and representation of minority groups where race and ethnicity are central variables in considering differences and equality (Lapeyronnie, 1993; Hargreaves, 1995; Bleich, 2005).[5] With reference to another border, the exclusive ethnic *jus sanguinis*-based German citizenship provides the other historical contrast to the French inclusive and *jus soli*-based citizenship[6] (Dumont, 1994; Schnapper, 1991; Brubaker, 1992; Kastoryano, 1997; Amiraux, 2001). The dichotomy between France and the United Kingdom is grounded in antinomic philosophies, narratives, political projects and social practices concerning both nationality and citizenship (Kepel, 1994; Bleich, 2003; Joly, 1994; Garbaye, 2000). The different terminology used in each context makes it more obvious: 'In the English-speaking world, such people are commonly referred to as "ethnic minorities" or "minority ethnic groups", and a large part of what the French call "immigration" is commonly known as "race relations". In France, such terms are taboo' (Hargreaves, 1995: 1–2). The central role of race, used in analogy with colour in the British context, contrasts with the denial of its relevance in French political and juridical terminology. France is a secular republic where race and ethnicity as well as religious belonging are not considered legitimate categories with which to think about differences among individuals

(Amiraux and Simon, 2006). In summary, the indivisible Republic stands as the counter-model to multicultural communalism.[7] In this comparative perspective, it appears clear today that the questions raised by the presence of migrant populations are, however, similar across countries. The divergences stem from the responses to these similar questions, also in terms of theoretical orientations and the culture of scholarship. For instance, British scholarship on migration pays particular attention to community issues, ethnicity and collective group initiatives; while the French tradition gives priority to the analysis of public policies and central attention to the state first, before considering the subjects of these policies (Rea and Tripier, 2003). Following the London bombings in July 2005, Kepel stated that 'the combined results of secularism, conscious integration and a preventative security policy in France – the inverse terms of multiculturalism – has meant that the country has been spared terror attacks for a decade' (Kepel, 2005). In the German, British and French contexts, citizenship regimes are grounded on grammars of ethnicity that are strictly opposed to each other. This historical opposition has been naturalized in policymakers discourses,[8] in the media, and in public reports dealing with the public management of diversity, social cohesion and integration.[9] In the French republican secular context, groups may exist and live a communal experience, but with no rights attached to this belonging.

> In opposition with the Anglo-Saxon tradition that puts community and voluntary groups at the core of the socio-political organization, the Republic constituted herself against intermediary bodies (states, orders, churches, corporations, trade-unions) and ideally instituted the direct confrontation between the nation and the citizen, i.e. the individual with no specific belongings, being religious, ethnic, family, professional or geographic. (Ion, 1999: 68)

Notwithstanding this short comparative and historical insight, the current debate on integration is still very much configured by two related issues: first, the historical ideological heritage of the Third Republic (Hazareesingh, 1994) and the central role played by school in the process of unifying the nation, educating active citizens (popular sovereignty) and transmitting its values; second, the development of *laïcité* as the embodiment of the republican ideal. It is the virtue (in the normative moral dimension) of the citizen to be fully faithful to these historical elements, still perceived as constituting the essence of the nation.

Secularism and French society

The prevailing institutional arrangement on citizenship in France has a long history. The philosophy of integration and the republican tradition that has developed and been applied more extensively over the last three decades of the twentieth century is rooted in a combination of Enlightenment principle, Revolutionary ideas and intra-European conflicts. Popular democracy, social justice, civil equality and sovereignty are central to the composition of the integration model. Historically, post-revolutionary republicanism is grounded on the need to 'privatize' cultural and religious elements of identification in order more easily to achieve an egalitarian treatment of all citizens in the public space. Freedom of conscience, reciprocal non-interference between political and religious spheres, equal state treatment of religions and beliefs were among the core elements.[10] The centrality of the individual intertwined with a claim for universalism is made possible through the constitution of a secular public space in which school operates as the central institution for the diffusion of principles, values and norms of national belonging.

Laïcité[11] – which I would here briefly define as freedom of belief and equality of all citizens independent of their belief or religion – constitutes the space that makes tolerance possible (Kintzler, 2007). '*Laïcité* represents primarily a freedom granted to everyone and not a constraint imposed on all' (HCI, 2008: 191). In this *laïc* public arena, absolute priority is given to individual rights over group ones. The cohesion of the French nation is rooted in the expression of the citizens' desire to live together, without any collective belief being imposed on individuals. This free will is supported by the fact that individual freedoms and public order are protected by the neutrality of the public space. As for republicanism, *laïcité* needs to be historicized. It cannot be taken for granted and also needs to be updated in the face of a changing society. Before March 2004 and the introduction of the law on the wearing of religious symbols in public schools, *laïcité* was (and to a certain extent remains) a principle, defined in a complex grammar of legal texts and decrees related to different sectors of social life. It has been a constitutional principle since 1946, confirmed in the 1958 Constitution. To a certain extent, *laïcité* was first a political tradition in the republican discourse to support and make possible the integration of society. It is only very recently that it has turned into an ideological concept.

In the republican *laïc* context, intimacy and private beliefs do not affect the way the central state administrates its citizens. The realm of intimacy and privacy is where religion belongs in this secular society. In summary, *laïcité* in the French context stems from a liberal project of protection of, first, individual freedoms and, second, various conceptions of the good that coexist in plural societies. Inside this secular project, religious freedom, equality of all citizens and the neutrality of the state are placed in a common institutional setting. *Laïcité* is thus a regulating principle in the politics of difference, and the framework for recognition or accommodation of pluralism (Laborde, 2001). In France, two elements are central: one, the role of institutions in implementing equality and neutrality (the rule of separation being the main pillar of the institutional setting; see Baubérot, 2005); two, the public doctrine of conscience that prescribes codes and norms of behaviour in public to both individual believers and religious organizations. Both types of actors are expected to 'behave' in public so far as their religious convictions are concerned. The contemporary reading of what a *laïc* regime should be goes far beyond the principle of separation between religion and politics as instituted by the Separation law of 1905. It is at the infra-political level that justice and tolerance are seen to be achieved, not only through a strict implementation of the law, but also through ethical and political culture. In 2008, the text of a draft charter on *laïcité* in public services (that is, not only in public schools) states: '*laïcité* … is the famous "French exception"' (HCI, 2008: 17) There is a need, says the text, to reference the meaning and the practices attached to the 'republican rule'.[12]

Schools play a central role in the implementation of the integration project of migrants and children of migrants, as they had when peasants were made into Frenchmen (Weber, 1979). So far as the secularization of French political culture is concerned, they have been made the exclusive sites for the civic education of individual citizens in a secular system (Deloye, 1995). Since the French revolution, public education has been about teaching French, the sharing of cultural values and instilling patriotic principles. It is also about individually assisting children to free themselves from any form of patriarchal influence on their rationality. Schools are the guarantee of access to universalism and emancipatory values: all pupils are equal and no differentiation among them should occur by any means. Jules Ferry's laws secularized the public space in the 1880s. This period, labelled by Baubérot the 'second threshold of secularization', culminated in 1905 with the approval of the Separation law (Baubérot, 2005). This separation of Church and State leads back to the centrality of equality among citizens in respect of freedom of belief (that is, the right to believe or not believe). The notion of 'sanctuary', regularly cited in parliamentary discussions preceding the vote on the March 2004 law, is a relevant illustration of the historical weight that characterizes this institution. Abstracted from social context, the notion of sanctuary connects school with a form of socialization unrelated to territory or ground: 'As with the Church, school is out of the world. It is morally unified. It is a sanctuary exempted from social divisions' (Dubet, 2002: 26, author's translation). Thus, the institutional programme[13] transmitted to pupils inside public schools not only mobilizes values that reflect society: it is because school is external to social context that it is able to act voluntarily to protect children and to 'snatch them … from the common and familiar experience of their own world' (Dubet, 2002: 27). The extraterritorial dimension of schooling is what makes equality possible among all citizens. Kintzler evokes the suspension of community ties as making the constitution of the political possible (Kintzler, 2007). In this project, recognition seems to be the keyword.

Schools have been, on two occasions at least, designated as the main place for illustrating the so-called 'failure of integration' in France. As in the headscarf controversies, public schools are considered to be in danger of overexposure to ethnic cleavages and their related effects. Lastly, in October 2005, urban riots took place in Clichy-sous-Bois. Two teenagers of North African and sub-Saharan origin electrocuted themselves, trying to escape police, by hiding in a power substation. This tragic event was the starting point for three weeks of riots in different cities all over the country. In November 2005, the right-wing government imposed a curfew in most of the cities involved, reactivating a 1955 law initially introduced for the purpose of controlling the insurrection during the Algerian war of independence. Several minors were arrested during these three weeks (Bertossi, 2007). Many issues were publicly discussed during and after the riots: the spatial segregation of specific populations (of migrant origin, young, male); the incapacity of central institutions such as schools to achieve equality and upward social mobility. During that specific episode, public educational institutions were designated as the main site of production and reproduction of social inequalities, in particular at the intersection of spatial segregation and ethnic-religious identification of populations.[14] The youngsters involved in the three-week riots fought against the symbols of their relegation into territories where republican equality did not reach, notably the institutional symbols of French society – the police, firemen, schools, and so on. They did not contest the principles of French citizenship. They claimed their legitimate place within it.[15]

The process of secularization of French society and state has taken place step by step through a long history of conflict (Baubérot, 1990, 2004). It is no surprise that even today it lies at the heart of contro-versy, and that schools are still systematically the place where debate starts. Since March 2004, the requirement to behave as a *laïc* citizen has been enforced inside public schools and punished by exclusion if the principles and the law are not respected.[16] *Laïcité* finally reached the status of a 'moral fact' in the sense that it is a rule of behaviour that can be punished if it is not respected, and is mandatory regardless of conscience or whatever belief people in society hold. To a certain extent, the passage of the March 2004 law and the intervention of the legislator indicates the incapacity of educational institutions to perpetuate their position as a sanctuary. *Laïcité* appears also as a unique resource for managing and regulating religious diversity at school, and the neutrality of the state therefore becomes the main indicator to assess the capacity of the *laïc* Republic to address a new type of claim and request (Koussens, 2009).

The integration paradigm

Integration as a doctrine emerged in the 1950s in relation to the decline and failure of the assimilationist colonial project. It only became a proper political project and the subject of public policies applying to migration in the 1980s, more specifically when immigration became a central item on the political agenda in the aftermath of Mitterrand's election to the presidency. However, integration in the French context is never completely dissociated from assimilation (Schnapper, 1991), defined as a process of reduction, through acculturation, of the cultural distance of an individual from the French society (Tribalat, 1995; Noiriel, 1996). During the 1980s, the opposition between *droit à la différence* (right to be different) and *droit à l'indifférence* (right to be treated with indifference) epitomized what was at stake in defining a French avenue for integration. The Marceau Long report of the Commission on Nationality (Long, 1988) stated a new agenda in the mid-1980s by stressing the causal connection between emerging forms of ethnic visibility, the need to reform the conditions for acquiring French nationality and the weakening of the institutions that had co-produced republican citizenship. The Haut Conseil à l'Intégration (High Council for Integration, hereafter HCI) was created as a follow-up to the report, with the mission of advising the Socialist government on how best to integrate migrants into French society. The report suggested shifting from a policy of social and economic insertion of migrants and their children to a politics of integration, referring to the idea of national identity and integration (Favell, 1998). Integration was thus institutionalized through the creation of the HCI in 1989, the year of the commemoration of the 200th anniversary of the French Revolution. In 1993, the HCI report proposed a definition of integration, referring to a specific process of active participation of individuals in national society, giving priority to a logic of equality, not of minorities or recognition. In this context, the first elements of a claim for reciprocal recognition emerged, driven by a demand to be treated as individual citizens with a migrant background on equal terms with 'native' ones. The hypothesis of a causal link between the failure of integration and the visibility of cultural distinction remains strong in the French context (Costa-Lascoux, 2006). Globally, the HCI's reports during the 1990s set out a project of integration that combines voluntary participation and adhesion to the core values of the national identity, but also point to the existence of cultural specificities that are not disqualified.

In this 'integration design' as public policy, the definition of national boundaries is a central issue that has concentrated, in the French case, on the question of access to nationality. How does one become French? Reform of the Nationality Law started in the second half of the 1980s and introduced the idea of a *jus soli* that, while still maintained as heritage of the Revolution, is coupled with the expression of the individual desire, of the personal will, to become French. This proposal of the Long Report was enacted by the Pasqua Laws in 1993. The notion of rules to be accepted and respected, and of the duties of the potential applicant for French nationality, was further politicized after 2000. The implementation of a *Contrat d'accueil et d'intégration* (hereafter CAI) in 2002 by President Chirac, later mentioned by the HCI report (2004), follows a constant oscillation between assimilationism and openness to multicultural influences. It reiterates the idea of a reciprocity between rights and obligations as incorporated in the practice of citizenship (Costa Lascoux, 2006). The CAI has been mandatory since 1 January 2007. The new formula of integration policy places strong emphasis on the empowerment of women and reinforces policy aimed at disadvantaged youth. In the public documents and the reports of the various authorities in charge, the statements are converging around the idea that the 'problems of integration' cannot be reduced to ethnic and national/cultural issues, but have to be seen in the light of other variables (family or economic problems, spatial segregation, etc.).

If the notion of 'integration' was the dominant reference for public policies and social scientists until the end of the 1980s, the concept has been highly contested since the 1990s by many actors, in particular by the main subjects of integration policies, the children of first-generation migrants. The end of the 1990s saw a major shift in the discourse on the republican capacity for integration. The emergence of a discourse on discrimination following the transposition of the European directives in November 2001 (except the provisions related to data collection and monitoring) introduces the idea of a reciprocal responsibility for the perpetuation of inequality in multiethnic societies. The emphasis on potentially unequal treatment based on specific variables (gender, ethnicity, race, religion, etc.) opens up the hypothesis of the possible existence in the republican French context of forms of inequality, attributable either to institutions (and some bureaucratic practices) or to individuals. The change from a perspective on integration to an anti-discrimination policy is the result of the intersection of various dynamics during the second half of the 1990s. The first dynamic arose in 1998 with the publication by the HCI of a report devoted to discrimination. Fassin underlines two dimensions of this major shift. First, the HCI report suggests looking differently at the process of integration: its success, says Fassin, would be conditional on a proper capacity on the part of French society and institutions to deal with issues of discrimination. The major change in this report is that it advances the hypothesis that it is not only the individual with a migrant background who is responsible for his/her 'non-integration' (because of cultural practices, inadequate educational achievement, socio-economic characteristics), but the way French society produces discriminatory situations and practices (often without being aware of it), a proper 'French model of discrimination' (*Mouvements*, 1999). Second, nationality is said in the report to be 'irrelevant' as people suffering from inequalities of treatment may be French citizens but associated with specific colour or ethnic backgrounds (Fassin, 2002). A second dynamic can be associated with the Socialist government's move on this issue, probably motivated by internal party debate and a real concern about racism and discrimination. Several initiatives were launched between 1997 and 2000 by the prime minister (Lionel Jospin) and other leading figures of the Socialist Party and the government (Martine Aubry, Jean-Michel Belorgey, Jean-Pierre Chevènement), at local, regional and national levels. A third dynamic is of European origin and has certainly affected the national political process by giving it more legitimacy. Two directives were adopted in 2000, namely a 'race directive' combating discrimination on the ground of race or ethnicity in a number of areas (e.g. housing, employment, education and training, the provision of goods and services) and a directive combating all forms of discrimination in employment.[17] In 2004, the HALDE (Haute Autorité de Lutte contre les Discriminations et pour l'Égalité) was created to centralize the handling of individual claims and initiatives for policy implementation and the use of legal recourse. Its prerogatives were extended in March 2006 when the law on equal opportunities legalized testing procedures to prove discriminatory practices. The outcomes in the French context were the development of a new perception of sources of inequality and discrimination and the introduction in the French context of terminology that had been largely developed in the British context. Through this new issue of discrimination, thinking about ethnic and racial inequality in the republican secular context acquired new value in the integration agenda.

Last but not least, political interest in the question of 'national identity' has been growing since the rhetoric of the National Front built upon it.[18] The creation in 2007 of a Ministère de l'identité nationale et de l'immigration by the newly elected President Nicolas Sarkozy established a link between immigrants (as a problem) and a national identity in need of reaffirmation and protection from the state. This association of integration and immigration is not new; it can be traced back to the HCI reports. The problems created by this new institution are, however, more troubling. First, because it naturalizes a causal link between the presence of migrants in France and the decline of French national identity. Second, because it assigns to the state the responsibility for organizing a 'shared national identity' as a measure of democratic life in the country. Several prominent scholars publicly expressed their disapproval of this initiative, while others even started to elaborate the notion of 'state xenophobia':

> By using the word 'xenophobia', we include all discourses and decisions that make foreigners a problem, a risk or a threat for the host-society, that try to keep them at a distance from this society, wherever these foreigners are located (already living in the host-country for a while or still abroad and potentially willing to come). Starting with this definition, we can identify a state xenophobia with its own history, specific features, that is different from the extreme-right xenophobia on the rise in the European contexts for the last two decades. (Valluy, 2008: 12, author's translation).

What happens to individual identities in the course of social interactions? What are the collective expressions of belonging in the secular public space? What is the place of culture in national identity? This set of questions overlaps with the past two decades of controversies that have regularly confronted the historical myth of French republicanism with its current transformation, a 'rationalist universalism, rooted in the philosophy of the eighteenth-century Enlightenment, [which] now looks more and more like a form of European ethnocentrism, and thus like a form of domination rather than liberation' (Jennings, 2000: 579). The main challenge seems to be the hypothesis that citizen's ways of identifying and social and political participation could be better articulated. In that discussion, *laïcité*, as we have seen, is a central concern. Criticism has mainly come from the political and civic spheres and has followed two lines of thought. On the one hand, universalism as indifference towards cultural particularism have been accused of constituting an ideological mystification maintaining post-colonial structures of domination (Laborde, 2001). The Indigènes de la République and the activists from the MIB (Mouvement de l'Immigration et des Banlieues) represent this tendency quite well. On the other hand, since culture is part of individuals' identity, the notion that a society that would exclude any aspect of cultural belonging from public life and political participation appeared to be a complete illusion. In a sense, criticism of republicanism suggests a more multicultural conception of social integration and cohesion in which the recognition of the cultural elements of diversity would be part of an egalitarian public space. Several events and public debates have made clear this development and illustrated the gap between the republican principles of universal citizenship and social practices. 'Like liberalism, republicanism has in the past two decades or so been internally reconfigured (albeit in a different way to liberalism) by its confrontation with new questions relating to cultural identity – both national and subnational' (Laborde, 2001: 717). On the one hand, a cultural nationalism hostile to multiculturalism grows more cohesive, creating systematic positions on any public discussion, such as those related to religious symbols. On the other hand, cultural identities in the public sphere are being ascribed greater significance, giving more importance to ethnicity in civic life (Fassin and Fassin, 2006).

Contemporary challenges and the reflexive turn

In the first section, I described some of the main features of the political republican horizon that have historically structured official reflections on integration and national identity. In this second section, I will illustrate the most recent episodes that have challenged this strong national tradition, and the ideology of 'integration' defined as a 'process in which immigrant characteristics uniformly converge toward the average characteristics of French society' (Safi, 2008: 5). Four recent 'episodes' symbolize the limits of French republican integration and citizenship, and question the very core of the model: the general discussion on post-colonialism; the headscarf controversies that ended with the approval of the March 2004 law banning visible religious symbols from public schools; the November 2005 urban riots; and the 2007 discussion of the legitimacy of using ethnic statistics. Of course, these do not all have the same trajectory, involve the same actors or refer to identical situations. But they all share the fact that they have been the justification for broader heated discussion addressing the 'limits' of the capacity of French republicanism to cope with French diversity. To sum up, the French tradition of integration has been contested for its promise of equality (November 2005, the urban riots), of neutrality towards cultural and religious differences (the headscarf affairs since 1989 and the passage of the March 2004 law), of the legitimacy of maintaining colour and race blindness (the 2007 ethnic statistics discussion). The principles of republicanism and *laïcité* have faced profound challenge, which raises the question: should France grant more space to ethnic differences in the public sphere?

Two dimensions can be distinguished in the recent emergence of criticism of the historical political tradition of French republicanism. The first can be described as a general difficulty in coping with the need to implement a policy which does justice to social diversification and fragmentation, the segmented modes of incorporation into French society. To illustrate this first dimension, I offer two examples. First, what proxies have been deployed in local policies to promote equal access to specific goods (social housing for instance) whilst behaving as if colour and race blind? How are French authorities dealing with anti-discrimination policies and the absence of statistics to guide the quantitative assessment of places and types of recurring discrimination? The second dimension I would sum up as a reflexive turn. It incorporates the upsurge of post-colonialism in both academic and political cultures. I will elaborate in particular on the link between post-colonialism and the politics of memory that has been the subject of passionate political discussion since 2000 and that underlines the difficulty of bringing ethnicity and colour into the discussion of pluralism and recognition.

Official discourse and concrete practices

Facing new challenges presented by the increasing diversity of French society, the view of integration politics as indifference on the part of the Republic towards citizens' origins and belongings had become an anti-discrimination policy by the end of the 1990s (Fassin, 2002; HCI, 2006). Not all differences are equal, and the introduction of affirmative action policies in France is mostly the result of discussion around parity and equal opportunity, rather than a consequence of mobilization by ethnic groups. 'Women were therefore granted advantages from affirmative action measures that other politically excluded categories could not claim because their difference was not "different" – that is, "universal"' (Lépinard, 2008: 98). Notwithstanding the implementation of legal means to fight against discrimination and the political discourse to explain it to a larger public, multiculturalism never became a social and political project in the French context – that is, it was not incorporated within specific institutions.[19] This statement should of course be qualified, as many indicators, notably in social housing (Kirszbaum, 2008), or more recently regarding access to higher education (Sabbagh, 2002), show how a language and proxies have been invented to permit ethnicity to enter into the French tradition without modifying the global philosophy. In general, in recent French public social policy, territory has played the role assigned to ethnicity in other contexts where affirmative action has 'come out'. In France, that is, it has been done without leaving the closet.

In the 1990s, the trend among policymakers was towards being more specific when dealing with integration issues, and more generally to begin to factor in, albeit implicitly, the ethnic dimension of integration policies. The designation of certain neighbourhoods as specific targets of public policies because of their educational shortfall (*Zone d'éducation prioritaire*) or the development of a more active policy of social diversity (*mixité sociale*) are among the best known examples since the implementation in the 1990s of the *Loi d'orientation sur la ville*. The accumulation of administrative categories with which to discuss the most socially and economically segregated parts of the largest French cities has contributed to widespread depictions of these neighbourhoods as dangerous and hopelessly bound up with the failure of public institutions to 'integrate'. But these categories also reveal the ambiguity of a political project: mixing people to achieve social harmony and create networks of socialization. In the 1990s, the priority was not only to support social diversity, but also to lay in the desegregation of those parts of the major cities where immigrants have remained concentrated in high proportions. In July 1991, the law passed by Parliament mentions the 'right to the city' (*droit à la ville*) as the right for diverse social categories to coexist. The project consisted in the regulation of the dispersion of people of low socio-economic status in order to mix multiple social categories in one area. Officially, there is no mention of the ethnic belonging of the population in question; rather, social status combined with location is the euphemism for ethnic categorization. The objective, through the strong control of access to social housing, should be to avoid the dominance (over-concentration) of any ethnic minority in a given area (Kirzbaum, 2004).

The rigidity of the model has been softened through this invention of proxies to isolate specific groups of population without naming them as ethnically or racially distinct from the majority society. The creation of an anti-discrimination frame was stimulated by European dynamics, in particular following the adoption of two central directives on that issue in 2001. The new European legal settings constituted another incentive for French public authorities to rely on ethnic and community repertoires and categories without modifying the official philosophy (Geisser, 2005; Guiraudon, 2006). In the autumn of 2007, a passionate debate occupied first academics and political leaders, then a larger audience, over the possibility of collecting so-called 'ethnic statistics'. This debate constitutes in a way the quintessence of the global republican dilemma about differences and ethnic/racial/colour blindness: how can we name something we do not recognize? The idea that race may be a legitimate criterion for categorizing people because it can be a subjective or socially constructed category is generally rejected, since its historical association with unacceptable political practices make it a non-starter in contemporary liberal European democracies. Ethnicity is no more acceptable. The notion of classifying people does not fit well with the egalitarian republican project of integration based on an idea of the nation as the product of a voluntary contract among free men. This is, for instance, what the 1789 Declaration of the Rights of Man is all about. The Republic conceives of citizens in relation to the situations they are embedded in, not as categories of population. This abstract universalism draws very strong boundaries between what is considered to be legitimate and what illegitimate in the public space. So racism is discussed without mentioning race. The figure of the foreigner in the 1980s, of the migrant in the 1990s, has become the category subsuming all other potential terms to evoke those who are living in France but have a migration background. In public statistics, the republican paradigm leads to the use of the nationality of origin of migrants as the proxy for race, ethnic origin and religion (Fassin and Simon, 2008). Ethnic identification is controlled at different levels. From a constitutional perspective, article 1 of the Constitution explicitly states that distinction by racial or ethnic origin is forbidden. This was supplemented by the 1978 law (*Informatique et libertés*) defining ethnic data as sensitive and subject to control for the sake of privacy. The main argument for rejecting the use of statistics on ethnicity is the risk that they could be deployed as a source of power against certain communities; this combined with the belief that these objective and essentialist categories do not help to understand social attitudes and phenomena (Stavo-Debauge, 2003).

The question of whether it was necessary to develop more so-phisticated statistical categories to monitor discrimination of specific population groups was revived after the adoption of the European directives into national legislation. EU legislation not only permits ethnic data collection but even encourages it as central to a well-informed fight against discrimination. Statistics serve first to describe society. They eventually may help political action. The discussion is not new. Controversy arose over this issue in the late 1990s, pitting two of the most prominent French demographers, Hervé Le Bras (and others, such as Alain Blum, Jean Luc Richard, Sandrine Bertaux) and Michèle Tribalat (Tribalat, 1995), against each other. In 1995, Tribalat had published the results of a large-scale survey (*Mobilité Géographique et Insertion Sociale*, conducted between 1987 and 1992; hereafter MGIS). This survey focused on the relevance of the French model of integration for immigrants and their children. In comparison with previous work on similar issues, MGIS was the first large-scale scientific work disconnecting the question of integration from 'foreigners' as a category. To describe the passionate controversies that again emerged with the preparation of a new major survey 'Life Stories' (*Histoires de vie*) in 2003, Fassin and Simon evoke the 'national ideological novel' and the paradox of a 'national paradigm that is both political and academic' and that faces the following dilemma: can we name and categorize something (racial discrimination) for which we have no label? (Fassin and Simon, 2008).[20]

The answers to this question fall into two camps (for a recent account of the French discussion, see Felouzis, 2008; Peer and Sabbagh, 2008). Some say No in the name of privacy and data protection, claiming that there is a risk of misuse of files with such data (*la peur des fichiers*), that statistics should not become a resource for racist discourse. Some say Yes, generally referring to other European countries and arguing that producing ethnic categories is necessary in order to assess evidence of discrimination and implement efficient policies to combat it. Creating statistical data and producing work based upon it means transforming individual experiences and personal trajectories into facts, thus enabling concrete action. The defenders of ethnic categories do not uphold multiculturalism or a politics of recognition of differences in the public space (Stavo Debauge, 2003). Tribalat, for example, favours the use of data on the origins of migrants, but considers the French assimilation model threatened by the public expression of identities (Kaltenbach and Tribalat, 2002). In the 2007 discussion, the controversy focused on the use in an academic survey (TeO, *Trajectoires et origines*, trajectory and origins) of subjective criteria used by individuals to define themselves or be defined by others. Skin colour, for instance, would be used in that context as a socially constructed category, not as a phenotypical datum. How can we look at something that has no name? (Fassin and Simon, 2008).

Recently, black people have become both a rediscovered object for the social sciences and a new visible group bearing specific claims for recognition and justice (for instance through the activities of the CRAN, Conseil représentatif des associations noires en France, Representative Council of Black Associations in France, created in 2005 for 'better equality'). They constitute, just as Muslims do on another level, a perfect illustration of the unresolved tension inside republicanism: on the one hand, they ask to be individually invisible through the privatization of cultural identities promoted in the name of a universalistic dimension of liberal neutrality ('l'éloge de l'immigré invisible', Noiriel, 2007). On the other hand, they are engaged in a process of recognition in the name of equal treatment and the fight against discrimination. But as race is of no social and political significance, some populations have been locked out, denied recognition and kept invisible. J. Stavo-Debauge, speaking of black people in France, refers to

> experience of humiliation, contempt and denial of recognition. Indeed, being invisible means not being counted among full and authorized members of a community, or a situation. It is also not being considered as a full participant capable of a potentially distinct contribution that could be welcomed by other members of the community. (Stavo-Debauge, 2007)

Post-colonial discussions and the politics of memory

Speaking up about the colonial past is a recent endeavour for French policymakers compared with the politics of memorial representation, which led the way to democracy in the immediate aftermath of the Second World War. The French discussion of post-colonialism started much later than among its counterparts in the English-speaking world. The year 2005 was a turning point, not so much because of the urban riots that took place in November, but because of the publication of a collective text in January by a group called Les Indigènes de la République that established a parallel between the situation of the elders (their parents or grandparents at the time of the French domination of North Africa) and their own position in French society as youngsters with migrant origins. As Hargreaves recalls, this evocation of a parallel between migrants and people living under French domination in the colonies was not invented in 2005 but had been exploited in literature and fiction already in the 1970s (Hargreaves, 2007). The post-colonial debate in France engages both activists and academics; as such, since the 1990s, it has illustrated well the way the historical legacy of republicanism has been criticized for its irrelevance when faced with contemporary social problems. For certain observers, post-colonialism would be everywhere but always presented as a political accusation (as by Les Indigènes de la République). For others, the current attention paid to colonial history and the close link to discussion about racism and discrimination follow the hypothesis that 'contemporary forms taken by the social question are racial because they originate in colonial practices and ways of thinking' (Stavo-Debauge, 2007). Denouncement (of amnesia, of culpability) dominates the post-colonial discourse at large, as if the native and the migrant were two extremes of the same moment of history. Colonial fantasy serves the politics of memory that mobilizes both a sense of guilt for past atrocities and exoneration from self-criticism (Merle and Sibeud, 2003).

Two other factors can complement our hypothesis of the 'post-colonial politics of memory' as a way to introduce multiculturalism and the emergence of race and ethnicity in the French politics of difference. On 21 May 2001, 'Taubira's Law' was approved, declaring the slave trade a crime against humanity, and in May 2006, a national day commemorating the abolition of the slave trade was established. On 23 February 2005, law no. 2005-158 'recognizing the contribution of the Nation and French nationals' to the colonies (Algeria, Morocco, Tunisia, Indochina) was approved. Article 4 of this law was widely criticized, for stating that the positive role of the colonizers should be recognized 'by law'. Reaction to this article was immediate and virulent. Most of the criticism concentrated on the close connection between how the memory of colonialism was conveyed in 'positive terms' and its impact on the current stigmatization of segregated populations. Article 4, it was argued, would amputate part of colonial history and deprive the parents of the second and third generations of children of their history; they would be French citizens but still considered as deviant and marginal populations. Yet the elaboration of a common memory of colonialism appeared to most commentators to be a necessary step in achieving a comprehensive reflection on the conditions of equality and the practice of citizenship.

As Muslims have been 'going more public' since 2001,[21] questions of representation and of the difficulty (in terms of social cost) of self-presentation as Muslim are indeed a constant reminder of the need to historicize this process of stigmatization, particularly in relation to the colonial period, which has long remained at the periphery of French historiography. I do not wish to reduce and limit the complexity of colonial experience to a causal responsibility in producing contemporary forms of racism. There is indeed no possibility of scientifically proving such a direct univocal causal link between colonial racism and the contemporary discrimination of French citizens with Muslim and North African origins (Saada, 2006: 64). But similarities in public discourses can be observed in the way hierarchies are established, categorized and justified, and in the obsession with strictly controlling the visibility of certain cultural belongings (i.e. religious ones). Suspicion of Muslims and Islam as a faith, for instance, is a republican tradition that dates back long before 9/11 (Geisser and Zemmouri, 2007). A reading of the administrative vocabulary provides evidence (Le Pautremat, 2003; Laurens, 2004; Simon, 2007). In a recent ethnographic study of the ceremony with which nominal decrees of naturalization were distributed to new French citizens in the city of Doucy, Mazouz describes what she calls the 'constitutive antinomy of this republican ceremony'. The ritual becomes a real test for assessing if the new Frenchman/woman is really qualified for his/her new position:[22] 'Exactly as this ceremony indicates the integration, even the assimilation, of new naturalized people, it reminds them and shows them how different and illegitimate they are' (Mazouz, 2008: 89).

Here the internal tensions of the republican project are visible. The French colonial empire was clearly conceived as reproducing abroad what was implemented on the metropolitan territory of the young French Republic. In practice, the colonial adventure ended up being less than faithful to these republican ideals. In continental France, the Third Republic implemented a process of democratization integrating the diverse components of French society. In the colonies, exception became a way of ruling. These contradictions culminated in

Algeria. Egalitarian universalism in particular led to the coexistence of contradictory practices, the most infamous being the hierarchy of status among citizens in French Algeria. The status of *Français Musulmans d'Algérie* (French Muslims from Algeria) is the most typical illustration of the bifurcation between citizenship and nationality in the French colonial context. The Indigenous People Code (*Code de l'indigénat*) was created in Algeria in 1881 and remained in force until 1946. The Muslim natives were French by nationality but with no citizenship and became French Muslims (Spire, 2003). Algerians, though of French nationality, did not have the right to vote and were thus, to use the contemporary word, denizens. This denial of citizens' rights applied, while race and ethnicity were not legitimate categories in the matter of civic rights. Whereas after 1946 French citizenship was extended to all persons living on French territory, the distinction between civil and personal status survived in colonized Algeria, and 'French Muslims' were those individuals in Algeria who did not renounce their religion but were French citizens. Algeria, a French department, was where 'French Muslims from Algeria' and 'French from the continent' referred to two categories of a unique regime of citizenship, 'making citizenship irrelevant as criterion of national identity' (Kepel, 1994: 135, author's translation).

Colonial practices regarding religion worked within the same type of paradox, the policy 'at home' being different from practices in the colonized territories. The 1905 separation law is a central part of a colonial rhetoric that pursued the dream of equality through the secularization of institutional settings and society. It turns out to have also been a tool for control and coercion in the colonial domination of people and lands. Indeed, the 1905 law was never applied to the Muslim associations that were created in 1907 following the publication of a decree transposing the 1905 law in Algeria: 'Ulamas made it clear that the French Republic was contradicting itself, making *laïcité* a dogma in continental France and changing its nature when transposing it in Algeria because the control of the local population was at stake' (Achi, 2007: 65, author's translation). Overall, there was never a homogeneous policy towards Muslims living in the colonized territories. The tensions between the republican project and the complex and inegalitarian architecture of the colonial administration became more complex with the expansion and the conquest of new places (Egypt, Morocco, Tunisia, Algeria). Facing these different contexts, a French Muslim policy emerged around 1890.[23] Its main argument was the idea that Islam is potentially subversive and puts the Empire at risk. Muslim policies logically moved into enterprises of control aimed at protecting the republican colonial project against the 'Islamic threat'. Muslim policy, a sort of 'police of the souls' (Lyauzu, 1994: 61), articulated academic expertise with public administration of the colonial territories (Laurens, 2004).[24] Muslim councillors, created in 1931, were seen as intermediaries capable of translating the claims and needs of Muslim populations. They were also meant as a channel for developing better trust of the metropolitan authorities and illustrating the non-hostility of the Republic towards Muslims (Laurens, 2004).

The obsession with control and regulation of Islam as a faith that has characterized Interior Ministry policies since 1989–1990 is thus not new (Amiraux, 2008). From 1989–90 until the creation of the French Council of Muslim Faith (*Conseil français du culte musulman*, CFCM) in 2003, the institutionalization of Islam as one of the main French religions still bore elements of colonialism (see Laurence and Vaisse, 2006: 135–62; Zeghal, 2005). For instance, in January 2000, when Muslim leaders were invited to join the discussion, they were asked to sign a Declaration of Intent concerning the rights and duties of Muslim believers in France (*Déclaration d'intention relative aux droits et obligations des fidèles du culte musulman en France*) that no other member of a minority religion had ever had to sign. The ministerial advisers in charge of policy on Islam since 1989 were either ideologues wishing to 'civilize the Muslims' or pragmatists aware of 'the sociological and demographic realism' that placed the question of Islam on the agenda (Geisser and Zemmouri, 2007: 71–99). Some of the youngest leaders taking part in this process of representation of Islam took the minister's invitation as a 'paternalist colonial injunction'. The *Homo islamicus* that emerged as a public figure through the process of institutionalization has two faces. The first responds to the institutional expectations of the Republic and is a mixture of civic virtue and loyalty to the Republic. The second is marked, rather, by resistance to the normative pressure that Muslim leaders are experiencing by taking part in the negotiations. Rather than a proper neutrality, the history of the relationship between the French state and Muslims, as a colonial and a post-colonial state, has been a process of tutorship and interference. While state interference may be necessary to protect common liberties, it should never be achieved through arbitrary measures or stigmatization of vulnerable populations.

The politics of difference and the governance of bodies

The tension between principles and ideals, on the one hand, and practices and concrete initiatives, on the other, can be observed daily in the expression of hostility towards differences and Otherness. The institutional level and that of the social production of discourses and representation do not operate at the same scale. A good illustration of individuals' difficulty in coping with subjective behaviour related to ethnic and religious differences lies in the development of what I call a public iconography of patterns that deviate from republicanism. These deviant patterns often intersect with gender, religious and ethnic belonging. The fantasy about the Other is now embodied in instances of deviant behaviour that link major controversies (over the headscarf, gang rape, the urban riots or global insecurity) to ordinary feelings of unease and difficult daily interactions between citizens. Whereas earlier I relied on history to demonstrate continuity of institutional practices (during and after the colonial empire), this emphasis on contemporary icons is rather ethnographic in its focus on the governance of bodies as the main sites for controlling the modes of social reproduction and transmission of good practices, and best virtues.[25] Many scholars have engaged in this type of analysis. The post-colonial tradition is a dominant approach in this field; analysis has included the colonial legacy of antithetic bodies such as the 'savage', the 'native' and the white civilized gentleman. One of the most performing faces of the colonized *indigène* can be found in one of contemporary France's dominant types: the figure of the militarily gifted North African warrior (Bancel et al., 2003) has been domesticated by the republican political sphere. The violent nature of these men, their uncontrolled instincts, belong to a historical trajectory of stigmatization of their apparent ineducability. Islam is here a sign of the absence of culture and manners. In that context, the 'Arab

boy' of North African origin, extensively publicized as responsible
for the insecurity of society at large, but also of the women of his
own community 'seems to be a ghost from the colonial past ... like
a clone of the *indigène* that turned into first an immigrant then a
Muslim' (Guénif, 2006: 118). The historical figure of the cruel Arab
is updated in new scenes of confrontation and crime, nowadays often
relating to deviant sexual practices (on gang rape, see Muchielli, 2005;
on the stigmatization of the Arab male as *voleur, violeur et voileur*
– 'thief, rapist and veiler' – see Guénif and Macé, 2004) or violent
radicalization (Deltombe, 2005). The Arab Muslim man remains
this historical stereotype of an individual unable to 'interiorize in
their bodies the rules of good manners and civility that had forever
governed the relationships between men and women and constituted
per se the French exception' (Guénif, 2005: 204).[26] In analysing the
2003–04 controversies over the headscarf, Guénif has described the
different patterns of integration that were synthesized by iconic
figures such as *la beurette* and *le musulman laïc*, placed in opposition
to their negative counterparts, the radical Muslim and the Muslim
girl wearing a headscarf (Guénif and Macé, 2004: 111). I would add
that in the current context, these 'integrated individuals', however
integrated they may be, are still largely perceived as potentially at
risk of bad behaviour or to fall prey to 'rebound effects of their
origins'. They are potentially transgressive rather than conformist.
As Guénif observes, 'the integration deficit of these post-colonial
Frenchmen and women comes not from their social inadequacy or
from their inadequate position on the job market. It can be located
in their body, in their incapacity to submit to the rules imposed by
the process of French civilization' (Guénif, 2006: 120).

The stigmatization of the Islamic headscarf since 1989 illustrates a
governance of bodies that is again very much anchored in the republican tradition of control of private space (Iacub, 2008). The public
obsession with the headscarf results from the convergence of first the
politicization and then the judicialization of the debate (Amiraux, 2007;
Bowen, 2006; Lorcerie, 2005; de Galembert 2008). Schools are no
longer sanctuaries. Reading the headscarf controversies as a 'normative
account of the relationships between citizenship and identity' (Laborde,
2001: 718), the 2003–04 consensus emerged over a shared conviction

that the headscarf is harmful both to the Republic and to individuals. It contravenes principles such as equality and neutrality and inserts private indicators of intimate conviction into the public sphere. The promoters of the March 2004 law claim that in public schools it breaches the principle of equality among pupils by being a clear element of distinction. It therefore creates obstacles to the civic mission of schools and brings religious authorities back into the education system and into competition with teachers. Last but not least, it contradicts the religious freedom of other pupils (Laborde, 2005: 327–8). Laborde distinguishes two forms of criticism, mostly from the political left. On the one hand, culture-blind universalism is blamed for being an ideological mystification perpetuating the structure of post-colonial domination (Laborde, 2001). The type of discourse this criticism ends up producing can best be illustrated by the Indigènes de la République movement, or the MIB. On the other hand, culture should be understood as an integral part of individual identity that cannot just be left behind when discussing political participation. This second criticism of the French republican tradition pushes towards a more multicultural republicanism, considering the recognition of cultural elements of distinction as part of an egalitarian public sphere. For the defenders of the republican fortress, the headscarf embodies the threat to public order and the symbolic urban ecology through which citizens make sense of their experience. The governance of private manners and of modesty is not a new tradition of republicanism. Iacub, examining the secularization of civil law, illustrates how the erection of a 'wall of modesty/decency' between private and the public spaces in nineteenth-century France led state authorities to govern previously purely private issues of sexuality and modesty. This tension has been exacerbated with the passing of the March 2004 law on religious symbols in public schools: if religion should remain a private matter in the secular Republic, should the legislator and the state take care of it?

Conclusion

In recent years, French politics of difference have been a mixture of hesitation, inconsistency and faithfulness to historical ghosts and abstract principles. The most apparent elements in recent developments are the institutional responses by the state to integration-related issues in terms of anti-discrimination policy – greater use of categories and references to the law and to the European perspective – and a new visibility of collective mobilization around questions of recognition. The current context is illustrative of the tensions resulting from the temptation to maintain a high level of abstraction rather than switching to more local levels of observation of social difficulties. 'The citizen is not a concrete individual. One does not meet the citizen. It is a subject of law' (Schnapper, 2004: 27). There is a need to invent a new type of tie binding individual citizens to the political, since national belonging (citizenship) is increasingly disassociated from cultural belonging. Citizenship and nationality are not equivalent. Many scholars have used quantitative or qualitative approaches to illustrate this non-equivalence (Duchesne, 1997; Safi, 2008). The republican paradigm needs to be somehow updated, introducing elements of multiculturalism, starting with the recognition of the cultural and ethnic diversity of French society even in a statistical approach.

As this volume aims to provide a comparative perspective, it should be recognized that the current 'reflexive' moment does not seem to be that specific to the French context. Indeed, other national scenes have experienced this questioning of inherited historical models, and discussed how to proceed. In most countries, Muslims have been the main actors challenging official policies. Multicultural traditions must open up to discussion of the meaning of civic participation and identification. Assimilationist traditions, such as in France, must incorporate the notion of accommodation of both individuals and groups. More generally, there is no more self-sufficient 'model' (Modood, 2007) and national traditions are more complementary than exclusive. Convergence occurs not by arriving at a common position but rather by creating parallel avenues for addressing and responding to situations of tension by developing cultures of equality while combining equal treatment with respect for difference.

The present is nevertheless characterized by certain elements. First, state authorities are increasingly active in regulating the private religious mores of certain groups of people with migrant backgrounds and/or Muslims.[27] Second, the conjunction of international events (9/11) with top-down input from transnational political institutions (the European Union) in the implementation of equality of treatment of all religions accelerated in April 2003 the creation of a board of representatives of Islam as a religion (Godard and Taussig, 2006). However, even if this institutionalization of Islamic representation has granted more space to discussion of Muslim issues in the public sphere (Jonker and Amiraux, 2006), it has not 'neutralized' the stigmatization and racialization (Fassin and Fassin, 2006) of Islam-related elements of diversity that can be observed in today's France.

The historical permanence of hostility towards certain forms of diversity, even when purely part of the private life of individuals, echoes an unspoken nationalism. Anti-Muslim racism – common all over Europe – is in France based on republican universalism. A rigidity of ideas and principles when dealing with citizenry and 'what it means to be a Frenchman/woman' continue to inform the public image of the French nation, which perceives itself as universal and abstract. French MPs from different political backgrounds have voiced several positions in favour of an extension of the current March 2004 law to 'the public space' at large.[28] The discussion of how to be *laïc* in a pluralist France still has a long way to go.

I do not support the hypothesis of a 'failure' of the republican model. It would place far too much emphasis on the idea of the uniqueness of being a Frenchman/woman, placing the burden on the individual, while the current challenge is rather to perform a pluralist representation of the nation (integration being multidimensional) that takes into account the accountability of institutions. The culturalist turn of Anglo-American political theory has certainly impacted on the way French social scientists have started criticizing the French model of integration. One could even say that, 'like liberalism, republicanism has in the past two decades or so been internally reconfigured (albeit differently from liberalism) by its confrontation with new questions relating to cultural identity – both national and subnational' (Laborde, 2001: 717). On the one hand, republicanism has reinforced the internal coherence of cultural nationalism articulated through the rejection of multiculturalism (see the recurring petitions by the 'extreme republican' front represented by Badinter, Debray, Finkielkraut, Sallenave et al.). On the other hand, the new significance and value given to cultural identity has strongly influenced the relativization of the need for France to think of itself as culture-blind and opened possibilities for critical discussion of the role, for instance, of ethnic attachment in the individual citizen's life (Fassin, 2007). Jennings distinguishes between three basic positions in France: traditional republicanism that sees the nation under constant threat; a 'modernizing' republicanism endorsing some elements of cultural pluralism while sticking to key republican concepts; and a 'multiculturalist' republicanism calling for a pluralist conception of civic identity with a positive assessment of minority cultures (Jennings, 2000: 584–5). The inherited model is being reworked and transformed by different experiences, including the European one.

Notes

1. This chapter was drafted before the creation of the parliamentary mission on the wearing of the burqa on French territory (July 2009) and the launch of the discussion on national identity (September 2009–January 2010).

2. The 1791 emancipation of the Jews is a major implicit reference for all religious and ethnic minorities that have negotiated the institutionalization of worship. While becoming French, Jews were incorporated individually into French citizenship independent of their religious belonging (Benbassa, 2003).

3. In a recent Pew survey, France was the most secularized country in the European Union: only one person in ten said that religion is 'very important' in one's life and 60 per cent of interviewees said they never pray (Pew, 2008).

4. Dealing with equal opportunity policies in France, parity was as much a challenge to republicanism as race equality: it was about ensuring concrete, and not only formal, equality by making the distinction not only visible but recognized (Lépinard, 2008).

5. The positioning of the French tradition vis-à-vis the British one is not identical to the way the US counter-example is thought of. Much use is made, for instance, of America's own critiques of multiculturalism and the denunciation of the tyranny of minorities (Jennings, 2000). The US example worked in the early 1990s as a counter-model to strengthen a French national identity and an integration project that were considered to be in danger (Granjon, 1994). The so-called 'dictatorship of minorities' that led to the domination of a new politically correct moral order was the occasion in France of the reaffirmation of the validity of the universalistic egalitarian republican model, and the imperative of keeping distance from any attempt to import elements of multicultural policies into the integration project. For French intellectuals who discussed the failure of the US multiculturalist project, the central motive was related to the risk of ethnic and tribal fragmentation of national societies. The French perspective on

US multiculturalism is a never-ending discussion: the latter embodies a 'pluriculturalism' that the former considers the main danger to its national and territorial integrity (Garbaye, 2007).

6. French perpetuation of *jus soli* dates back to February 1851, the first law establishing an automatic link between place of birth and access to French nationality: all children born in France from a father born in France are French by birth. In 1893, the same legal provision was extended to the mother. Since the second half of the 1980s, the conditions for receiving French nationality have regularly been legally modified.

7. Communalism is a notion that dates back to the 1920s in British India and refers to the belonging to a community, either Muslim or Hindu. Initially, the connotation was rather negative, implying a hierarchy. Communalism became a positive concept later on when integrated in the electoral system in 1909 (Kepel, 1994: 130–33).

8. In 2006, the annual High Council for Integration (HCI) report summarized three years of integration policies saying: 'The model of integration *à la française* is often criticized. As for all ideal-types, it does not respond to a changing reality. We however remain convinced that we should not throw out the baby with the bath water, as the only alternative suggested would consist in the importation of an Anglo-Saxon type of model that officially supports communalism. This approach would contradict our values, our conception of social life. And such a shift would take a very long time to be implemented, while the situation is urging us to act quickly. Lastly, it would be paradoxical to rely on a formula whose main advocates deeply question its relevance, as the recent developments in Great Britain or in the Netherlands illustrate' (HCI, 2006: 18, author's translation).

9. One good illustration is the seminal work conducted by Beckford et al. on British and French prisons. While looking at the way Muslim prisoners are treated by the two administrative officers, they assess the impact of the two opposing integration policies on the way different populations among prisoners are mistreated on a daily basis, aggravating the marginalization and discrimination of Muslims inside prison (Beckford et al., 2005).

10. The 'classical republican ideology consisted of a basic commitment to the concepts of political liberty and equality of condition, and the foundation of a political order based upon representative institutions and the principle of popular sovereignty; these principles were reflected in the French Republic's motto of liberty, equality, and fraternity' (Hazareesingh, 1994: 65).

11. Historically, the first mention of the word dates back to 1871, in a text dealing with public education. Just as there is no definition of religion in the French legal tradition, there is no definition of *laïcité*, which is a notion that evolves through jurisprudence and exists mostly through specific interactions. For a discussion regarding the proper translation of the term, see Baubérot, 2007: 19–20.

12. The historical structural meaning of this distinction between what can be done in public and what cannot (which is also related to the assignation of a role to the state to exercise its control over social practices) is a wider

dynamic attached to the republican tradition of secularization of all domains of social life. Iacub illustrates this private–public dynamic in relation to the control of differences in public life by working on the way the republican post-revolutionary tradition supported the legal implementation of a governance of bodies through the control of private space (Iacub, 2008).

13. That is, 'the social process that transforms values and principles into action and subjectivity thanks to a specific professional competence'. From this emerges a socialized individual and autonomous subject (Dubet, 2002: 24).

14. In 2005, during riots, 500 British imams had published an anti-violence fatwa (legal ruling). The Union of Islamic Organizations of France (UOIF) published a fatwa against the French 2005 riots, urging the creation of neighbourhood patrols: 'All Muslims living in France, whether French citizens or guests of France, are entitled to insist on the scrupulous respect for each person, their dignity and their beliefs, and to act on behalf of greater equality and social justice. But this action, whether organized or spontaneous, must not be in contradiction with the above teachings and the law governing public life.' Available at www.uoif-online.com.

15. The best empirical analysis of the 2005 riots can be found in Jobard, 2009.

16. In September 2004, when the law was first applied in public schools, 47 expulsions took place.

17. Directive 2000/43/CE of 28 June 2000 and Directive 2000/78/CE of 27 November 2000. The Directives covered both direct and indirect discrimination and allowed scope for 'positive action'. The EU legislation is novel in the way it favours the achievement of substantive equality and expands the notion of indirect discrimination – defined as the fact that apparently neutral laws and practices disadvantage persons from specific groups. It introduces notions such as harassment and victimization. Finally, it sets up procedural guarantees for making those rights effective (e.g. shifting the burden of proof in procedures) and requires the creation of national equality bodies to promote anti-discrimination initiatives and monitor implementation.

18. Chirac himself, in June 1991, issued polemical declarations, the most famous of which was made on commercial radio about *les bruits et les odeurs* (the racket and smell) coming from migrants living in poor neighbourhoods and disturbing the 'honest French worker returning home in the evening'.

19. The classical distinction between types of multiculturalism (as political project, as descriptive terminology, as pragmatic policies) has been extensively worked out recently in the context of the 'crisis' of multiculturalism (Modood, 2007; Malik, Chapter 1 of this volume)

20. This text was drafted before the Committee for the Measurement of Diversity and the Evaluation of Discriminations (COMEDD) began its work, and the publication of its report in February 2010.

21. 'Going public' refers here to the simultaneous intensification of discourses on the incompatibility of Islam and democracy, Islam and secularism, the increased designation of Muslims as potential suspects following 9/11, the politicization of Islamophobia, and the double-standard discourse regarding Muslim mobilization in European contexts at large. See Amiraux, 2006.

22. It is no surprise that most of the abusive interpretations of the application of the March 2004 law prevented women wearing a headscarf at such ceremonies as receiving their decree of naturalization. See, in this respect, the deliberation 2006-131, 5 June 2006, HALDE.
23. In October 1870 (the Crémieux Decree), Jews native to Algeria became French citizens.
24. The *Bureaux Arabes* (Arab offices) since 1833 in Algeria and the Commission interministérielle des affaires musulmanes (CIAM), created in June 1911, were meant to relay central French policy to networks of local partners (Le Pautremat, 2003).
25. For a parallel reading of the stigmatization of body practices linked to religion (prayer, headscarf) and sports, see Silverstein, 2004; Guénif, 2005.
26. On a totally different stage, but one I consider related, Zinedine Zidane's headbutt during the 2006 World Cup finals, while a public violation of sporting norms and practices, was also proof for some of an inability to control his personal emotions, and a failure to live up to the nobility expected in high-level sport. Yasmin Jiwani draws attention to the Orientalist and specifically animal imagery employed by the international press to describe and interpret the event, which drew the conclusion that the player had failed to integrate (Jiwani, 2008). Media coverage of the event also contained the same construction of a racialized image of the figure of the heterosexual Arab (or here, Kabyle) man, one of whose duties is to defend the honour of his family's women, insulted by a player from the other team.
27. One thinks, for instance, of the hardening of the laws dealing with family reunification, of the public campaigns against 'forced/arranged marriages' (two practices that are definitely not synonymous but are still confused), of the unanticipated effects of new migration policies in Europe.
28. See, for example, the draft Law no. 1121 proposed on 23 September 2008 by Jacques Myard banning burqas in public.

References

Achi, Raberh (2007) '"L'islam authentique appartient à Dieu, 'l'islam algérien' à César". La mobilisation de l'association des oulémas d'Algérie pour la séparation du culte musulman et de l'État (1931–1956)', *Genèses* 4(69): 49–69.
Amiraux Valérie (2001) *Acteurs de l'islam entre Allemagne et Turquie. Parcours militants et expériences religieuses*, Paris: L'Harmattan.
Amiraux, Valérie (2006) 'Speaking as a Muslim: Avoiding Religion in French Public Space', in G. Jonker and V. Amiraux (eds), *Politics of Visibility*, Bielefeld: Transcript Verlag, pp. 21–52.
Amiraux, Valérie (2007) 'Religious Discrimination: Muslims Claiming Equality in the EU', in Christophe Bertossi (ed.), *European Anti-discrimination and the Politics of Citizenship: France and Britain*, Basingstoke: Palgrave Macmillan, pp. 143–67.
Amiraux, Valérie (2008) 'De l'Empire à la République: à propos de l'islam de France', *Cahiers de recherche sociologique* 46, September.

Amiraux, Valérie, and Virginie Guiraudon (2010) 'Discrimination in Comparative Perspective: Policies and Practices', *American Behavioral Scientist* 53(12).

Amiraux, V., and P. Simon (2006) 'There Are No Minorities Here: Cultures of Scholarship and Public Debate on Immigrants and Integration in France', *International Journal of Comparative Sociology*, 47(3/4): 191–215.

Bancel, Nicolas, Pascal Blanchard and Sandrine Lemaire (2003), *La Fracture Coloniale*, Paris: La Découverte.

Baubérot, Jean (1990), *La laïcité quel héritage? De 1789 à nos jours*, Geneva: Labor et Fides.

Baubérot, Jean (2003) 'Société civile et société politique. Une société multiculturelle jusqu'où?', *Cahiers français* 316: 27–33.

Baubérot, Jean (2004) *Laïcité 1905–2005, entre passion et raison*, Paris: Seuil.

Baubérot, Jean (2005) *Histoire de la laïcité en France*, Paris. Seuil.

Baubérot, Jean (2007) *Les laïcités dans le monde*, Paris: PUF.

Beckford, James, Danièle Joly and Farhad Khosrokhavar (eds) (2005) *Muslims in Prison: Challenge and Change in Britain and France*, London: Palgrave.

Benbassa, Esther (2003) *La République face à ses minorités. Les Juifs hier, les Musulmans aujourd'hui*, Paris: Mille et une nuits.

Bleich, Erik (1995) 'The Legacies of History? Colonization and Immigrant Integration in Britain and France', *Theory and Society* 34(2): 171–95.

Bleich Erik (2003), *Race Politics in Britain and France*, Cambridge: Cambridge. University Press.

Bowen, John (2006) *Why the French Don't Like Headscarves: Islam, the State, and Public Space*, Princeton NJ: Princeton University Press.

Brubaker, Rogers (1992) *Citizenship and Nationhood in France and Germany*, Cambridge MA: Harvard University Press.

Cole, A., P. Le Galès and J. Levy (2008) 'From Chirac to Sarkozy: A New France?', *Developments in French Politics*, New York: Palgrave Macmillan, pp. 1–21.

Costa-Lascoux, Jacqueline (2006) 'L'intégration "à la française": une philosophie à l'épreuve des réalités', *Revue européenne des migrations internationales* 22(2): 105–26.

Deloye, Yves (1995) *École et citoyenneté*, Paris: Presses de Sciences Po.

Deltombe, Thomas (2005), *L'islam imaginaire: la construction médiatique de l'islamophobie en France (1975–2005)*, Paris: La Découverte.

Dubet, François (2002), *Le déclin de l'institution*, Paris: Le Seuil.

Duchesne, S. (1997) *Citoyenneté à la française*, Paris: Presses de Sciences Po.

Dumont, Louis (1994) *German Ideology: From France to Germany and Back*, Chicago: Chicago University Press.

Fassin, Didier (2002) 'L'invention française de la discrimination', *Revue française de science politique* 52(4): 403–23.

Fassin, Didier, and Éric Fassin (2006) *De la question sociale à la question raciale. Représenter la société française*, Paris: La Découverte.

Fassin, Didier, and Patrick Simon (2008) 'Un objet sans nom. L'introduction des discrimination raciales dans la statistique française', *L'Homme, Miroirs transatlantiques* 187–188: 271–94.

Favell, Adrian (1998) *Philosophies of Integration: Immigration and the Idea of*

Citizenship in France and Britain, Basingstoke: Macmillan.

Felouzis, Georges (2008) 'L'usage des catégories ethniques en sociologie', *Revue française de sociologie* 49(1): 127–62.

de Galembert, Claire (2008) 'Le voile en procès', *Droit et Société* 66.

Garbaye, Romain (2000) 'Ethnic Minorities, Cities, and Institutions', in Ruud Koopmans and Paul Statham (eds), *Challenging Immigration and Ethnic Relations Politics, Comparative European Perspectives*, Oxford: Oxford University Press, 2000, pp. 283–311.

Garbaye, Romain (2007) 'Crossing Paths? The British and French Experiences with Racial and Ethnic Diversity since 9/11', presented at 'Multiculturalism and Its Discontents', University of Colorado at Boulder, 23–25 April.

Geddes, Andrew, and Virginie Guiraudon (2006) 'The Europeanization of Anti-discrimination in Britain and France', in C. Bertossi, *European Anti-discrimination and the Politics of Citizenship: France and Britain*, Basingstoke: Palgrave Macmillan, pp. 125–42.

Geisser, Vincent (2005), 'Ethnicité républicaine versus République ethnique?', *Mouvements* 38, March–April.

Granjon, Marie-Christine (1994) 'Le regard en biais. Attitudes françaises et multiculturalisme américain (1990–1993)', *Vingtième Siècle. Revue d'histoire* 43, July–September: 18–29.

Guénif, Nacira (2005) 'La réduction à son corps de l'indigène de la République', in Nicolas Bancel, Pascal Blanchard and Sandrine Lemaire (eds), *La fracture coloniale*, Paris: La Découverte, pp. 199–209.

Guénif, Nacira (2006) 'La Française voilée, la beurette, le garçon arabe et le musulman laïc. Les figures assignées du racisme vertueux', in N. Guénif (ed.), *La République mise à nu par son immigration*, Paris: La Fabrique, pp. 109–132.

Guénif, Nacira, and Eric Macé (2004). *Les féministes et le garçon arabe*, Paris: Éditions de l'aube.

Guiraudon, Virginie (2006) 'L'intégration des immigrés ou la politique de l'esquive. Réformer sans changer de modèle', in P. Culpepper, P. Hall and B. Palier (eds), *La France en mutation: 1980–2005*, Paris: Presses de Sciences Po.

Hargreaves, Alec (1995) *Immigration, 'Race' and Ethnicity in Contemporary France*, London: Routledge.

Hargreaves, Alec (2007) 'Chemins de traverse. Vers une reconnaissance de la postcolonialité en France', *Mouvements* 3(51): 24–31.

Hazareesingh, Sudhir (1994) *Political Traditions in Modern France*, Oxford: Oxford University Press.

HCI (Haut Conseil à l'Intégration) (1998) *Lutte contre les discriminations : faire respecter le principe d'égalité, rapport au Premier ministre*, Paris: La documentation française.

HCI (2002) *Les parcours d'intégration*, Paris: La documentation française.

HCI (2004) *Le contrat et l'intégration*, Paris: La documentation française.

HCI (2006) *Le bilan de la politique d'intégration 2002–2005*. Paris: La documentation française.

HCI (2008) *Charte de la laïcité dans les services publics et autres avis*, Paris: La documentation française.

Iacub Marcella (2008) *Par le trou de la serrure. Une histoire de la pudeur publique XIX–XXIè siècle*, Paris. Fayard.

Ion, Jacques (1999) 'Engagements associatifs et espace public', *Mouvements* 3, March–April.

Jobard, Fabien (2009) 'Rioting as a Political Tool', *Howard Journal for Criminal Justice* 48(3).

Jennings, Jeremy (2000) 'Citizenship, Republicanism and Multiculturalism in Contemporary France', *British Journal of Political Science* 30(4): 575–97.

Joly, Danièle (1994) 'Is "Multiculturalism" the Answer? Policies on Ethnic Minorities in Britain', in Grigoriou Panayotis (ed.), *Questions de Minorités en Europe*, Brussells: Presses Interuniversitaires européennes.

Jonker, Gerdien, and Valérie Amiraux (2006) *Politics of Visibility: Young Muslims in European Public Spaces*, Bielefeld: Transcript Verlag.

Kaltenbach, Marie-Hélène, and Michèle Tribalat (2002) *La République et l'Islam. Entre crainte et aveuglement*, Paris: Gallimard.

Kastoryano, Riva (1997) *La France, l'Allemagne et leurs immigrés: négocier l'identité*, Paris: Armand Colin.

Kastoryano, Riva (ed.) (2005) *Quelle identité pour l'Europe? Le multiculturalisme à l'épreuve*, Paris: Presses de Sciences Po.

Kastoryano, Riva (ed.) (2006) *Les codes de la différence*, Paris: Presses de Sciences Po.

Kepel, Gilles (2005) 'Europe's Answer to Londonistan', *Opendemocracy*, 24 August, www.opendemocracy.net.

Kepel, Gilles (1994) *À l'ouest d'Allah*, Paris: Le Seuil.

Khosrokhavar, Farhad (1996) 'L'Universel abstrait, le politique et la construction de l'Islamisme comme forme d'altérité', in Michel Wieviorka (ed.), *Une société fragmentée? Le multiculturalisme en débat*, Paris: La Découverte, pp. 113–51.

Kirszbaum, Thomas (2008) *Mixité sociale dans l'habitat. Revue de la littérature dans une perspective comparative*, Paris: La documentation française.

Kirszbaum, Thomas (2004) 'Discours et pratiques de l'intégration des immigrés. L'exemple des Grands projets de ville', *Annales de la recherche urbaine* 97.

Kintzler, Catherine (2007) *Qu'est ce que la laïcité*, Paris: Vrin.

Koussens, David (2009), 'Neutrality of the State and Regulation of Religious Symbols in Schools in Québec and France', *Social Compass* 56(2): 202–13.

Kriegel, Blandine (1998) *Philosophie de la République*, Paris: Plon.

Laborde, Cécile (2001) 'The Culture(s) of the Republic: Nationalism and Multiculturalism in French Republican Thought', *Political Theory* 29(5): 716–35.

Laborde, Cécile (2005), 'Secular Philosophy and Muslim Headscarves', *Journal of Political Philosophy* 13(2): 139–47.

Lapeyronnie, Didier (1993) *L'individu et les minorités. La France et la Grande-Bretagne face à leurs immigrés*, Paris: PUF.

Laurence, Jonathan, and Justin Vaisse (2006) *Integrating Islam: Political and Religious Challenges in Contemporary France*, Washington DC: Brookings Institution Press.

Laurens, Henry (2004) *Orientales II. La IIIème République et l'Islam*, Paris, CNRS éditions.

Le Pautremat, Pascal (2003) *La politique musulmane de la France au XXème siècle. De l'Hexagone aux terres d'Islam*, Paris: Maisonneuve et Larose.

Lépinard, Éléonore (2008) 'Gender and Multiculturalism: The Politics of Difference at a Crossroads', in A. Cole, P. Le Galès and J. Levy (eds), *Developments in French Politics 4*, New York: Palgrave, pp. 92–110.

Lloyd, Cathie (1999) 'Race and Ethnicity', in Malcolm Cook and Grace Davie (eds), *Modern France: Society in Transition*, London: Routledge, pp. 33–52.

Long, Marceau (1988) *Être français aujourd'hui et demain: Rapport de la Commission de la nationalité*, Paris: La documentation française.

Lorcerie, Françoise (ed.) (2005) *La politisation du voile: l'affaire en France, en Europe et dans le monde arabe*, Paris: L'Harmattan.

Mazouz, Sarah (2008), 'Une célébration paradoxale. Les cérémonies de remise des décrets de naturalisation', *Genèses* 70, March: 88–105.

Merle, Isabelle, and Emmanuelle Sibeud (2003), 'Histoire en marge ou histoire en marche? La colonisation entre repentance et patrimonialisation', http://histoire-sociale.univ-paris1.fr/Collo/usages.htm.

Modood, Tariq (2007) *Multiculturalism*, Cambridge: Polity Press.

Mouvements (1999) 'Un modèle français de discrimination, *Mouvements* 4.

Muchielli, Laurent (2005) *Le scandale des 'tournantes'. Dérives médiatiques, contre-enquête sociologique*, Paris: La Découverte.

Noiriel, Gérard (1996) *The French Melting Pot: Immigration, Citizenship, and National identity*, Minneapolis: University of Minnesota Press.

Noiriel, Gérard (2007) *Immigration, antisémitisme et racisme en France (XIXe-XXe siècle) - Discours publics, humiliations privées*, Paris: Fayard.

Ollier, Fabien (2004) *L'idéologie multiculturaliste en France. Entre fascisme et libéralisme*, Paris: L'Harmattan.

Peer, Shanny, and Daniel Sabbagh (eds) (2008) 'French Colour-blindness in Perspective. The Controversy over "Statistiques Ethniques"', *French Politics, Culture and Society* 26(1).

Perreau, Bruno (2004) 'L'invention républicaine. Eléments d'une herméneutique républicaine', *Pouvoirs* 111: 41–53.

Pew (2008) *Unfavorable Views of Jews and Muslims on the Increase in Europe*, Pew Global Attitudes Project, http://pewglobal.org/2008/09/17/unfavorable-views-of-jews-and-muslims-on-the-increase-in-europe/.

Rawls, John (1993) *Political Liberalism*, New York: Columbia University Press.

Rea, Andrea, and Maryse Tripier (2003) *Sociologie de l'immigration*, Paris: La Découverte.

Rioux, Jean-Pierre (2002) 'Vivacité du récit français des origines', *Vingtième Siècle. Revue d'Histoire* 76, October–December: 131–7.

Saada Emmanuelle (2006), 'Un racisme de l'expansion. Les discriminations raciales au regard des situations coloniales', in Didier Fassin and Eric Fassin (eds), *De la question sociale à la question raciale? Représenter la société française*, Paris: La Découverte, pp. 55–71.

Sabbagh, Daniel (2002) 'Affirmative Action at Sciences Po', *French Politics, Culture, and Society*, 20(3): 52–64.

Safi, Mirna (2008) 'The Immigrant Integration Process in France: Inequalities and Segmentation', *Revue française de sociologie* 49(5): 3–44.

Schnapper, Dominique (1991) *La France de l'intégration. Sociologie de la nation en 1990*, Paris: Gallimard.

Schnapper, Dominique (1999) 'Traditions nationales et connaissance rationnelle', *Sociologie et Société* 31(2).

Schnapper, Dominique (2004) *Guide Républicain*, Paris: La documentation française.

Schor Paul, and Alexis Spire (2006) 'Les statistiques de la population comme construction de la nation', in Riva Kastoryano (ed.), *Les codes de la différence*, Paris: Presses de Sciences Po, pp. 91–146.

Silvermann, Maxim (1992) *Deconstructing the Nation: Immigration, Racism and Citizenship in Modern France*, London: Routledge.

Silverstein Paul (2004), *Algeria in France*, Bloomington: Indiana University Press.

Simon, Patrick (2003) 'Les sciences sociales françaises face aux catégories ethniques et raciales', *Annales de démographie historique* 1: 111–30.

Simonin, Anne (2008) *Le déshonneur dans la République: une histoire de l'indignité*, Paris: Grasset.

Spire, Alexis (2003) 'Semblables et pourtant différents. La citoyenneté paradoxale des "Français musulmans d'Algérie" en métropole', *Genèses* 53: 48–68.

Stavo-Debauge Joan (2007) 'L'invisibilité du tort et le tort de l'invisibilité', *Espacestemps.net, Actuel*, 19 April, http://espacestemps.net/document2233.html.

Stavo-Debauge Joan (2003) 'Prendre position contre l'usage de catégories "ethniques" dans la statistique publique. Le sens commun constructiviste, une manière de se figurer un danger politique', in Pascale Laborier and Danny Trom (eds), *Historicités de l'action publique*, Paris: PUF, pp. 294–327.

Taguieff, Pierre-André (2005) *La République enlisée*, Paris: Seuil.

Taguieff, Pierre-André (1989) *La force du préjugé. Essai sur le racisme et ses doubles*, Paris: La Découverte.

Tribalat, Michèle (1995) *Faire France*, Paris: La Découverte.

Valluy, Jérôme (2008) 'Xénophobie de gouvernement, nationalisme d'Etat', *Cultures & Conflits* 69.

Walzer, Michael (1997) *On Toleration*, New Haven CT: Yale University Press.

Weber, Eugen (1979) *Peasants into Frenchmen: The Modernization of Rural France 1870–1914*, London: Chatto & Windus.

Weil, Patrick (2002) *Qu'est-ce qu'un Français? Histoire de la nationalité française depuis la Révolution*, Paris: Grasset.

Weil, Patrick (2005) *La République et sa diversité. Immigration, intégration, discriminations*, Paris, Seuil.

Wieviorka Michel (ed.) (1996) *Une société fragmentée? Le multiculturalisme en débat*, Paris: La Découverte.

Zeghal, Malika (2005) 'La constitution du Conseil Français du Culte Musulman: reconnaissance politique d'un Islam français ?', *Archives de sciences sociales des religions* 129.

3

The German Sonderweg: multiculturalism as 'racism with a distance'

Stephan Lanz

In West Germany, the debate on multiculturalism first emerged in the left-wing political scene and in pedagogical circles. It was then taken up by politicians concerned with social and labour market affairs, before achieving the decisive media exposure and becoming a political issue in the late 1980s. The German debate adopted basic concepts from earlier discourses on multiculturalism that had developed, for example, in Canada and Australia. In these countries, multiculturalism had already become a 'state doctrine' (Nassehi, 1997) by the end of the 1970s. However, in Germany the discourse on multiculturalism was adapted within the specific German norms regarding immigration.

Hence, the German model of multiculturalism cannot be properly understood without taking into account the context and history of German immigration policies. Therefore multiculturalism in (West) Germany will be analysed here as an ambiguous political concept and tool with which to deal with immigration at different levels: in public discourse, and in national as well as regional politics, with the city state of (West) Berlin as a particularly interesting and telling example. Berlin was the first West German state to pursue its own multicultural integration policy. Further, the city has for decades been used as a key reference point, both by advocates and by opponents of multiculturalism in Germany.

As will be shown, 'multiculturalism' has proved to be an extremely flexible concept for German politicians, compatible with various political ideologies. At the same time, one can identify a specific German model of multiculturalism which to this day, a quarter of a century after its emergence, still has a substantial impact on political debate concerning the whole complex issue of immigration.

The historical continuity of German immigration policy

After the West German government had signed the first treaty with Italy on the official recruitment of migrant labour in 1955, similar agreements were reached with Spain and Greece (1960), Turkey (1961), Morocco (1963), Portugal (1964), Tunisia (1965) and Yugoslavia (1968). Several million so-called 'guest workers' had emigrated to the Federal Republic of Germany by 1973.

These treaties guaranteed foreign employees the same wages as their German counterparts, and provided for a rotation system by restricting their residence permits to a maximum of one year and by linking them to a single employer. As members of the European Economic Community (EEC) only Italians were exempt from this regulation. These measures showed a remarkable continuity with the preceding three political systems (German Reich, Weimar Republic, Nazi Germany), unmasking the official narrative of a new beginning for Germany's post-war immigration policy as a fiction (Herbert 2001: 201). Rather, one might reasonably conclude that the government wanted to attain 'extensive control over the presence of foreigners' (Schönwälder, 2001: 219). Already in the early 1950s, the National Socialist 'foreigners police decree' (*Ausländerpolizeiverordnung*, APVO) from 1938 and the 'decree on foreign employees' from 1933 had been reinstated, although, according to the Ministry of the Interior of Schleswig-Holstein in 1948, their 'explicit xenophobic character' and their 'removal of all legal guarantees' for non-German residents were well known (Schönwälder, 2001: 219). With the introduction of a 'central register of foreigners' (*Ausländerzentralregister*) in 1953, the national government began recording personal data on immigrants (while similar data storage for German citizens was prohibited by law) as well as possible objections to their entry into Germany (Dietrich,

2005). Around the same time, 'aliens were too often stigmatized with an embarrassing lack of historical awareness as undesirable, or even criminal and antisocial' (Schönwälder, 2001: 220). Displaced persons, in particular, most of them former inmates of the National Socialist concentration camps, became the victims of such verbal attacks. Thus the discursive structures that would dominate political debate in West Germany for decades to come had already been put in place, before the number of 'guest workers' expanded significantly at the beginning of the 1960s, and the 'general labelling of foreigners as a menace, the notion of immigration as a permanently growing danger, as illegal, as "infiltration" or a "flood"' (Schönwälder, 2001: 224).

Accordingly, the German foreigners law (*Ausländergesetz*), which passed on a broad vote across all political parties in 1965 was influenced by an authoritarian understanding of the state, consistent with traditions of the APVO. Its aim was to enable the government to register and closely control all residents of foreign nationality and deport them immediately if required (Dohse, 1981; Ha, 2003). The protection of the individual civil rights of migrants was subordinated to 'concerns and interests of the German state', and the granting of a residence permit remained an act of mercy (Dietrich, 2005: 293). Administrative discretion provided for a flexible system that was used to supply the West German labour market with the manpower needed for the economy (Herbert, 2001: 211). By that time, even lesbian relationships among recruited workers, disturbance of the industrial peace, troubling the authorities or insufficient integration were considered to be offences against the public interest and ranked among the reasons for deportation. Furthermore, different legal interpretations of the law insisted that certain groups of migrants violated the interests of the Federal Republic because they were seen as unable to adjust to the German way of life. Although it was never declared an official policy, due to reasons of image, the national post-war German governments adopted highly selective strategies towards immigrants, based on ethnic origin and skin colour. In most instances, so-called 'Afro-Asians' (*Afroasiaten*) were excluded from obtaining a residence permit, on the grounds that their customs appeared 'too strange' to Germans. The term 'Afro-Asian' merged all subjects with an African or Asian origin, becoming a general category for incompatible strangers (Schönwälder, 2001). Notwithstanding this discrimination, the German foreigners law was considered to be liberal, as it guaranteed long-term immigrants more favourable terms than did preceding laws.

The recruitment of migrant workers was accepted as an economic necessity and won widespread approval within German society. Not only the legal instruments but also the general assessments by political and media elites were similar to those of the Wilhelminian Empire and the Weimar Republic. The deployment of migrant labour was considered to be beneficial for the country because the workers were young and therefore very efficient, and generated no educational or follow-up costs. Moreover, they prevented the need for wage in-creases for low-skilled workers and made it possible for Germans to rise to better positions. In addition, immigration was regarded as anticipatory of European integration. These 'encounters between Europeans', however, was not that of equals. Rather, most Germans saw themselves – informed by colonial discourses – as educators and 'development workers', doing 'guest workers' a favour. Immigrants were regarded as children in need of support and attendance, and at the same time perceived as uncivilized but sexually potent Mediter-ranean types (Schönwälder, 2001: 166). The media emphasized time and again – often as an attempt to promote more tolerance and empathy – the neediness especially of female migrant workers. This was not an openly hostile but rather a paternalistic gesture that sharply distinguished between 'us' and 'them'. In public discourse the presence of migrants was for the most part linked with labour market issues and crime. The stereotype of the impulsive and violence-prone 'southerner' characterized an overall category of the 'foreign worker' which did not make a distinction between ethnic origins and cultural affiliations.

In the wake of the recession in 1966 more than 400,000 migrant workers left West Germany. By then, many Germans had started to question the economic usefulness of the guest worker system. Gradu-ally, a public discourse emerged and intensified that claimed there was a 'problem caused by foreigners' (*Ausländerproblem*). Its central elements were 'their difference', language and communication prob-lems and the lack of assimilation. As migrants assumed an increasing visibility in certain urban neighbourhoods, officials worried about the formation of 'ghettos' and cautioned against social and political (communist) 'alien elements' and thus the disintegration of society. A decisive aspect of the discourse on the 'immigrant problem' was the idea that the growing number of strangers in Germany would take over the national economy and culture. 'This imagined threat, which has been a very powerful influence on German nationalism since the end of the nineteenth century, was obviously still firmly rooted in German society and not disavowed through history' (Schönwälder, 2001: 200). By the 1960s, debates on 'assimilation' and 'integration' had become more common and were dominated by the notion of a temporary integration of immigrants who would later return to their home country. Assimilation, understood as the detachment from identity, roots and customs, was rejected by most politicians, especially by conservatives, who believed that it would be a hindrance to the returning home of the so-called 'guests'. A spokesperson of an employers' association (cited Schönwälder, 2001: 207) defined integration on behalf of many others around that time as the 'adaptation to our social life, our idea of order, our lifestyle and our mentality'. In this understanding, nationalistic notions of nationality and ethnicity as values on their own merged with rather instrumentalist intentions to keep the idea alive that immigrants had to go back to their countries of origin when their labour was no longer needed.

Former political conceptions of integration: Berlin

In 1971, the Social Democratic senate in Berlin set up an initial planning committee supposed to develop measures for a 'harmonious integration of foreign employees and their families' (Der Regierende Bürgermeister, 1972: 2). It formulated the so-called 'demand-oriented integration model', motivated by the goal to regulate and control immigration in accordance with German interests: namely economic growth and the maintenance of law and order. A political model to foster non-transient immigration was explicitly rejected, however, with the argument that this would facilitate 'foreign infiltration' and 'thus pose a threat to Germany's constitutional system and its democracy as well as to public security and order' (Der Regierende Bürgermeister,

1972: 2). The 'demand-oriented integration model' was supposed to allow for a 'selective process by which the state could single out those migrant workers who were deemed willing and capable of integration, while the vast majority were relegated to the rotation system' (Der Regierende Bürgermeister, 1972: 13). For the few chosen ones, this model was meant to provide for reliable future prospects in Germany and various support services to assist them with integration, while at the same time motivating 'loyal behavior towards German society' and leading, in the medium term, to a process of 'normalization'. Some migrant families were seen as capable of melting into 'German culture', whereas the rest of them were supposed to return to their home countries.

This model of integration was the first example of an immigration policy which for decades tried to profit from the recruitment of migrant labour, while shying away from dealing with the political and financial consequences of a multi-ethnic population structure. Its ultimate goal was to exploit the potential of migrant workers at optimal cost. German immigration policies were from now on characterized by two double binds: on the one hand, the majority of immigrants were required to conform to German society, while at the same time they were asked to prepare for their return home at the end of their employment contracts. On the other hand, the cultivation of the presumably alien national character of the 'guest workers' was both encouraged by the government and stigmatized as a potential danger and proof that they lacked the will to integrate. Thus, the local state simultaneously introduced German lessons for immigrant children and promoted classes where they were to learn about their countries of origin (*Heimatunterricht*), in order to prevent their 'national estrangement' and not jeopardize a return (Der Regierende Bürgermeister 1972: 41ff.).

The recruitment ban and its results

The social–liberal coalition under Chancellor Willy Brandt, which took over the federal government in 1969, at first tied its immigration policy to other social and democratizing reforms. Since an increase of migrant workers was regarded as indispensable for the economy, the new government considered an integration policy via naturalization. The intention was to fight social evils and better protect minorities, a concern that was raised particularly by Willy Brandt. Initially, the general optimism regarding social reform was successful in pushing back nationalistic sentiment. Nevertheless, the main aim of integration policy in the 1970s continued to be the adjustment of immigrants to mainstream social behavioural norms. It was dominated by the patronizing notion of migrants as temporary 'fellow citizens' in need of special attendance and care. Historically familiar and still powerful resentments, and perceptions of Germany as an ethnically homogeneous society, in combination with apprehensions concerning possible economic crisis, all added to a political climate that fostered a growing rejection of further immigration, even by trade unions and various welfare associations. Cultural plurality as a potential model was not even discussed at that time: human beings were seen as irrevocable parts of a homogeneous nation (*Volk*); 'cultural exchange and change were interpreted in purely negative terms, as uprootings' (Schönwälder, 2001: 525).

The years 1972–73 marked an important turning point in German immigration policy. In November 1973, the recruitment of 'guest workers' came to an end. A political conception had steadily gained ground which defined immigrants as an incalculable expense for the national economy and as a general social burden. In the meantime, the broad discretion German authorities had exercised when dealing with the rights of non-citizen residents had been restricted by various EC regulations and by the fact that an increasing number of long-term immigrants had settled for good in Germany. The hostage-taking and killings during the Olympic Games in Munich in 1972, carried out by a Palestinian organization, also contributed to the more negative perception of non-German residents. The image of 'foreigners as victims of abuses and social evils' that had prevailed until then was replaced by a general bias, based on the portrayal of foreign students and immigrants as potential terrorists. Immigration policy was again more commonly discussed as a matter of national security. Whereas even undocumented migrants – at least for a short period – had formerly been described as victims of economic exploitation, public discourses and media reports on immigration to Germany were now swamped with terms like 'tidal wave', 'invasion' and 'battalions of foreign workers'. All of a sudden, it was claimed that the 'boat was full' and that the 'capacity of the country to absorb' was exhausted. The inadequate provision in many urban neigbourhoods of basic social services was no longer interpreted as a problem caused by a lack of infrastructure but as the product of too many 'foreigners'. In 1973, dramatic reports on the explosive situation in urban areas, including warnings of 'ghetto fires' and open street battles, reached a peak. The term 'negro', whch was by now associated with civil unrest in US cities, as well as the term *Fremdarbeiter*, which was used in Nazi Germany to describe forced labour, resurfaced in public discourse, portraying immigrants as dangerous alien elements and as 'walking time bombs'. In this context, some very influential media branded a spontaneous strike of thousands of migrant workers against dismissals and unreasonable working conditions in the Ford Motor Company of Cologne as 'Turkish terror'. The category 'Turk', which until then had been a somewhat neutral term, became ideologically charged and a synonym for the 'communist threat' (Kleff, 2004). This was particularly true during the Cold War and in the frontier city of Berlin, where the Turkish Socialist Association, founded in 1967, was already viewed with suspicion by officials (Özcan, 1993).

Following the official recruitment ban by the federal government, which intended the return of non–EC-citizens to their home countries to be an irreversible decision, many tried to get their families to Germany and relocate on a permanent basis. Hence the numbers of non-German residents started to grow. As the increasing number of children and family members lowered the proportion of employ-able adults in the migrant communities, the term 'guest worker' was gradually replaced by the term 'foreigner'. In the course of their irreversible settlement in Germany, foreigners were no longer regarded 'as useful members of society who help us to maintain or to increase our gross national product' (Social Democrat MP Schmidt in 1975, cited in Morgenstern, 2002: 251). The term 'foreigner' served, rather, to highlight their alien character, by focusing on descent and different cultural roots. The term 'ghetto' advanced to become a dominant metaphor, branding foreigners as dangerous and suspicious elements. Many politicians held immigrants responsible for the spread of urban 'ghettos', identifying their assumed desire to physically separate themselves from Germans as the main problem. In Berlin, the Kreuzberg district developed into a nationwide symbol for ideological battles around the immigration issue, as the following statement by the Christian Democrat MP Mick during a debate in the Bundestag illustrates (15 May 1975, cited in Morgenstern, 2002: 251): 'When I wander through Berlin–Kreuzberg and feel like I'm in Ankara, something must have gone wrong. We believe something must have gone wrong not because we dislike foreign workers, but rather because we don't want to create new ghettos, because we want to integrate them.' Eventually, the federal government and local officials enacted various ordinances (*Zuzugssperren*) prohibiting new immigrants moving into certain urban areas. In Berlin, non-German residents were not allowed to settle in the inner-city districts of Kreuzberg, Wedding and Tiergarten. A corresponding instruction was placed in their passports, and they could be expelled for failure to abide by the ordinance. This local immigration ban, which many considered unconstitutional, was in effect from 1975 until 1989.

In the late 1970s, an official 'report on the situation of foreigners in Berlin' found that the majority of them had settled permanently in Berlin and, in the meanwhile, had built up a dense entrepreneurial infrastructure. In Kreuzberg alone, the report recorded more than 200 businesses run by immigrants. Other West German cities registered similar developments. Against this background, the first so-called foreigners' representative (*Ausländerbeauftragte*) of the federal government, Heinz Kühn, launched a paper in 1979 which outlined a new policy for dealing with immigration. This 'Kühn Memorandum' confirmed, on the one hand, the official position that Germany was not an immigration country. On the other hand, it demanded for the first time serious efforts by the government to assist immigrants in integrating – even if this meant abandoning the requirement to return to their home country – and the right to naturalization for those who were born in Germany. However, this position did not find favour, and the report had no political consequences (Meier-Braun, 1988). Henceforth, educational inequality and high unemployment among second-generation immigrants became the main focus of integration policies. In 1979, the senate in Berlin set up new 'guidelines and measures for the integration of foreigners in Berlin', which confirmed the previous dual strategy of improving 'integration', while calling for better protection from uncontrolled immigration and the return of unwanted alien residents: 'The senate will do everything to prevent … an additional influx of foreigners' (Meier-Braun, 1988: 12). For the first time, an official paper warned of a 'burdensome asylum-seeker problem'. Moreover, the document claimed that the senate was 'the first local government [in Germany] to recognize immigration … as an irreversible fact' (Presse- und Informationsamt, 1980: 1).

From a homogeneous society to multiculturalism

Until the end of the 1970s, the dominant public discourse in West Germany perceived migrants as a homogeneous category of 'guest workers' and distinguished them from ethnic Germans. In this ideological concept, belonging to a nation or people (*Volk*) was conceived of as a natural community of common descent (*Abstammungsgemeinschaft*) whose biological reproduction was of prime importance, and that was bound by shared physical, spiritual and cultural features. By separating 'our own' from 'the other', foreign nationals were defined as temporary 'guests'. According to Christine Morgenstern (2002: 264), this ideological formation can be interpreted as 'racism without races'. During the 1970s, the fundamental contradiction between this ideological consensus and the reality of migration to Germany became increasingly evident. Especially in urban areas with a growing number of immigrants, everyday life duly produced new forms of acceptance and exclusion, with some groups no longer considered strangers, while others were further stigmatized. By this time, German law and the authorities were already differentiating between citizens of the EC and nationals from other European and Third World countries. With the rapidly growing transnationalization of migrant and refugee movements – due to poverty and political oppression in many countries in the South – a new classification system was established in Europe to deal with the increasing number of asylum-seekers; this was based mainly on cultural and ethnic distinctions. Initially, conservative politicians, in the main, linked the so-called 'integration ability' of migrants to their culture and origins. But eventually it became the aim of the conservative–liberal government under Chancellor Helmut Kohl, which came to power in 1982, to reduce significantly the number of immigrants and asylum-seekers. During the sixteen years of the Kohl administration the main responsibility for immigration policy was exercised by the Ministry of the Interior, marking a shift in focus from regulating the labour market to matters of national security. Part of this shift was a growing concern with asylum-seekers. The official position on immigration in that period was characterized by a generally defensive attitude and a lack of programmes aimed at promoting integration; at the same time, politicians exploited immigration issues in their election campaigns (Bundesministerium, 2000: 41).

By the middle of the 1980s, alarming and aggressive debates 'on the menacing flood of millions from Turkey' (Herbert, 2001: 259) had reached their climax, when – as a result of the EC Treaty – the freedom of movement for Turkish workers finally made it onto the political agenda. The presumed inability, particularly of Turks, to in-tegrate and adjust to German society was increasingly ascribed to their specific national and cultural identity. This identity was said to be part of a 'spiritual and mental inheritance' (Morgenstern, 2002: 315), and was believed to determine the lifestyle, language and religion of every person. Understood as a prerequisite for the well-being of individuals, communities and societies, the conservation of cultural identities came to be seen as essential. Before members of the Green Party were elected to the Bundestag for the first time in 1983, there was an agreement among all political parties in the German parliament that a further influx of immigrants with differing cultural backgrounds had to be avoided to prefent serious conflict. The main concern was Turks and non-European asylum-seekers. At the same time, immigration policy emerged as a controversial and partisan subject. Arguments on both sides – on the one hand, by advocates of immigration and integration; on the other, by conservative politicians who favoured the return of immigrants and advocated separation – grew more confrontational (Herbert, 2001: 254). The Greens characterized the plans of the national-conservative federal minister of the interior, Friedrich Zimmermann, for a new immigration law (*Ausländergesetz*) as an expression of racist thinking, and introduced for the first time the notion of a multicultural society. The conservatives still claimed the existence of an ethnic homogeneity in German society which they wanted to preserve. In very drastic terms, they cautioned against the dangers of a 'multicultural and multi-ethnic state' that would blur all differences. The privileged treatment of ethnic Germans with Soviet or Polish nationality – the so-called *Aussiedler* – whose immigration numbers skyrocketed with the political liberalization in Eastern Europe, illustrated the nationalistic character of this ideology. However, since most social democrats and liberals had given up on the centrality of categories of descent and ancestry, and in the meanwhile acknowledged the multicultural reality of German society, the immigration policy of the conservatives lost sway.

Social-democratic and liberal conceptions of a multicultural society, though, still differentiated between immigrants who were deemed capable of integration and those from cultures that were considered to be too alien; this led to demands for restrictions on the immigration of the latter category (Morgenstern, 2002). Even in the Green version of multiculturalism, the existence of different categories of people, based on origin and cultural identity, was not questioned. It defined 'culture' as the quasi-natural environment of a person which cannot be left behind. Due to very heated public debate and the aggressiveness of national-conservative rhetoric, it went unnoticed for a long time that

> the major difference between the homogeneous and the multicultural
> model of society was the assumption of the latter that cultural
> differences could and should be tolerated. After all, culturalistic
> concepts, beliefs and basic ideas had gained so much ground that the
> most antagonistic positions both referred to them. A new ideologi-
> cal concept gradually began to displace the by then already outdated
> 'racism without races' as the foundation of a general political con-
> sensus: culturalistic racism. (Morgenstern, 2002: 349).

The Christian Democratic Party (CDU) did not begin to distance itself from nationalistic ideologies based on the idea of ethnic homogeneity until Wolfgang Schäuble replaced Friedrich Zimmermann as minister of the interior in 1989. Schäuble's draft of a new immigration law (*Ausländergesetz*) was compatible with the new ideological formation, allowing for a compromise that was acceptable to the majority in the German parliament. The law that came into effect in 1990 was in fact still based on the ideological assumption that Germany was a non-immigration country and that German identity, in the end, had to do with a specific ancestry. However, it was no longer aimed at the preservation of a national culture and an ethnic homogeneity, but codified the actual status quo of immigration and removed certain repressive regulations. At the same time, according to the official justification of the new law, the understanding of integration had been broadened and now included the 'adaptation to local legal, social and economic circumstances' (cited in Treibel, 1990: 51).

Conceptions of multiculturalism in 1980s' West Germany

All concepts of multiculturalism start out from the fundamental premise that immigrants are nationally, ethnically or religiously distinct and should have the right to a certain cultural autonomy. Thus the resulting cultural plurality has an overall positive connotation (Welz, 1996: 106). However, whereas in Canada, the United States and Britain, the concept of multiculturalism has been linked with political demands for equal treatment and measures of anti-discrimination by representatives of ethnic minorities, the German discourse has been almost completely left to the majority; it has highlighted cultural differences and thereby legitimized, often unintentionally, social disparities and inequities. Conflicts and tensions associated with immigration that are the consequence of power relations and social and economic inequalities have been treated as questions of pedagogy (Kürşat-Ahlers, 2002: 329). This German *Sonderweg* is, essentially, the result of a specific notion of German nationality, based on ethnic-cultural conceptions, and on the dominant public discourse, which denied the reality of immigration in Germany for decades.

Nonetheless, considerable differences can be identified within the German discourse on multiculturalism in the 1980s. Back then, conservative and liberal positions fiercely confronted each other in the debate. Moreover, both camps contained competing positions and concerns (cf. Fanizadeh, 1992; Rommelspacher, 2002). The label 'multicultural society' served 'well-meaning xenophiles as well as fascist xenophobes' (Nassehi, 1997: 189). The opponents of a multicultural society interpreted multiculturalism as the coexistence of several national cultures enjoying equal rights, and regarded it therefore as a threat to a German national and cultural identity based on ethnical homogeneity. Conservatives frequently used openly cultural–racist terms in their bitter attacks on multiculturalism. Some approved of multicultural concepts, but used them – as did many right-wing extremists – to oppose any form of immigration or intermixing, since cultures are constructed as essential or intrinsic unities that require a spatial separation in order to be protected.

Typical of conservative discourses in the 1980s was another more instrumental and utilitarian approach linking immigration with demographic issues (Radtke, 1991). In particular, liberal representatives of the Christian Democrats, such as Heiner Geißler, became advocates of a multicultural society, or – in the words of a Christian Democrat strategy paper – of a 'coloured cultural society' (see Leggewie, 1993), providing the 'intellectual and economic resources' that were needed for the regeneration of the country (Geißler, cited in Fanizadeh, 1992: 14). Geißler demanded dual citizenship for migrant workers to meet the demands of the German economy. He thereby rejected 'German origin' as a criterion for affiliation to the nation, which provoked the conservative mainstream. Nevertheless, his formula of 'foreigners ... as utilizers and benificaries of a system that produces a surplus of jobs and acommodations' (15) defines a form of multiculturalism that remains within existing relations of power and economic exploitation.

In contrast to conservative approaches, three liberal concepts of multiculturalism can be distinguished: a tolerant pluralistic model; a pedagogical model; and a model that is grounded in political liberalism. The first model defines cultural diversity as an enrichment of the host culture. This implies a politically naive form of multiculturalism which ignores the challenges and conflicts associated with bargaining processes around issues of and claims for cultural recognition. Moreover, it takes for granted that cultural diversity as such fosters social life and interaction (Neubert et al., 2002: 20). As early as 1989, Thomas Schmid – an early proponent of liberalism – had already criticized this 'harmonizing' form of multiculturalism, claiming that politicians, from both the Green and the Social Democratic parties, had tried to sell multiculturalism as a 'great street party'. According to Schmid, this approach trivializes the 'other' in order to incorporate it into the majority, since its advocates – not much different from right-wing extremists – are incapable of facing up to and accepting real difference (Treibel, 1990: 50). The main arguments of pedagogical approaches to multiculturalism, initially popular in alternative circles until they entered the mainstream social/educational work of churches and welfare organizations, tend to be somewhat moralistic. This does not mean they were not applied as techniques to deal with immigrants. In particular, social welfare organizations and schoolteachers distinguished different groups of immigrants according to their culture. This differentation was meant to make the handling of these new clients easier, by creating manageable and clear-cut categories (Radtke, 1991: 83). In practice, this form of pedagogical multiculturalism presented a social technology for interaction with, and management of, ethnic minorities that corresponded closely to the traditional German paternalism towards immigrants that had emerged during the era of colonialism. The third conception of multiculturalism, based on political liberalism and rooted in Anglo-American discourses, received only minimal attention in West Germany in the 1980s; it is not further discussed here.

However, it is important to stress that in those years any concept of multiculturalism in Germany was grounded in an extremely problematic, unhistorical and essentialist concept of culture, based on the assumption that the identity of any ethnic group is defined by a stable system of cultural homogeneity and a clearly separable set of practices and values. It implies that there is a natural and unchangeable link between culture and ethnicity, and that ethnic groups are self-contained communities of common descent. Therefore all members of these communities share one 'culture', which determines customs and individuals' patterns of interpretation and guides their actions (Bommes and Scherr, 1991). By connecting diversity to ethnic or national origin, this type of multiculturalism defines ethnicity as an anthropological factor (Radtke, 1991: 91). Thus, it remains 'on the track of nationalism, even if it changes direction' (Radtke, 1996:

13). The argument that culture is an individual's second nature is one that barely differs from biological racist theories. Hence, Slavoj Žižek has referred to this form of multiculturalism as 'a disavowed, inverted, self-referential form of racism, a "racism with a distance" – it "respects" the other's identity, conceiving the other as a self-enclosed "authentic" community, towards which he, the multicultural-ist, maintains a distance rendered possible by his privileged universal position' (Žižek, 1997: 44). Thus Žižek emphasizes the issue of power relations concealed within German concepts of multiculturalism. In German debates, which are characterized by paternalistic positions, advocates of multiculturalism usually form the majority. This raises the questions of who defines 'culture' and who uses this term. Very often, the interests of conservative elites, both of the majority and of the minorities, overlap: while the former try to outdistance ethnic mi-norities or even exclude them, the latter try to consolidate their power within immigrant communities, which are defined as quasi-natural groups (Rommelspacher, 2002). At the same time, multiculturalists tend to take the most conservative values of minorities as representa-tive of their authentic character. This is because these values appear to be farthest away from their own (Erel, 2004).

In arguing against this position, cultures cannot be understood as stable and essential unities but rather as brief products of dynamic and never-ending processes of construction. 'Therefore, the drawing of lines between different groups that are called ethnic is based not on traditions, but on positions continuously renegotiated between self-definitions and definitions by other actors, between inclusion and exclusion' (Welz, 1996: 114). Cultures are discursive fields (Schif-fauer, 1997) or representations (Sökefeld, 2004) grounded in specific interests and represented by different claims to power. They change constantly and are open, without strict borders. Therefore culture does not determine the actions of individuals but instead originates from individual and collective action. Furthermore, ethnic groups do not exist per se but are socially constructed within a process of ethnification, which is driven at least initially by the majority: 'In this process, immigrants become objects of classification and analysis by administrative, legal, scientific and everyday discourses, which separate them from the national population and emphasize their cultural difference' (Ronneberger, 1997: 225). At the same time, migrants often ethnicize themselves within the context of their situation in the country of immigration. Here, ethnic distinctions are secondary processes that can become functional in certain social situations (Bukow, 1993). Thus it is no coincidence that in the West German context interpretations of migration as a problem of ethnic-cultural differences emerged at around the same time that rising unemployment could no longer be coped with 'by means of the social-technical manipulation of migration streams' (Bommes and Scherr, 1991: 299). On the other hand, migrants of the second and third generations took over the cultural attributions and labels from the majority and adopted the cultural perspective of their opponents. They demanded more tolerance for their 'cultural group' or defined their self-organization in ethno-cultural ways. Thus ethnicity can also have an instrumental dimension that can be used by elites, which define themselves as ethnic, politically on behalf of their interests. Moreover, at the individual level it can provide for orientation and relief (Dittrich and Radtke, 1990). The ethnic-cultural identity of migrants is thus 'less a problem before migration but a result of migration' (Nassehi, 1997: 192). A concept of culture, however, which addresses individuals in an essentialist manner and does not allow for multiple affiliations, can easily evolve into an 'object of imperatives of exclusion' (196). To sum up, discourses on multiculturalism dating from the 1980s must be credited with having brought up positions that are more sensitive and accept differences, while at the same time they must be held responsible for the negative consequences that go along with culturalist understandings and definitions of the character and essence of migrants (Mecheril, 2003).

'Real existing' multiculturalism in 1980s' West Berlin

The conservative Christian Democratic Union (CDU) came to power in West Berlin in 1981, a year before the Kohl administration assumed office. In its election campaign in Berlin the CDU had focused on immigration issues, especially on the populist slogan that the 'capacity of the country to absorb' was exhausted. The position of the new CDU senate on the local regulation of immigration coincided with changes in urban and social policies: there was a shared rejection of modernistic conceptions of a comprehensive state planning system in favour of small-scale entities and identities, along with the growing involvement of the business community and civil society. Immigration policy, which until then had been understood as a problem of governmental planning, was now organized around a system of 'representatives and commissions' (Schwarz, 1992, 2001). In 1981, Berlin, the first West German state to introduce the position of 'foreigners' representative' (*Ausländerbeauftragte*), whose main task was to develop and coordinate local immigration policies. From the beginning, this office was well equipped with the necessary staff and skills. Conservative immigration policies in the 1980s basically followed the well-known dual strategy, promoting the return home of unwanted migrants and the integration and adaption to German ways of life of those remaining. Richard von Weizsäcker, who was elected mayor of Berlin in 1981, defined integration in his inaugural address as 'the will and decision to become a German in the long run'. Whereas the parliamentary representatives of the Social Democratic Party (SPD) in Berlin demanded that foreign 'fellow citizens' have 'equal opportunities and treatment in all legal, social and political matters' (SPD Berlin, 1981: 9), the CDU-majority senate cared more about aspects of well-being and culture. The type of multiculturalism implemented by the foreigners' representative in West Berlin added to the traditionally repressive elements of conservative immigration policy new aspects of a socio-cultural identity policy: 'People with different national backgrounds should live together free of tensions ..., feel comfortable with each other and at home', and become accustomed to the 'idea of naturalization' (Senator für Gesundheit, 1982: 6). Social rights were not even mentioned. 'Foreigners' were called upon to accept and adopt democratic principles along with the 'basic points of view and customs' of locals. Integration efforts on the part of the majority were reduced to the willingness 'to accept the other in his otherness' (6). For the first time, though, it was officially acknowledged that 'the coexistence of various customs and cultures ... can be also experienced as an enrichment through more diversity. Therefore, the Berlin senate prefers integration programmes which leave enough space for the cultural autonomy of foreigners'

(6). In a declaration issued after taking office, Eberhard Diepgen, who in 1985 followed Weizsäcker as governing mayor, stressed: 'A metropolis like Berlin profits from its diversity, heterogeneity and from its immigrants' (Presse- und Informationsamt, 1985: 30). On the one hand, Diepgen praised the decline in the number of migrants of Turkish descent in the city as a positive outcome of conservative policies. On the other hand, immigrants were no longer to be judged solely according to their economic performance, but were praised for their contribution to a culturally diverse and lively metropolis. This discourse is representative of broader transformations in the perception of large cities: from the social-democratic 'Fordist' conception that focused on a standardized culture and social equality, to the postmodern model of a 'metropolis'. As urban lifestyles and social environments became increasingly pluralized and diverse, social and cultural contrasts which were formerly regarded as undesirable and a reason for state intervention were increasingly portrayed as quasi-natural components of a metropolitan culture.

The senate introduced a new programme which especially supported self-help groups, including immigrants' organizations. Social and cultural work gradually converged programmatically and conceptually:

> This policy was launched as being communicative, close to people's way of life, generous and tolerant: ... It assists Turkish community and counselling centres and folkloric groups, providing the latter with rehearsal rooms and engagements. A special advertising campaign promotes sympathy and greater acceptance of foreign workers. It creates the positions of so-called women's and foreigners' representatives.... It introduces one million programmes for self-help projects.... It experiments with new conceptions of urban renewal, which are less aggressive and more open to grassroots interests. This kind of identity politics is concerned with creating a socio-cultural climate in which citizens are supposed to feel and act as self-dependent, unique and competent subjects. (Homuth, 1987: 101f)

The foreigners' representative played a crucial role within this 'ideological penetration of the informal sector' (Homuth, 1985: 84). Until then, governmental aid to migrants had been limited to various social services provided by established German welfare associations. Policies or studies which were concerned, for instance, with 'inclinations and barriers towards the integration' of Turks in Berlin (EMNID, 1983) had either ignored their self-organizations completely or had defined them as a phenomenon conducive to ghettoes. Now Barbara John, the foreigners' representative of West Berlin, began actively to involve associations of migrants in her policy. By 1987, almost fifty groups with a migrant background were supported financially by the local government. The temporary 'accentuation of a specific ethnic identity' in the course of 'the conflict-riddled self-discovery process within German society' was no longer automatically regarded as an obstacle to integration. However, not all forms of self-organization were accepted: 'A critical limit ... is reached when the emphasis on cultural peculiarities is accompanied by the deliberate retreat to an ideological ghetto and insulation, creating hostility towards the outside world and an aggressive inward pressure to conform and show solidarity to one's own community' (cited in Schwarz, 1992: 134).

This 'policy of notabilities' followed conservative traditions (Schwarz, 2001), while it perceived immigrants for the first time as independent subjects, and no longer as destitute victims. Increasingly, it addressed such social problems as being due to insufficiently educated adolescents or to rapidly growing unemployment among the immigrant population, which accompanied the process of de-industrialization. In 1982, the unemployment rate among immigrants was already 40 per cent higher than the rate among native Germans (Senator für Gesundheit, 1982). Local government instrumentalized the social commitment of nonprofit organizations for their own benefit by promoting more and more self-help programmes. Therefore the number of such groups grew considerably. 'The bare existence' (Schwarz, 1992: 146) of ethnic organizations often rendered them worthy of financial support by the government. One reason for the encouragement of their activities was to compensate for the exclusion of immigrants from the political system. Thus the organizational structure within minority communities changed. Organizations which had started out as solely political initiatives now founded neighbour-hood centres or projects for young people in order to fulfil funding guidelines and receive money from the local state. Another new element of conservative social policy at the beginning of the 1980s was to introduce workfare measures for welfare recipients and test them first in the refugee community. Asylum-seekers were forced to perform community service, 'to send a signal', according to one official. Later on, participation in workfare programmes became compulsory for all recipients of welfare payments (Grottian et al., 1985: 49).

After the Kohl era: political reforms of the red–green government

Unification in 1989 generated an instrumental 'self-ethnification' of German national identity, combined with widely discriminatory policies and attitudes towards immigrants (Bommes and Scherr, 1991: 331). Thus, at the beginning of the 1990s the concept of multi-culturalism disappeared from the main political agenda. According to Claus Leggewie, an early advocate of the concept 'for the time being, multiculturalism was in the political index' (1993: 1). It was still alive, though, in programmes of the representatives of foreigners and social workers dealing with immigrants. The end of the 1990s marked another important turning point, at both national and local levels.

In 1998, the SPD and the Green Party formed a governing coalition at the national level, with Gerhard Schröder becoming chancellor. In the election campaign both parties had advocated an extensive liberalization of immigration policies. They duly introduced a major reform of German citizenship law at the beginning of 2000, although it turned out to be a compromise between the governing parties and the conservatives. Shortly before that, the CDU had gained power in the state of Hesse thanks to a campaign against the plans of the red–green federal government to grant immigrants dual citizen-ship. Nevertheless, the citizenship law constituted a break with the ethno-national principle, according to which one could not become a German but had to be one by origin and birth (Bade and Oltmer, 2004: 129). It added to the prevailing *jus sanguinis* central elements of the *jus soli*. Thus the Wilhelminian law of 1913 was replaced (see Grenz, 2000). For the first time in German history, it was officially declared that 'Germany became an immigration country a long time ago' (cited in Meier-Braun, 2002: 98). Although other promised reforms of the foreigners' law, such as the right of residents from non-EU countries to vote in local elections, failed, the federal government had initiated a debate on the principles of German immigration policy (see Angemendt and Kruse, 2004).

By 1999, the Social Democratic minister of the interior, Otto Schily, howeer, still claimed that the 'capacity of the country to welcome and absorb immigrants' had already been exceeded. Shortly after that, a new political agreement recognized that for demographic and economic reasons Germany had to recruit highly qualified foreigners. Even within the national conservative wing of the CDU a major U-turn was evident: whereas formerly it had rejected all immigration, it now supported immigration that was beneficial to the German economy. Responsible for this change of heart was a bold initiative by Chancellor Schröder: the 'Green Card'. In February 2000, during the technology trade fair CeBIT, Schröder announced that the German government would bring much needed foreign computer specialists into the country by issuing a so-called 'Green Card'. The subsequent 'Green Card decree' arranged for the immigration of 20,000 highly qualified information technology specialists, linking their residence permit to an employment contract, restricted to five years – basically, a modernized version of the recruitment of 'guest workers'.

Whereas this recruitment policy would have been possible without a 'Green Card', it introduced a new idea into German discourse which tied immigration issues to economic competitiveness. 'At that time, the label "Green Card" had the potential to link the hype around the glorious "New Economy" to the unpopular topic of immigration'; now it was about 'immigration in "our" interest' (Ette, 2003: 48). The federal government used the new climate to set up an independent commission under the direction of the liberal conservative politician Rita Süssmuth, which was assigned to produce a new immigration law. The CDU reacted with the creation of its own commission. Representatives of the business community, in particular, had pushed the conservatives to give up their opposition to a modern immigration law.

The so-called 'Süssmuth Report' urged for a 'paradigm shift' in immigration and integration policies. It advocated a system of comprehensive support and services to assist with integration, recommended simplifying the foreigners' law, and proposed the introduction of a points system to select suitably qualified migrant workers (Unabhängige Kommission, 2001). The report of the CDU commission, for its part, proposed a similar model for the regulation of necessary migration. Thus a general agreement between the government and the opposition began to effect what was described as a 'paradigm shift in immigration policy' (Hailbronner, 2001: 7). The consensus view accepted the reality of immigration and allowed for controlled immigration in the economic interest of Germany. At the same time, the intention was to restrict other forms of immigration, and require immigrants in Germany to redouble their efforts at integration. By summer 2001, the draft of a new immigration law, coordinated by the minister of the interior and conservative politicians, had postponed the option of a points system for migrant workers to a far-off future. Instead, it tightened the laws on asylum-seekers by expanding the reasons for deportation, and thereby returned, according to statements issued by numerous welfare organizations, 'to an integration model of rotation hostile to "guest workers"' (cited in Meier-Braun, 2002: 110). The events of 9/11 also had a major impact on public opinion. Once again, traditional discourses on national security prevailed, and Muslim immigrants were suspected of representing a potential risk. By autumn 2001, the all-party consensus on immigration policy had fallen apart. Whereas members of the governing coalition disputed the restrictive character of the bill, the conservatives criticized the fact that it did not provide for sufficient control of unwanted immigration. They pursued a course of confrontation, which caused the law to be rejected by parliament in spring 2002.

After a new round of negotiations between the red–green government and the conservatives, a more restrictive version of the original bill was passed and came into force at the beginning of 2005. The main focus of this 'immigration law' (*Zuwanderungsgesetz*) lay in effective regulation and a limitation placed on immigration. According to the law, the government finally recognized Germany as a country of immigration, but the initially proposed immigration options were simply dropped. The law, in principle, allows only for the legal entry and settlement of highly qualified experts and entrepreneurs. It relaxes the residency rules and contains some improvements based on humanitarian concerns. Migrants are now obliged to attend newly set up integration courses and to learn the German language. So-called 'hate preachers, for instance, "agitators" in mosques' (Meier-Braun, 2005: 247) can be expelled much more easily than before. Applications for naturalization have to pass initial scrutiny by the Federal Office for the Protection of the Constitution (one of Germany's intelligence services). All the new restrictions in the law are premissed on the supposed clash of cultures between the West and Islam.

Good cultures, bad cultures:
Berlin as a multicultural metropolis

At the end of the 1990s, another factor proved decisive for the dual shift in national and local immigration policy: a specific political interpretation of social–spatial processes within German cities. Particularly in Berlin, contradictory trends can be observed: on the one hand, a revival and modernization of the concepts of multiculturalism that had emerged in the 1980s; on the other hand, a political and ideological relapse into ideological concepts of a 'national German culture' (*Leitkultur*) to which immigrants must assimilate.

Throughout the 1990s, the reunited city of Berlin – which again became the German capital – was run by a CDU–SPD coalition, under the governing mayor Eberhard Diepgen (CDU). The coalition pursued a radical growth policy, the main goal of which was to make Berlin a 'global city' within only a few years. This policy was based on an absurdly optimistic and unfounded boom scenario. Because the senate ignored the real economic and social situation of the city, Berlin soon faced an economic and fiscal crisis of gigantic proportions. The city lost two-thirds of all its manufacturing jobs within a couple of years. By the end of the 1990s, unemployment had reached almost 20 per cent. The unemployment rate of the second and following genera-tions of most immigrant groups, who had come to Berlin mainly as low-skilled industrial workers, levelled off around 40 per cent. The racist structures of the German educational system contributed to the fact that in most instances children of the first generation of im-migrants did not experience any upward mobility, but were relegated to the low level of education of their parents (see Gomolla and Radtke,

2002; Terkessidis, 2004). Many immigrants experienced a downward trend, which included lasting exclusion from the labour market as well as persistent impoverishment and social marginalization.

The economic decline of Berlin was in contrast to the increasing international attention paid to the dynamics of its urban cultures. In the period immediately following the fall of the Wall, a temporary legal vacuum and the availability of large amounts of derelict land in the centre of East Berlin provided ideal conditions for the spread of various subcultures. In the space of a decade, they had developed into one of the few instances of economic potential in the city. In addition to the media and music industry, tourism was regarded as another hope for economic growth. By the end of the 1990s, crisis-ridden Berlin and its establishment began to lay claim to urban (sub)cultures as one of the few marketing opportunities for the city. Multicultural facets of the urban landscape of cultures were an important part of this strategy. Efforts to style Berlin as a cosmopolitan metropolis and the growing 'festivalization' of urban policy began to incorporate specific elements of immigrant cultures. Public discourse henceforth increasingly distinguished 'good' (utilizable) from 'bad' (potentially disturbing) cultures.

In particular, the 'Carnival of Cultures' evolved into a symbol for the economic and social potential of the multicultural metropolis: for the first time, in May 1996, this street parade took place in Berlin–Kreuzberg. Since then it has developed into an annual mega-festival and international tourist attraction. Today, several thousand participants and up to a million visitors take part in the parade and the numerous accompanying parties and club events; even larger numbers watch the festival live via the Internet and television. An amazingly broad coalition of participants welcomes and uses the carnival as a metaphor for a peaceful and very lively display of multiculturalism. The carnival began as a 'workshop of cultures' set up by the foreigners' representative Barbara John (CDU) as a sign of 'the growing cultural variety of Berlin' (John, 2005: 9). According to the organizers, who for the most part once belonged to the alternative scene, the objectives of the carnival are to fight 'xenophobia' or 'fears of foreign infiltration', to demonstrate diversity and to provide migrants with the opportunity to express their cultural identity (Frei, 2003). From its beginnings, it expressed a moral, and indeed explicitly anti-racist, commitment as well as supporting the idea of 'multicultural coexistence' in urban society (Klausner, 2005; Glindemann, 2005).

However, the carnival is above all embedded in an overall policy of culturalization and ethnic representation, and is thus part of an 'ambivalent space where self-perceptions and external perceptions are constructed and negotiated' (Färber, 2005: 12). The multicultural idea embodied in the carnival is still grounded in the German tradition of a clear distinction between different and coexisting cultures, notwithstanding the tolerance of hybrids and the fact that nobody is excluded. Ethnologist Michi Knecht (2005: 27) discovers in the 'Carnival of Cultures' the 'ubiquity of a pedagogical concept of multiculturalism' whose symbolic structure easily delegitimizes opposing views: 'Those who do not want to join in tend to be accused of being too religious, backwoods, uneducated, intolerant or inferior in some other way.'

The latent selectivity distinguishing between desired and suspect cultures becomes obvious when one considers the composition of the actors and participants and the public perception of the carnival. Body conscious, colourful and exotic dance groups, specifically inasmuch as they feature 'samba, Rio de Janeiro and half-naked women' (Frei, 2003: 165), are clearly overrepresented. At the same time, the rather limited participation of 'Turks' or 'Arabs' – that is, Muslims – receives critical attention. These are perceived not as musicians but rather as representatives of their religion or their nation, being too traditionalistic and lacking in the happy-go-lucky required of a carnival (see Früh and Schmidt, 2005). Since only the exotic seems to appeal to the public, the carnival serves and reproduces cultural clichés, even when it pretends to strengthen intercultural possibility. This is true also for the immigrants whose 'identity management' (Welz, 1996) follows the precept 'folklorize yourself or die!' (Diederichsen, 1995: 130) that is communicated to them in a more or less subtle way by the majority. For most, the main reason for their participation is the economic benefit of the carnival. It also provides an opportunity to become visible, make contacts, exchange information and socialize. Thus, the category culture allows for an advancement of personal status. 'Therefore, the very logic of the participants to define their living space culturally can be understood as a way to position themselves within the social order of the majority' (Frei, 2003: 168f). However, at the same time the insistence on cultural instead of political strategies of adjustment leads to stereotypical and traditional behaviour instead of modern forms of adaptation. So how is the huge success of the carnival to be explained? First, it belongs to the category of urban events which on a global scale represent the city as an attractive cosmopolitan consumer zone. Accordingly, it is a counterpart to the dominant representation of the multi-ethnic metropolis as a zone of disintegration and social problems. This not only serves the interests of the growth coalition in symbolic economies – culture, media, tourism – which encompasses all relevant political, media and economic forces of the city; it also suits players in the multicultural milieu, who believe that such festivals foster a climate more tolerant of immigrants and less vulnerable to racist positions. If one takes a closer look at the carnival, it becomes apparent that its policy of culturalization leads to classifications of cultural diversity; this serves to privilege certain practices, while others remain invisible. Its success results from its ability to serve two dominant codes of ethnic representation in Berlin today: the code of 'consumption of ethnic cultures' and the 'code of an integrating space, transforming ethnic culture into socio-culture' in order to cover up social problems (Färber, 2005: 12f). The first code follows an exoticism focused on immigrants; the latter leads to an instrumentalization of culture for social purposes and the political objective of integration. Culture, on the one hand, is politically charged with 'nearly utopian expectations of salvation' (Greve, 2003: 404) and, on the other hand, is symbolically downgraded to second-rate status by virtue of its use as a means of integration in socio-cultural work.

The West and the rest: Muslims as the 'Other'

Parallel to the success story of the 'Carnival of Cultures', which began to offer a positive and living example of multiculturalism, one could witness among Muslims a discursive and political relapse into the negativity of earlier decades, as a result of the increasing social problems experienced by numerous immigrant milieux, on the one hand, and the discursive consequences of 9/11, on the other hand. Increasingly, state-sponsored studies had revealed that spatial and social structures, especially in big cities, had become increasingly fragmented and polarized. This is to say that groups that had originally migrated as 'foreign workers' and lived in the immigrant quarters of the inner cities were noticeably more impoverished. Muslim immigrant groups seemed to be particularly affected by these processes of social exclusion. As a result, discourses on the integration of these 'other'/excluded groups of immigrants blended with discourses on new forms of urban poverty. 'Integration' was now increasingly perceived as a failure, or at least threatened by failure. In line with the historically dominant integration discourse in Germany, which had always focused on immigrants as a potential danger to national security or the social peace, exclusion was picked out as a central topic, primarily from a point of view which interpreted them above all as a threat to society.

Because discourses of 'failed integration' mainly blaimed the 'culture' and behaviour of the affected groups for this failure, such groups were constructed as dangerous classes. Muslim youngsters in particular were accused of deliberately separating themselves from the majority. After the 9/11 attacks, a West–Islam conflict scenario began increasingly to dominate debates on immigration and integration. However, it was the murder of Theo van Gogh – whose films and publications had attacked the idea of a multicultural society and accused Islam and Muslim immigrants of not being compatible with Western societies – by a young Islamist on 2 November 2004 that caused a 'discursive bursting of a dam':

> Obviously, an already tense mood found a valve in this murder; the attack was just the last straw of it. In a wild acceleration, all debates that had emerged since 9/11 culminated here: terrorism and fundamentalism, the constitution of the European Union and the admission of Turkey, multicultural society or the German Leitkultur. (von Lucke, 2005: 10)

'Holland is everywhere' ran the headlines not only in the most popular and highest circulation tabloid *Bild* (15 November 2004), and the radical right-wing paper *Junge Freiheit* (19 November 2004) but also the acclaimed weekly magazine *Die Zeit* (16 December 2004). However, none of them referred to concrete incidents in Germany.

Features pages of influential newspapers discussed the 'battle around Europe' (Gilles Kepel in *Welt am Sonntag*, 21 November 2004) and the 'bankruptcy of multiculturalism' (*Frankfurter Algemeine Zeitung*, 23 November 2004). Fierce criticism countered such opinions by declaring instead the 'simple-minded reasoning of a monoculture' as a failure (*Frankfurter Algemeine Zeitung*, 15 November 2004), defending the 'experiment of multiculturalism' against the 'panic mood of a religious world war' that had grasped the West since 9/11 (*Südeutsche Zeitung*, 12 November 2004). Nonetheless, the headline of the conservative German news magazine *Focus* condensed the prevailing discourse in its headline 'Uncanny guests. The counter-world of Muslims in Germany' (22 November 2004). In doing so, it abandoned the distinction between Islam and Islamism, and 'racialized' Muslims as an ethnocultural group incompatible with Western societies. Moreover, it excluded Muslims from society and relegated them to their original status of 'foreign workers', irrespective of nationality. Hence, their life was declared a 'counterworld'. 'The stigmatizing suggestion is clear: in the Muslim "counterworld" lurks the stranger, the unknown, in short the bad' (von Lucke, 2005: 10). At that time, the notion of a parallel society evolved into a fashionable concept counter to 'multicultural society' (Butterwegge, 2005: 200). This set off a nationwide debate, which found its concrete object of discussion in the Berlin district of Neukölln. The mayor of Neukölln, Heinz Buschkowsky (SPD), contributed heavily to the discussion by emphasizing the structural similarities in the failure of migrants to integrate in Rotterdam and Neukölln. He accused Arab and Turkish 'main minorities' of being unwilling to integrate. He claimed the existence of a parallel society with its 'own binding behavioural norms' and, hence, declared multiculturalism to have failed (first in *Die Tagesspiegel*, 13 November 2004). This debate on Neukölln and interviews with Buschowsky in several newspapers received nationwide media attention.

It is worthwhile examining the statements of this Social Democratic mayor more closely. Neukölln is a borough of Berlin associated with social problems and heterogeneous immigration. The middle classes have been moving out in much larger numbers than from any other district of Berlin or from any other city in Germany. Buschowsky's statements not only demonstrate the persistent continuity of a particular German understanding of multiculturalism, but also refer paradigmatically to important discursive shifts. Like 'integration', the term 'multiculture' functions within German immigration discourse as a concept open enough to include all kinds of contents and political positions. It is almost impossible to assign advocates and opponents of multiculturalism to traditional political camps. Hence, the fiercely debated thesis of the failure of multiculturalism raises the question, what is multiculturalism all about? What are the concepts of a 'multiculture' that form the foundation of this debate? How do they relate to traditional currents and to contemporary conceptions of integration policies? To which images of an immigration society do they relate?

The public statements of Mayor Buschkowsky sum up the type of multicultural discourse based on the objective of assimilation that is dominant in the contemporary debate. In one interview, he compares two versions of multicultural society: 'In my view, a multicultural society consists of many cultures peacefully living together in one country. Other people say that in a multicultural society many people introduce their own conceptions of life and culture into a community and in that way create a new multicultural identity' (*Kommune*, January 2005: 16). He goes on to say that because the latter model would deny that people feel secure only in their own familiar culture, a multicultural society in that form could not exist. According to Buschkowsky, this idea led to the formation of 'areas of social and ethnic segregation ... in our cities'. However, a 'multiethnic society, which peacefully lives in a common democratic legal order with shared values is possible. This is what I aim for' (*JF*, November 2005). These two opposing versions of a multicultural society basically correspond to the two ideological models of assimilation in American immigration debates: the 'melting pot' and cultural pluralism. These debates have a long tradition in the United States; however, both concepts are outdated and have never really related to the historical reality of racial and ethnic discrimination and segregation in the country. The concept of a 'melting pot' suggests that the cultures and origins of immigrants should meld into a new national identity. The concept of cultural pluralism maintains that 'ethnic groups should be integrated into American society under the protection of their culture and in a way that allows them to live together peacefully and be treated equally' (Han, 2005: 324). Since Mayor Buschkowksy understands culture as the second nature of individuals with a determining role, the melting pot for him must exist as an ideological notion that is not realizable. Furthermore, since his concept of culture is linked automatically to ethnicity, there remains only one option in dealing with the reality of immigration: either the apartheid model of an unconnected coexistence of ethnic groups, or cultural pluralism – diversity within unity, in which coexistence conforms to a given order of shared values. Such a constellation is described by the term 'salad bowl', a metaphor in which the ingredients of the salad are still individually identifiable but are supposed to harmonize with each other. This reveals that Buschkowsky agrees precisely with the basic points of those proponents of a multicultural society against which he so vehemently fights. According to Daniel Cohn-Bendit and Thomas Schmid, the German conception of multiculture is based on the thesis that 'the melting pot is a failed model' (1993: 316). They do not agree with the position that advocates 'diversity instead of homogeneity.... Democracy requires a common understanding of binding values on which common agreement is needed' (319).

At the heart of this discourse is a concept of immigration and integration that separates the ethnocultural self from the other self by defining both with the help of distinct sets of cultural attributes. The self that defines social normality and thus binding values either embraces only those groups that identify with a German ethnoculture, or integrates in a broader sense all subjects which identify themselves as members of a Western community with shared values. Immigrants are thus split into two large groups: those that accept Western values, and thus are not targeted by the integration discourse; and those defined as 'others' that have to be 'normalized'. According to Stuart Hall (1994), the latter category corresponds to the 'rest' beyond the 'West', and is today characterized primarily by its affiliation to Islam. This discourse does not just reveal historical continuities –'the West and the rest' discourse or an essentialist concept of culture – but also marks an evident move away from German tradition. For the first time, national-conservative positions also basically accept the reality of immigration and now direct their 'patriotic appeal' (Balibar, 1993) also to immigrants. Hence, they follow the new principle of citizenship that was introduced by the red–green federal government: one does not necessarily have to be a German by descent; even an immigrant can become a German. Nevertheless, this finds its limits where cultures are assumed to clash. An integral part of this differential thought and speech is the discourse of cultural assimilation, which imagines society as a salad bowl in which various 'cultures' have to conform without conflict to an order of shared values dictated by the majority.

Because this discourse addresses immigrants as members of essentially different ethnocultures, it stands in the tradition of German multiculturalism and must therefore, to cite Slavoj Žižek, be considered as 'racism with a distance'. However, we can again identify a significant shift from this period. The early concepts of multiculturalism of the 1980s positioned themselves against a prevailing integration discourse that demanded that foreigners adapt culturally to the majority. This majority was perceived as homogeneous. By demanding recognition of the cultural peculiarities of immigrants, early multiculturalism was talking mainly to the majority. The present, implicit multiculturalism, however, takes the opposite perspective by demanding that immigrants integrate the central values of the majority into their own 'cultures' and identify with them. This current form of German multiculturalism thus contains the imperative of cultural dominance, similar to the traditional integration discourse against which it was originally directed. Thus, in time, it has moved from the left to the right wing of the political spectrum. Since 9/11, more and more leading politicians, and also journalists, formerly of the left, have joined the ranks of those articulating this discourse. This is especially true of politicians from the Green party. The antagonistic construction of the West as secular and democratic and of Islam as backward and undemocratic seems to be successfully separating the majority from Muslim immigrants.

'The hype about hybridity': diversity-recognizing multiculturalism

Far from the culture-clash debates, however, diverse concepts of multiculturalism have emerged within the last decade, which at least in Germany can be considered as new to the political stage. It appears that two discourses confront each other in the current debate. They differ in distinct ways. The first concept, assimilative multiculturalism, is consistent with traditional German notions of multiculturalism and constructs differences between cultures as essentialist; the second concept assumes a dynamic diversity in society. In doing so, it moves beyond the traditional German model. Whereas the former concept interprets cultural differences as a potential threat to social cohesion and aims at a specific variation of cultural assimilation, the latter is based on the thesis of social normality built on a dynamic cultural diversity that needs to be accepted by everyone.

In particular, Berlin's 'integration programme' (*Integration-skonzept*), which was passed in the local parliament under the slogan 'Promote plurality – strengthen cohesion' in August 2005, embodies the diversity model of multiculturalism in Berlin politics. This is the first official document that expresses explicitly the intention to implement an integration policy on different political levels. It is the foundation of the integration policy of the Berlin government which since 2001 has been constituted by a Social Democratic–Socialist coalition under the governing mayor Klaus Wowereit (SPD). The integration programme no longer reduces plurality and diversity to the dimensions of 'ethnic groups' and 'culture'. Rather, 'pluralization is [regarded as] an irreversible process of modern societies': plurality is interpreted as 'social wealth', and accordingly 'does not restrict itself to ethnic plurality, but takes the whole complexity of modern urban societies as a starting point' (Abgeordnetenhaus, Dr. 15/4208, 2005: 6). The red–red senate pursues the approach of diversity which aims for a 'neutral' public sphere and adopts measures to counter cultural forms of discrimination. One example is the 'package of measures to create the ideological–religious neutrality of the state, better integration and protection against the discrimination of migrants' (Presseinformation der Fraktionen SPD und PDS, 31 March 2004). The senate established these policies in 2004 in the wake of a nationwide political debate which centred on the demand to prohibit the wearing of the headscarf in public institutions such as schools and courts. In the meantime, an anti-discrimination office was created with a 'representative for migration and integration' as its head, which has replaced the former position of foreigners' representative.

This office is conceived 'as a contact point for everybody who feels discriminated against on ethnic, religious and ideological grounds'. 'Its main objective is to strengthen and encourage a culture of acceptance towards persons of other religions and other ethnicities', the senate announced in February 2005 (Der Beauftragte, 2005). Furthermore, new policies include a 'neutrality law', according to which civil servants are no longer allowed to wear any 'visible religious or ideological symbols' (Gesetz- und Verordnungsblatt für Berlin, 2005). However, the conservatives, for their part, demanded prohibition of only the headscarf while allowing Christian religious symbols in public institutions. The CDU thus demonstrated that its official policy remains rooted in the idea of cultural assimilation (see Abgeordnetenhaus, Dr. 15/2122, 2005).

The liberal strand within the conservative camp, however, has taken up a position in favour of diversity, thereby demonstrating that the dividing line on multiculturalism does not run straightforwardly between conservative and progressive parties. At the same time, it turns out that only representatives of the majority advocate an assimilative multiculturalism. Therefore, a central reason for the emergence of pro-diversity positions in public discourses in Germany has to do with the fact that representatives of immigrant minorities have started to become much more visible and have achieved a stronger voice in national politics.

The difference between the pro-diversity and the assimilative position is that the former does not construct ethnocultural groups and set up an antagonism between 'us' and 'them'. Hence, this constellation dismisses the historically hegemonic German immigration discourse that had defined national affiliation ethnoculturally as a community of common descent and culture, and conceived of culture as the determining second nature of an individual. In contrast, this new notion of a pro-diversity multiculturalism defines culture rather as a dynamic set of everyday practices and discourses that neither strictly determine the actions and identities of individuals nor can be applied as an overall explanatory category for social and individual problems and conflicts. It neither marks non-Western immigrants as fundamentally Others, nor establishes exclusionary borders against them. The centrality of the West–Islam conflict scenario in contemporary immigration discourse is obvious, as the main focus on Muslim immigrants illustrates. The emphasis on religion in this debate makes clear how much these positions differ from the assimilative ones. Assimilative positions define problematic phenomena such as the oppression of women within patriarchal family relations as typical of Islam. By doing so, they put Muslims – whether they are immigrants or not – generally under suspicion and stigmatize them. In contrast, pro-diversity positions can address such problems within the concrete context of each case and do not interpret and ascribe a value to religious groups as imaginary cultural communities. Rather, a dynamic diversity of national, ethnic, religious and (sub)cultural affiliations is perceived as an essential, given feature of contemporary societies. Such diversity is seen not as a fundamental problem but instead as desirable and worthy of being fostered. This view is not concerned with potential collisions or disharmonies between cultures, because society is not understood as a given community with a common destiny and all-embracing norms and values. Instead, society is seen as functionally, socially and culturally diverse, held together primarily by the quality of its institutions. Thus, this discourse disengages from the logic of cultural apartheid that used to characterize German concepts of multiculturalism, and promotes dynamic processes of cultural hybridization that often also follow economic interests.

The integration programme of the senate in Berlin, for instance, establishes a connection between 'cultural plurality' and the economic competitiveness of the city, disclosing in the process the progressive and emancipative, but also the utilitarian, character of its policies and intentions. According to the integration programme, 'the positive handling of plurality promotes intercultural competence, a certain vitality and the capacity to act on behalf of the city, and leads to advantages in the international competition of cities thanks to its attractiveness for its people and business community' (Abgeordnetenhaus, Dr. 15/4208, 2005: 71). From this point of view, Berlin ranks among the globalizing cities, 'where new influences merge with traditions to produce new forms of cultural expression' (71). The postulate 'plurality is a strength' is presented as a major 'principle of modern business philosophies' that could also hold true for Berlin. 'Migrants contribute to this strength': their traditions and cultures mix with 'cultural and traditional aspects of the receiving society ... [and] foster the emerge of new hybrid cultures which have become symptoms of modern urban societies' (5).

This text reveals a phenomenon which the political scientist Kien Nghi Ha (2005) calls the 'hype about hybridity': today, processes of cultural penetration are reinterpreted in a positive way. This is not necessarily an obviously emancipatory project and a liberation from the binary modern logic of either/or. Rather, the concept of hybridity seems to be quite compatible with the cultural dominant logic of postmodern capitalism (see Harvey, 1989; Lanz, 1996). In so far as the global economy becomes increasingly 'cultural' and flexible, the difference of the Other is perceived less and less as a dangerous breeding ground of marginality, but rather as a resource likely to foster productivity and as a 'lifestyle and consumption model in the market of possibilities' (Ha, 2005: 59). According to Ha, the classical German concept of multiculturalism, which wanted to preserve absolute differences, is beginning to be replaced by a model of society that puts hybridity and transculturality at its centre. In this model, ethnic and cultural mixtures are seen as producing desirable results. Such a logic, for example, can be found in the *BerlinStudie*, which was commissioned by the mayor in search of a vision for the future of Berlin. This report assigns to immigrants the role of a dynamic avant-garde whose job it is to remove the 'mental barriers' of an ossifying society by introducing and spreading more entrepreneurial behaviour. Thus immigrants are seen as an important resource that should develop within one or two generations into a 'new elite' (Der Regierende Bürgermeister, 2000: 68). However, this instrumental 'hype about hybridity' makes it necessary to detach the threatening parts of the construction of the Other from the desired ones and to domesticate the unpredictable moments of cultural transformation. Here, another shift can be observed. Traditional concepts of multiculturalism accepted the 'difference' of other cultures so long as it offered some form of exoticism that appealed to the majority society and was manageable. This is a mechanism that can still be found in festivals such as the 'Carnival of Cultures', where exoticism is celebrated as an enrichment of society. However, today the incentive of multiculturalism is primarily the economic potential of cultural diversity, which is perceived as a competitive advantage in a globalized economy.

Between frontier fortification and hybridity

This overview on the contemporary formation of discourses on multiculturalism in Germany has illustrated the existence of two main positions: a cultural 'frontier fortification and hybridity' (Terkessidis, 2000: 202). On the one hand, the political focus narrows down to the assumed cultural fundamentalism of Muslim immigrants who are constructed as radical 'others' and are increasingly excluded from an imagined community of the 'self'. On the other hand, a positive reference to cultural plurality and hybridity has evolved. Minorities not only appear as an additional participant in the consumer market, but, particularly in Berlin, are also valued as a relevant social resource for the future. In some instances, minorities are even represented as an economic and social avant-garde that facilitates the shift towards a neoliberal society. At the same time, the pedagogical socio-multiculturalism which had characterized a great deal of the integration policy of the municipal authorities since the 1980s seems to have become obsolete.

References

Abgeordnetenhaus (2003) Dr. 15/2122, *Berlin sagt Nein zum Kopftuch im öffentlichen Dienst*, 22 October, CDU.

Abgeordnetenhaus (2004) Dr. 15/3254, *Antidiskriminierungs- und Integrationsfördermaßnahmen für Berlin 'Einrichtung einer Senatsleitstelle gegen Diskriminierung aus Gründen der ethnischen Herkunft, der Weltanschauung und der Religion'*, 23 September, SPD, PDS.

Abgeordnetenhaus (2005) Dr. 15/4208, *Ein Integrationskonzept für Berlin*, 2 May SPD, PDS (Drucksache 15/3929); Mitteilung zur Kenntnisnahme (Folgedokument), 23 August (Drucksache 15/4208).

Angemendt, Steffen, and Imke Kruse (2003) 'Der schwierige Wandel. Die Gestaltung der deutschen und euroäischen Migrationspolitik an der Wende vom 20. zum 21. Jahrhundert', in Jochen Oltmer (ed.), *Migration steuern und verwalten. Deutschland vom späten 19. Jahrhundert bis zur Gegenwart*, Osnabrück, pp. 481–98.

Bade, Klaus J., and Jochen Oltmer (2004) *Normalfall Migration. Herausgegeben von Bundeszentrale für politische Bildung*, Bonn.

Balibar, Étienne (1993) *Die Grenzen der Demokratie*, Hamburg.

Bommes, Michael, and Albert Scherr (1991) 'Der Gebrauchswert von Selbst- und Fremdethnisierung in Strukturen sozialer Ungleichheit', *Prokla* 83(21): 291–316.

Bukow Wolf-Dietrich (1993) *Leben in der multikulturellen Gesellschaft. Die Entstehung kleiner Unternehmer und der Umgang mit ethnischen Minderheiten*, Opladen.

Bundesministerium für Familien, Senioren, Frauen und Jugend (2000) *Sechster Familienbericht. Familien ausländischer Herkunft in Deutschland. Leistungen – Belastungen – Herausforderungen*, Berlin.

Butterwegge, Christoph (2006) 'Migrationsberichterstattung, Medienpädagogik und politische Bildung', in Christoph Butterwegge and Gudrun Hentges (eds), *Massenmedien, Migration und Integration*, Wiesbaden, pp. 185–234.

Cohn-Bendit, Daniel, and Thomas Schmid (1993) *Heimat Babylon. Das Wagnis der multikulturellen Demokratie*, Hamburg.

Der Beauftragte für Integration und Migration des Senats von Berlin (2005) Senatsbeschluss zur Einrichtung einer Senatsleitstelle gegen Diskriminierung vom 25. Februar 2005.

Der Regierende Bürgermeister von Berlin (ed.) (1972) *Eingliederung der ausländischen Arbeitnehmer und ihrer Familien. Abschlußbericht*, Berlin.

Der Regierende Bürgermeister von Berlin (ed.) (2000) *Die BerlinStudie. Strategien für die Stadt*, Berlin.

Diederichsen, Diedrich (1995) 'Wie aus Bewegungen Kulturen und aus Kulturen Communities werden', in G. Fuchs, B. Moltmann and W. Prigge (eds), *Mythos Metropole*, Frankfurt am Main, pp. 126–42.

Dietrich, Helmut (2005) 'Ausländerpolitik in der Bundesrepublik Deutschland', in Kölnischer Kunstverein et al. (eds), *Projekt Migration*, Cologne, pp. 290–97.

Dittrich, Eckhard J., and Frank Olaf Radtke (1990) 'Der Beitrag der Wissenschaften zur Konstruktion ethnischer Minderheiten', in Eckhard J. Dittrich and Frank Olaf Radtke (eds), *Ethnizität. Wissenschaft und Minderheiten*, Opladen, pp. 11–40.

Dohse, Knuth (1981) *Ausländische Arbeiter und bürgerlicher Staat. Genese und Funktion von staatlicher Ausländerpolitik und Ausländerrecht. Vom Kaiserreich bis zur Bundesrepublik Deutschland*, Königsstein/Ts.

EMNID-Institut (1983) *Türken in Berlin. Lebensbedingungen, Kommunikationsverhalten und Integrationstendenzen. Im Auftrag des Senats für Gesundheit, Soziales und Familie*, Berlin.

Erel, Umut (2004) 'Paradigmen kultureller Differenz und Hybridität', in Martin Sökefeld (ed.), *Jenseits des Paradigmas kultureller Differenz. Neue Perspektiven auf Einwanderer aus der Türkei*, Bielefeld, pp. 35–52.

Ette, Andreas (2003) 'Politische Ideen und Policy-Wandel: die "Green Card" und ihre Bedeutung für die deutsche Einwanderungspolitik', in Uwe Hunger and Holger Kolb (eds), Die *deutsche 'Green Card'. Migration von Hochqualifizierten in theoretischer und empirischer Perspektive*, Osnabrück, pp. 39–50.

Fanizadeh, Andreas (1992) 'Die multikulturellen Freunde und ihre Gesellschaft', in Redaktion diskus (ed.), *Die freundliche Zivilgesellschaft. Rassismus und Nationalismus in Deutschland*, Berlin, pp. 13–24.

Färber, Alexa (2005) 'Vom Kommen, Bleiben und Gehen. Anforderungen und Möglichkeiten im Unternehmen Stadt. Eine Einleitung', in Alexa Färber (ed.), *Hotel Berlin. Formen urbaner Mobilität und Verortung. Berliner Blätter* 37, pp. 7–21.

Frei, Kerstin (2003) *Wer sich maskiert, wird integriert. Der Karneval der Kulturen in Berlin*, Berlin.

Früh, Anja, and Meike Schmidt (2005) '"Kreuzberg, Europa, die Welt." Ein Stadtteil und sein Fest', in Michi Knecht and Levent Soysal (eds), *Plausible Vielfalt. Wie der Karneval der Kulturen denkt, lernt und Kultur schafft*, Berlin, pp. 53–72.

Gesetz- und Verordnungsblatt für Berlin (2005) *Gesetz zur Schaffung eines Gesetzes zu Artikel 29 der Verfassung von Berlin und zur Änderung des Kindertagesbetreuungsgesetzes* (27 January 2005), 61(4), 8 February.

Gomolla, Mechthild, and Frank-Olaf Radtke (2002) *Institutionelle Diskriminierung. Die Herstellung ethnischer Differenz in der Schule*, Opladen.

Glindemann, Birgit (2005) 'Aneignungsprozesse oder: Wem gehört der Karneval? Vom soziokulturellen Abenteuer zur Institutionalisierung', in Michi Knecht and Levent Soysal (eds), *Plausible Vielfalt. Wie der Karneval der Kulturen denkt, lernt und Kultur schafft*, Berlin, pp. 32–52.

Grenz, Wolfgang (2000) 'Die Ausländer- und Asylpolitik der rot-grünen Bundesregierung', in Christoph Butterwegge and Gudrun Hentges (eds), *Zuwanderung im Zeichen der Globalisierung. Migrations-, Integrations- und Minderheitenpolitik*, Opladen, pp. 105–19.

Greve, Martin (2003) *Die Musik der imaginären Türkei. Musik und Musikleben im Kontext der Migration aus der Türkei in Deutschland*, Stuttgart and Weimar.

Grottian, Peter, Friedrich Krotz, Günter Lütke and Michael Wolf (1985) 'Die Entzauberung der Berliner Sozialpolitik', *Ästhetik und Kommunikation* 16(59): *Politik der Städte*, pp. 45–53.

Ha, Kien Nghi (2003) 'Die kolonialen Muster deutscher Arbeitsmigrationspolitik', in Hito Steyerl and Encarnación Gutiérrez Rodríguez (eds), *Spricht die Subalterne deutsch? Migration und postkoloniale Kritik*, Münster, pp. 56–107.

Ha, Kien Nghi (2005) *Hype um Hybridität. Kultureller Differenzkonsum und postmoderne Verwertungstechniken im Spätkapitalismus*, Bielefeld.

Hailbronner, Kay (2001) 'Reform des Zuwanderungsrechts. Konsens und Dissens in der Ausländerpolitik', in *Aus Politik und Zeitgeschichte, Beilage zur Wochenzeitung das Parlament* 43, pp. 7–19.

Hall, Stuart (1994) *Rassismus und kulturelle Identität. Ausgewählte Schriften 2*, Hamburg.

Han, Petrus (2005) *Soziologie der Migration. Erklärungsmodelle, Fakten, Politische Konsequenzen, Perspektiven*, Stuttgart.

Harvey, David (1989) *The Condition of Postmodernity*, Oxford.

Herbert, Ulrich (2001) *Geschichte der Ausländerpolitik in Deutschland. Saisonarbeiter, Zwangsarbeiter, Gastarbeiter, Flüchtlinge*, Munich.

Homuth, Karl (1985) 'Pädagogisierung des Stadtteils. Über die Bedeutung von "behutsamer Stadterneuerung", als präventive Sozialpolitik', *Ästhetik und Kommunikation* 16(59): 78–86.

Homuth, Karl (1987) Identität und soziale Ordnung. Zum Verhältnis städtischer Kultur und gesellschaftlicher Hegemonie, *Prokla* 68, 17(3): 90–112.

John, Barbara (2005) 'Vorwort: Noch eine Berliner Pflanze. Der Karneval der Kulturen', in Michi Knecht, and Levent Soysal (eds), *Plausible Vielfalt. Wie der Karneval der Kulturen denkt, lernt und Kultur schafft*, Berlin, pp. 7–12.

Klausner, Martina (2005) 'Im Dialog mit dem Fremden. Zur (Re-)Produktion kultureller Differenz', in Michi Knecht and Levent Soysal (eds), *Plausible Vielfalt. Wie der Karneval der Kulturen denkt, lernt und Kultur schafft*, Berlin, pp. 176–92.

Kleff, Hans-Günter (2004) 'Täuschung, Selbsttäuschung, Enttäuschung und Lernen. Anmerkungen zum Fordstreik im Jahre 1973', in Jan Motte and Rainer Ohliger (eds), *Geschichte und Gedächtnis in der Einwanderergesellschaft. Migration zwischen historischer Rekonstruktion und Erinnerungspolitik*, Essen, pp. 251–8.

Knecht, Michi (2005) 'Einleitung', in Michi Knecht and Levent Soysal (eds), *Plausible Vielfalt. Wie der Karneval der Kulturen denkt, lernt und Kultur schafft*, Berlin, pp. 13–29.

Kürşat-Ahlers, Elcin (2002) 'Aktuelle Wandlungen der Grenzziehung zwischen "Wir" und "Sie"', in Hartmut M. Griese, Elcin Kürşat-Ahlers, Rainer Schulte and Massoud Vahedi (eds), *Was ist eigentlich das Problem am 'Ausländerproblem'? Über die soziale Durchschlagskraft ideologischer Konstruktur*, Berlin, pp. 323–34.

Lanz, Stephan (1996) *Demokratische Stadtplanung in der Postmoderne*, Oldenburg.

Lanz, Stephan (2007) *Berlin aufgemischt: abendländisch – multikulturell – kosmopolitisch? Die politische Konstruktion einer Einwanderungsstadt*, Bielefeld.

Leggewie, Claus (1993) *multi kulti. Spielregeln für die Vielvölkerrepublik*, Berlin.

Lucke, Albrecht von (2005) 'Diskursiver Dammbruch', *Blätter für deutsche und internationale Politik* 1: 9–11.

Meier-Braun, Karl-Heinz (1988) *Integration oder Rückkehr? Zur Ausländerpolitik des Bundes und der Länder, insbesondere Baden-Württembergs*, Munich.

Meier-Braun, Karl-Heinz (2002) *Deutschland, Einwanderungsland*, Frankfurt am Main.

Meier-Braun, Karl-Heinz (2005) 'Einwanderungspolitik. Von einer Geschichte, die nicht zu Ende gehen wollte', in Wilhelm Heitmeyer (ed.), *Deutsche Zustände*, vol. 3, Frankfurt am Main, pp. 240–49.

Mecheril, Paul (2004) *Einführung in die Migrationspädagogik*, Weinheim.

Morgenstern, Christine (2002) *Rassismus – Konturen einer Ideologie. Einwanderung im politischen Diskurs der Bundesrepublik Deutschland*, Hamburg.

Nassehi, Armin (1997) 'Das stahlharte Gehäuse der Zugehörigkeit. Unschärfen im Diskurs um die multikulturelle Gesellschaft', in Armin Nassehi (ed.), *Nation, Ethnie, Minderheit. Beiträge zur Aktualität ethnischer Konflikte*, Cologne and Weimar, pp. 177–208.

Neubert, Stefan, Hans-Joachim Roth and Erol Yildiz (2002) 'Multikulturalismus – ein umstrittenes Konzept', in Stefan Neubert et al. (eds), *Multikulturalität in der Diskussion. Neuere Beiträge zu einem umstrittenen Konzept*, Interkulturelle Studien 12, Opladen, pp. 9–32.

Özcan, Ertekin (1993) 'Selbstorganisation der türkischen Einwandererminderheit', in Berliner Geschichtswerkstatt e.V. (ed.), '*...da sind wir keine Ausländer mehr*'. *Eingewanderte Arbeiter Innen in Berlin 1961–1993*, Berlin, pp. 66–74.

Presse- und Informationsamt des Landes Berlin (ed.) (1980) 'Leitlinien und neue Maßnahmen zur Ausländerintegration in Berlin und deren Durchführung', Landespressedienst, Aktuelles der Woche, Berlin, 22 May.

Radtke, Frank-Olaf (1991) 'Lob der Gleichgültigkeit. Zur Konstruktion des Fremden im Diskurs des Multikulturalismus', in Uli Bielefeld (ed.), *Das Eigene und das Fremde: neuer Rassismus in der Alten Welt?*, Hamburg, pp. 79–96.

Radtke, Frank-Olaf (1996) Fremde und Allzufremde. Zur Ausbreitung des ethnologischen Blicks in der Einwanderungsgesellschaft, in Hans-Rudolf Wicker, et al. (eds), *Das Fremde in der Gesellschaft: Migration, Ethnizität und Staat*, pp. 333–52.

Rommelspacher, Birgit (2002) *Anerkennung und Ausgrenzung. Deutschland als multikulturelle Gesellschaft*, Frankfurt and New York.

Ronneberger, Klaus (1997) 'Die Dienstleistungsgesellschaft zwischen Multikulturalismus und Ethnisierung', in Barbara Danckwortt and Claudia Lepp (eds), *Von Grenzen und Ausgrenzung. Interdisziplinäre Beiträge zu den Themen Migration, Minderheiten und Fremdenfeindlichkeit*, Marburg, pp. 219–34.

Schiffauer, Werner (1997) *Fremde in der Stadt*, Frankfurt am Main.

Schönwälder, Karen (2001) *Einwanderung und ethnische Pluralität. Politische Entscheidungen und öffentliche Debatten in Großbritannien und der Bundesrepublik von den 1950er bis zu den 1970er Jahren*, Essen.

Schwarz, Thomas (1992) *Zuwanderer im Netz des Wohlfahrtsstaates. Türkische Jugendliche und die Berliner Kommunalpolitik*, Berlin.

Schwarz, Thomas (2001) 'Integrationspolitik als Beauftragtenpolitik: Die Ausländerbeauftragte des Berliner Senats', in Frank Gesemann (ed.), *Migration und Integration in Berlin. Wissenschaftliche Analysen und politische Perspektiven*, Opladen, pp. 127–44.

Senator für Gesundheit, Soziales und Familie and Ausländerbeauftragter (1982) *Miteinander leben. Ausländerpolitik in Berlin*, Berlin.

Sökefeld, Martin (ed.) (2004) *Jenseits des Paradigmas kultureller Differenz. Neue Perspektiven auf Einwanderer aus der Türkei*, Bielefeld.

SPD Berlin (1981) 'SPD-Fraktion des Abgeordnetenhauses in Zusammenarbeit mit dem Landesverband Berlin' (ed.), *Zusammenleben mit ausländischen Mitbürgern*, Berlin.

Terkessidis, Mark (2000) 'Wir selbst sind die Anderen – Globalisierung, multikulturelle Gesellschaft und Neorassismu', in Christoph Butterwegge and Gudrun Hentges (eds), *Zuwanderung im Zeichen der Globalisierung. Mirgrations-, Integrations- und Minderheitenpolitik*, Wiesbaden, pp. 188–209.

Terkessidis, Mark (2004) *Die Banalität des Rassismus. Migranten zweiter Generation entwickeln eine neue Perspektive*, Bielefeld.

Treibel, Annette (1990) *Migrationen in modernen Gesellschaften. Soziale Folgen von Einwanderung und Gastarbeit*, Weinheim and Munich.

Unabhängige Kommission 'Zuwanderung' (2001) *Zuwanderung gestalten – Integration fördern. Bericht der Unabhängigen Kommission 'Zuwanderung'*, Berlin.

Welz, Gisela (1996) *Inszenierungen kultureller Vielfalt. Frankfurt am Main und New York City*, Berlin.

Žižek, Slavoj (1997) 'Multiculturalism, or, the Cultural Logic of Multinational Capital', *New Left Review* 64, September/October: 28–51.

4

Multiculturalism in Italy: the missing model

Stefano Allievi

From country of emigration to country of immigration

Italy has only recently become an immigration country. While Central and Northern European countries are already well-established labour-importing economies (most from at least the time of post-war reconstruction and the subsequent period of economic boom, some for longer), Italy was still, along with other Mediterranean countries such as Spain, Greece and Portugal, a sending country with a significant percentage of emigrants.[1] Only in the 1970s did the situation begin to reverse.

In one century, from the country's unification in 1861 until 1970, almost 27 million Italians were obliged to expatriate (Ascoli 1979), mainly in search of a job (a relatively smal number were political refugees during the Fascist period): an impressive number, considering that the entire population of Italy was, at the beginning of Italian history as a unified country, only 21 million (excluding the region of Veneto, not yet part of the country). Not all these migrations were definitive: net emigration – the difference those who emigrated and those who repatriated – was probably between 8 and 9 million (Birindelli, 1989). Today, around 5 million Italians (those holding an Italian passport) still live abroad; in addition to which perhaps 50 to 60 million people of Italian descent (migrants and their descendants) are estimated to live in outher countries – another Italy outside the borders of Italy. All it took was 'an increase in the prices of some necessary goods, a minor outbreak of cholera or a new malarial epidemic, a poor harvest, a controversy with the landlord, to oblige people, individuals or groups to leave' (Volpi, 1989); or indeed the need to flee the police and the law, an attempt to avoid military conscription or debts, an argument with parents, a failed love affair or the need to find money to marry: the letters and testimonies of migrants tell us the stories of the great migration epic.[2]

Contrary to common perception, the North of Italy has contributed to international migration more than the South: Veneto is the region with the most emigrants (around 3 million), followed by Campania (2.7 million), Sicily (2.5 million), Lombardy (2.3 million), Piedmont and Friuli (2.2 million each), Calabria (almost 2 million), and so on. But from the period of economic boom on (and to date), and particularly in the 1960s, the North received great waves of internal migrants from the South, making the South the part of Italy that has experienced the greatest emigration.

It is only since the 1970s that Italy has started to become, statistically, an immigration country. The symbolic turning point can be considered 1973, the first year in which ISTAT (the Italian Institute of Statistics) data show that, compared with 123,802 expatriates, there were 125,168 repatriates: albeit by 1,366 people, Italy was no longer, officially, an emigration country.

This marks the end of an era. The Italy of emigrants, the Italy of underdevelopment, the Italy with a fragile social structure despite its economic success, the Italy of boats to America, the Italy of cardboard suitcases, the Italy of millions of individual sufferings, the Italy of both a great popular epoch and historic national shame, seems now to belong only to the past, dissolving finally in the established national well-being. Despite the fact that the number of emigrants remains relevant (in this period it is annually still higher than the number of immigrants), and despite the fact that repatriation is often a bitter sign of personal defeat, a failed attempt, Italy can raise its head: Italians are no longer a poor and wretched people, forced by circumstance to make their way outside the country's borders, often stigmatized and treated badly in receiving countries.

The national rhetoric, after having carefully and deliberately concealed for more than a century what was probably the most important social phenomenon of Italian history (demonstrable by a quick glance at the minimal space devoted to emigration in history books, particularly textbooks), can finally claim that the phenomenon has vanished, has 'been put behind us'. The forgotten epoch can finally fade into oblivion.

Nevertheless, history sometimes plays games. In 1973 foreigners officially resident in Italy numbered 175,746, a group slightly greater than the Italians emigrating in a single year. This number appears insignificant, and most of them were Europeans, rather than the new wave of migration from the so-called Third World. But from that moment on, quickly, silently and unnoticed, the phenomenon became manifest. The new migration arrived, and a new cycle had started.[3]

The legislative process:
how the missing model was built

As we have seen, immigration in Italy is a recent phenomenon. This can explain the weakness of planning and the initial lack of experience. But it is not enough to explain how even the legislative process concerning migration has been constructed without model or reference: a house built without architect or engineer, and with little idea of the materials to be used – with some good intentions, particularly in the beginning, and a lot of work already done (some walls have been built, destroyed, rebuilt...), but facing at times substantial opposition, including the refusal of some to build anything at all. The Italian missing model has been the result of shifting majorities in coalition government, which, as we will see, continually altered the principles underlying the different laws approved, but also of internal contradictions, lack of clarity of purpose, the prevalence of tactical manoeuvring and political advantage-seeking (on both left and right) with regard to the need to solve empirical problems, the lack of experience and contact with the real world, or simply the absence of pragmatism and willingness to take risks.

The numbers, in the beginning, were modest. In 1970, permits of stay issued to foreigners numbered 146,989;[4] in 1975 they were 185,715;

but by 1980 the number had reached 298,749. However, Europeans held 61 per cent of permits in 1970, and they remained the absolute majority until 1986, the year of the first Italian migration law. It is only in more recent years that migration from developing countries has become more visible and appeared in statistics: according to the National Statistical Office (ISTAT) more than 1.3 million permit holders at the end of 2002, and 1.7 million at the end of 2003, 2.1 million in 2004, 2.3 million in 2005, 2.6 million in 2006, 3.1 million in 2007, 3.9 million in 2008. The most widely used estimates (Caritas, 2009; 2008 data) suggest an even higher number, 4.5 million (accounting for about 7 per cent of the current resident population of the country), including regular immigrants not yet registered and not included in the ISTAT statistics because they have not yet enrolled in the population registry.

In all this data the number of foreigners with no permit of stay – particularly important in Italy and cause of undesirable social phenomena and negative public perception – is not included. An estimate by the Caritas research group, based on specific research, was of 500,000 'irregulars' at the end of 2005. In 2006, there were 484,000 applications for an 'undeclared regularization', through the quota agreement (*decreto flussi*); even if some applications were rejected, this might partly explain both the increased number of immigrants and the diminishing number of irregulars. The ISMU report (Fondazione Ismu, 2007) estimates 760,000 irregulars in 2006, which probably makes Italy one of the countries with the highest percentage of irregulars in Europe, even though most of them (64 per cent according to 2006 Caritas estimates) are overstayers: people who entered Italy regularly, but became irregulars after a certain period, due either to the law – as we will see in more detail below – or, more often, to bureaucratic inefficiency.

The initially modest numbers of immigrants made it possible for Italian governments to overlook the new migration (from developing countries) for a long time. And when they did recognize this immigration, they seemed not only to reject it but to have learned nothing from a century of emigration. Not having reflected on the costs and consequences of emigration, having forgotten them, Italy (and, concretely, Italian government) has failed to understand immigration.

No lessons have been learned. There has been no thought of building a model to inform the legislative process. Conflicting approaches have alternately held sway, producing different laws. It is not by chance that practically all the important laws on migration have been linked to a *sanatoria* (regularization), discussed and approved often with the term 'emergency', and always with an emergency situation in mind, featuring in the accompanying political and media debate. Immigration has been understood more as a temporary pathology than as a progressively established natural trend.

The 1986 law: labour force and nothing more

To go back to the beginning: the first Italian Civil Code, approved in 1865 (shortly after the unification of the country and the proclamation of the Kingdom of Italy, which dates from 1861), contained a very liberal principle, almost inconceivable today and in light of current legislation covering all of Europe. Article 3 states simply: 'foreigners admitted enjoy the civil rights granted to citizens', practically granting equivalent status to citizens and foreigners, or rather abolishing the juridical consequences of any distinction, with the obvious exception of political rights, which were not universally granted in those years even to citizens (Nascimbene, 1988). In reality, as the rights of the citizen have been progressively defined, so has the contrasting juridical notion and status of a foreigner. Already in 1889, a law on public security had gone in a completely different direction; this was confirmed and aggravated during the Fascist period, with the passage the 1931 'Testo Unico delle Leggi di Pubblica Sicurezza' law, infamous among immigrants, who long suffered its consequences. This law remained in force in its entirety until a few years before the approval of the first 'modern' immigration law, and was only recently modified.

The first immigration law approved in Italy, as a parliamentary initiative, and which ended an embarrassing legislative silence unparalleled in the receiving countries of Europe, was Law 943 (officially published on 30 December 1986), entitled 'Legislation concerning the employment and treatment of extracommunitarian immigrants and against clandestine immigration', also known as *Legge Foschi* from the name of the MP who took the initiative.

The long title immediately reveals two things: (a) that immigrants from outside Europe form a specificity, called in the Italian bureaucratic jargon 'extracommunitarian';[5] (b) that the law considers only the aspect of presence in the labour market – the immigrant exists as a worker, and has no specificity or need outside this role.

The main purpose of the law was to make the foreign presence in the labour force visible, transforming a *de facto* presence in a *de jure* integration, shifting immigrants out of the informal economy, with its lack of rights, into the open where they would enjoy equal rights and social citizenship. These were, at least, the hopes that accompanied the very long process of drafting this law. However, the law was born under the wrong star: not so far as immigrants were concerned (rarely could one observe so many people wishing to be subject to a law, because although a law involves restrictions, sanctions and limits, it also guarantees certain rights, and thereby puts to an end a situation of total discretionality, uncertainty and irregularity), but because of public opinion. The first law on immigrants in Italy arrived when public opinion was already mobilizing against them. And that is not all: the first attempt to lobby for a draft law dates to 1980, when it was supported by the trade unions. But the real debate reached parliament in December 1985, immediately after the Palestinian attacks on Rome and Vienna airports, and the Ministry of the Interior increased the level of alert, proposing its own draft (titled 'Additional regulations to the current law for the control of foreigners'), contributing to the easy equation 'foreigner = terrorist'. In those days the syllogism argued that because the terrorists are foreigners, so immigrants are suspected of being close to terrorism entered into media language and political practice. But that was also a period in which the immediate reactions of trade unions, churches (particularly the Roman Catholic Church, which – directly and through the associations belonging to or depending on it – is the organization most involved in serving immigrants) and associations translated into a push for reform, some of which ended up as law.

Everybody wanted *a* law, possibly a complete and articulated one, but only one piece of it arrived, the part concerning employment, and only for waged and salaried work, not self-employment (the parts on residence permits, students, refugees, citizenship, and more generally on rights in society were announced but were not forthcoming). The immigrant was considered only as labour – consider the significance of the Italian expression *mano d'opera* (working hand), that is, just a *piece* of the migrant, the useful part in terms of work, not the whole person and its implications (the different level of needs, connectedness, including family ties, and so on).

The Martelli Decree and its consequences: a (temporary) positive perception of immigration

The second legal initiative on immigration was the fruit of a quite different situation, in the late 1980s. Immigration, already acknowledged, started to make its costs felt, along with the rights these costs *should* grant. It was a period of mobilization and activity by churches, trade unions, NGOs and other associations, and the adoption of a perspective of relative 'sympathy' towards migrants, not least as a consequence of dramatic episodes of violence that served to stigmatize migrants – but such sympathy rapidly vanished in the years that followed.

On the night of 24 August 1989, a young black South African immigrant, Jerry Essan Masslo, was shot dead in his hut in Villa Literno, a rural area in the region of Campania, where he was working in the poorly paid seasonal job of tomato harvesting. Masslo was a political refugee, who had fled the apartheid regime that had killed his father and daughter. It was probably just a 'normal' robbery, possibly the work of drug addicts. But this murder, which was followed by many similar acts of violence, clearly shows that Masslo was targeted because he was a vulnerable victim, defenceless and without protection: black, immigrant, poor. He was the first official victim of racist Italy.

The reaction across the entire country was massive, and television and newspaper coverage was unprecedented.[6] Masslo was very well known in the immigrant community: he had been a guest of the Community of Sant'Egidio, where he was videotaped in interview. Coverage and debate grew. Awareness thus emerged of a phenomenon hitherto considered marginal, if not non-existent, something that might happen elsewhere, but not in Italy. The vice-president of the Council of Ministers, Claudio Martelli, officially participated in the funeral, and the ceremony was given full coverage by the national broadcasting company.

Masslo's funeral marked the start of a reflection that led to the approval of a new law, *Decreto Legge* (a form of urgent decree) 416, of 30 December 1989, entitled 'Urgent legislation concerning political asylum, entrance and residency of extracommunitarian citizens, and the regularization of extracommunitarian citizens and stateless people already present in the territory of the State', widely known as the 'Martelli Decree', which became Law 39 on 28 February 1990, after parliamentary approval with some modifications.

The Martelli Decree reopened the debate about the presence of immigrants in Italy, and put it on new footing. There was in fact another, unofficial, reason for writing a new law that included a regularization (*sanatoria*): the unsatisfactory nature and inefficiency, if not the failure, of the previous one. Law 943 saw some 118,700 foreign workers regularize their position. This was far fewer than expected, even though the initial three-month application period was eventually extended to 21 months. Law 39 of 1990, with broader criteria for acceptance of applications, opened a six-month *sanatoria* that led to 217,700 regularizations. Another *sanatoria* followed five years later, with Decree 489 of 1995 (the so-called 'Dini Law', from the name of the minister who proposed it), which resulted in 246,000 regularizations, and again in 1998, with 217,000 regularizations.[7] At the end of 1999, the 566,000 immigrants living in Italy who were previously regularized through a *sanatoria* comprised 42 per cent of the 1,340,655 legal residents (Carfagna 2002). As the number of undocumented foreigners suggests, most of these legislative initiatives were emergency measures. The word 'urgent' is present in almost all the titles of these government decrees, which require the justification of necessity and exigency, in contrast to normal legislation, which is openly debated in parliament. There was no larger ambition to construct a full legal framework capable of regulating immigration, preventing its negative consequences, predicting its flows, helping with the integration of immigrants already present, and thereby escaping from this epiphenomenal logic. On the contrary, the same logic applied in the following years: the *sanatoria* (which bore a different name but the same mechanism) of 2002, the largest so far, led to 705,000 applications and 646,000 regularizations.[8] Thus, Italy promoted regularizations (regardless of the composition of the ruling coalition) in 1977, 1982, 1986, 1990, 1995, 1998 and 2002, with numbers of foreigners regularized going from 5,000 in 1982 to 646,000 in 2002 (Einaudi, 2007).

The Turco-Napolitano law: the first non-emergency legislative frame

The following period, notwithstanding the previously cited Dini Decree in 1995, a legislative initiative with limited ambitions (mainly a regularization), saw the first serious attempt to build a non-emergency legislative framework for immigration in Italy. This framework law, or *testo unico* (unified text), was Legislative Decree 286 of 25 July 1998, widely known as the 'Turco–Napolitano Law', from the names of the two ministers of the centre-left government (the first Prodi government, which took power after the election of 1996) who promoted it. The law set out a comprehensive proposal, entitled 'Unified text of dispositions concerning the discipline of immigration and norms on the conditions of foreigners'.[9] Although the law appeared somewhat ingenuous, with unclear objectives and internal contradictions, it did represent an attempt to lay the foundations for a coherent approach to immigration policy. It revealed, on the one hand, a genuine desire to grant individual rights and encourage solidarity and, on the other, a determination to provide a counterpoint to a repressive discourse emerging in public opinion and dominated by the right-wing parties. Nevertheless, the initiative was subsequently cancelled, without much protest, by the succeeding right-wing government.

The period was in fact already unfavourable to a law based on rights: wide sectors of public opinion were much more disposed towards the logic of repression and negation, openly promoted with evident success by political parties like the Northern League (Lega Nord) of Umberto Bossi, but sustained also by the traditional right of Gianfranco Fini's National Alliance (Alleanza Nazionale) and the 'new' right represented by Forza Italia, the party created by Silvio Berlusconi.[10] It must be said that the more openly xenophobic Northern League has been able to set the agenda also for the rest of the rightist coalition, and for a larger part of public opinion, including on the left. Giovanna Zincone notes that it was at the turn of the century that the Italian right, previously cited by foreign observers as a positive example of openness and respect towards migrants, moved in the direction of religious intolerance and xenophobic aggression, with an explicit anti-immigrant language (Bolaffi, 2001).

The spirit of the law was nevertheless realized, based not on an emergency logic but on a projection of what might happen in the future, in both the labour market and in society at large. Yet the law also paid more than lip service to the logic of repression of irregularity and to security policies widely demanded by commentators and public opinion. However, there were serious practical deficiencies, which made the law an easy target for the right. The Northern League used the ministers Livia Turco and Giorgio Napolitano's last names to comment ironically on the law's weaknesses: 'How could a good law on immigration come from a Turk and a Neapolitan?'[11] Nevertheless, the law had tried to reconcile the universalist (in terms of rights) and the solidarist approach (the law was sustained by the Catholic Church and the more active movements and organizations working on migrant issues, most of them Catholic), on the one hand, with the need for law, order and security, introducing centres for temporary detention (CPTs) and other measures, on the other. And in the eyes of the public it was probably the failure of the repressive part – meant to include repatriation of irregulars but never effectively applied – that was the main target of critics, thereby pushing the more positive integrative aspects into the background. Nevertheless, the Turco-Napolitano law deserved the chance to succeed, in contrast to the previous initiatives, among other reasons because of the several readmission agreements signed with source countries governing illegal migration, which had particularly successful in the cases of Albania, Tunisia and others.

The Bossi–Fini law and its consequences: a period of emerging ideologies

With the change in government following the victory in the April 2001 elections of the right-wing coalition – who campaigned on the

issue of immigration, and the need to regulate it or better to oppose it
– ideology triumphed completely, largely overwhelming the pragmatic
approach. Ironically, while it was particularly voters in the North who
voted for the right, it was entrepreneurs in the Northern regions who
asked for *more* migrants and a larger quota of them for their labour
market.[12] Law 189, of 30 July 2002 ('Modifications to the law concerning immigration and asylum'), bears the names of the two right-wing
leaders who had been the toughest on immigration, Umberto Bossi of
the Northern League and Gianfranco Fini of National Alliance. The
Bossi–Fini law was presented as the tool to regulate immigration and
eliminate irregularity. Ironically (and dramatically, in terms of the
conditions and the quality of life of migrants), because of its requirement that there be a direct link between the residence permit and a
regular job (so that if you lost the latter the former was revoked), the
Bossi–Fini law actually served to increase the number of irregulars
in the country, thereby paradoxically *producing* irregularity via the
legislation. It also led directly to an increase in the foreign presence
in Italian jails, with thousands imprisoned for crimes connected to
clandestine immigration (which was criminalized under this law)
or for non-compliance with expulsion orders (in excess of 10,000,
according to reliable estimates).

The Bossi–Fini law, widely considered an inappropriate tool for
the regulation of migration, has been from a certain point of view the
perfect law, successfully creating the target that was needed to rally
political support for law-and-order policies and their accompanying
political message, along with the creation of social anxiety that
could be exploited for political gain by the pedlars of fear (Bonini
and D'Avanzo, 2006; see also Allievi, 2007). This, then, has been
the triumph of ideology, with no consideration given to individual
rights, pragmatism and realpolitik (lacking attempts to regulate the
phenomenon, at least at the economic level), or to emerging social
and cultural problems.

It has been in this period that anti-Islamic discourses[13] have
emerged dramatically in the public space, particularly in the media
and in politics, reinforcing each other, making Italy one of the few
countries in Europe where Islamophobic discourses have been openly
promoted, or allowed to set the agenda, by *government* parties and

spokesmen, including MPs, political leaders, ministers, and even on occasion the head of the government. These anti-Muslim campaigns are described below.

In the 2006 elections, the centre-left came back to power, albeit with a very weak majority, for what turned out to be a short inter-regnum. The minister for social affairs, Paolo Ferrero, of the Communist Refoundation Party, wanted to introduce a significant change in immigration law, even though the minister of the interior, Giuliano Amato, intended to follow a more pragmatic approach, a sort of return to rationality.[14] With work proceeding in parallel on draft laws on immigration, citizenship and religious rights, a more open debate also on cultures seemed to become possible.[15] So, after twenty years of legislative attempts, even aspects outside the labour market entered the debate and were proposed.

On 24 April 2007, a new set of draft laws came under discussion, with the approval of a *Disegno di legge delega* presented by the two ministers of the centre-left coalition and bearing their names (Amato–Ferrero): 'Modifications of the discipline on immigration and on the norms on the condition of the foreigner'. The draft law, intended to become a definitive law within twelve months, represented a spectacular and ambitious change in respect to the previous 'philosophy', and was probably too radical a shift for public opinion.

The declared starting point was the failures of the Bossi–Fini law, which had concentrated disproportionately on illegal as opposed to legal immigration. The main objectives concerned common-sense goals, such as control of illegal immigration, its legalization, the repression of human trafficking, and the politics of integration. But at the same time a contrary ideological framework, in respect of the Bossi–Fini approach, seemed to be present: based, on one hand, on a pragmatic approach, with a different notion of rights and their universality; but, on the other hand, a 'progressive' perspective, very much a counter-tendency to what was and is happening in most countries of Europe, and also to majority Italian public opinion. One example of the turnaround was the draft law on citizenship, presented in August 2006,[16] which promoted a shift from a particularly strict policy (the result of which has been the insignificant number

– compared to most countries of Europe – of no more than 200,000 citizenships granted in decades of immigration) to an unusually liberal one, with the possibility of obtaining Italian citizenship after five years permanence.[17] The same can be said for other parts of this raft of laws.[18]

What is problematic in every project of legislative modification is that it is closely linked to the ruling majority. This is very clear in analysis of the perception of immigrants,[19] which differs significantly according to political affiliation. Those who consider that 'Immigrants are a danger for our culture, our identity and our religion' account for (in 2007) 34.6 per cent of the population, 24.4 per cent of centre-left voters, and 43 per cent of centre-right voters. With reference to cultural issues, those who think that 'the presence of immigrants favours our openmindedness' account for 46.4 per cent of the population: 60.2 per cent of centre-left voters and 35.6 per cent of centre-right voters. These statistics, which are reflected by politicians, became the basis of arguments in electoral campaigns and – less directly – of political decisions. The result of this polarization, not unique in Europe but differing significantly from the position in many other countries, means that a new majority can completely destroy the legislative building constructed by another majority, without provoking significant protest. This is precisely what happened with the transition from the Berlusconi to the Prodi government, and again following the internal crisis of the centre–left government headed by Prodi in April 2008, when it lost its majority and the president of the Republic was obliged to call new elections. The centre–right coalition returned to power, with a large majority, and turned the clock back to the Bossi–Fini law. The only change is that the present government can be much tougher on immigrants, given the power obtained by the Northern League, which holds the Ministry of the Interior.

The intentions of Northern League members of the government have already become evident: at the cultural level, they have energetically promoted anti-immigrant and specifically anti-Muslim campaigns, both locally (particularly at mosques and other places of worship) and nationally; at the legislative level, they have actively promoted laws and regulations intended to make life as difficult as possible for immigrants in general, and for illegal immigrants and overstayers in particular. An example is the law approved in February 2009 in which the main emphasis is on issues of security and protection of native Italians, with no reference made to rights, including the cultural rights, of immigrants. Meanwhile legislation on immigration remains strictly focused on labour issues and policies (Chaloff, 2004; Sciortino, 2009), with no commitment to intervene in other domains. In particular, cultural, multicultural and intercultural debate and politics remain entirely separate from legislative activity. There have been many initiatives, a plethora of conferences, forums and debates, and even a significant amount of documentation and analysis, not to mention the impact on the school system and local initiatives to encourage cultural and religious dialogue. But all this activity has had no influence on the political debate, or on legislative activity, both of which point in the opposite direction: there is little recognition of cultures, and, where there is, it follows a logic of conflict rather than one of dialogue – more a 'clash of civilizations' paradigm than that of sociological analysis at an empirical level, with successes and failures measured, and the seeking of solutions to perceived problems.

This duality regarding the recognition of cultures, and even more the recent shifts in politics that have been previously described, serve to highlight for discussion a tendency often taken for granted: that, in the long run, more rights are gradually granted to immigrants, and their existence is progressively taken into account both in the realm of politics and in terms of policy (possibly more the latter, particularly at the local level), while laws are progressively consolidated in legal practice. This probably remains true in the long run, but there is a pattern of strong counter-tendencies in the short term.

Recognizing cultures through a religious lens?

Today immigrants represent at least 6,5 per cent of the population (Caritas/Migrantes, 2009), but the figure is double that in some cities; for example, foreigners account for 14 per cent of residents in Milan and 10.9 per cent in Rome. Several provinces, mainly in the North, have significant proportions of immigrants. Indeed, the top ten provinces by immigrant presence in the population are in the North, with the exception of Rome (Caritas/Migrantes, 2006): Prato 12.6

per cent, Brescia 10.2 per cent, Rome, 9.5 per cent, Pordenone 9.4 per cent, Reggio Emilia 9.3 per cent, Treviso 8.9 per cent, Florence 8.6 per cent, Macerata and Trieste 8.1 per cent. In total, 59.5 per cent of all immigrants are located in the North, 27 per cent in the central region, and 13.5 per cent in the South. In terms of regions (Caritas/Migrantes, 2008), Lombardy leads, hosting 23.9 per cent of all the immigrants in Italy. These figures do not, however, take into account the significant presence of undocumented foreigners, of which estimates vary, though they are quite high, and are subject to context (and sometimes the political and religious opinions of researchers).

The leading source countries for immigrants at the end of 2008 (Caritas/Migrantes, 2009) were: Romania (800,000; up 27 per cent compared to 2007), followed by Albania (440,000; up 10 per cent), Morocco (400,000; up 10 per cent), China (170,000; up 9 per cent), Ukraine (150,000; up 16 per cent), Philippines (114,000), Tunisia (100,000), Poland (99,000), India (91,000) and Moldova (89,000). These are followed by Ecuador, Peru, Egypt, Moldova, Serbia and Montenegro, Senegal, Sri Lanka, Bangladesh, Pakistan, Nigeria, Germany and Ghana, all nationalities accounting for at least 1 per cent of the immigrant population. These data clearly show the recent change in migration flows, where migration from Eastern Europe (and, partly, Asia) has been greater than that from North Africa and the Middle East, combined with a constant increase that has changed the cultural and religious landscape of migration. And there has also been a progressive concentration: the first two countries listed account for about one-third of the immigrant population, and the first five countries for half of it.

Curiously enough, it is not immigrants from the most numerous nationalities (Eastern European/Orthodox Christian) who are the most debated. Arabs, and particularly Muslims, remain at the centre of cultural debate over immigration (Allievi, 2005a, 2005b), even as their relative weight is shrinking (and, notably, immigrants from Muslim countries have never represented more than one-third of the total).

This simple observation leads us to the core of our argument: the legislative process concerning migration has not really raised – and even less solved – the problem of the ongoing process of the cultural pluralization of Italy, whether interpreted in terms of multiculturalism (with its different meanings in different contexts) or in any other way. The laws on migration simply have not contained any reference to cultures, and the European and Western debate on (for or against) multiculturalism has played no part in the legislative process. This is all the more surprising since the debate on cultures, and on Islam particularly, has been visibly and violently raised, overtly exploited politically, and widely covered, if not fuelled, by the media.

The (anti-)Muslim debate started from what we can call the 'black September' of Islam in Italy – not September 2001, but the previous year, when three important events occurred at different levels. On the political plane, the Northern League started the most aggressive and pervasive anti-Muslim campaign ever seen in Italy, which still continues.[20] At the religious level, Cardinal Biffi, Archbishop of Bologna, gave voice to Catholic anti-Muslim opinion, with a letter addressed to his parishioners but intended for national readership, which has achieved significant visibility.[21] At the cultural level, a political scientist, Giovanni Sartori, with no specific expertise on the subject, published a pamphlet arguing against multiculturalism (Sartori, 2000). Sartori was already well known to the media, and his text, although superficial, polemical and ill-informed, was treated as if it were rigorous, and it enjoyed great success and earned considerable attention in the political milieu. Sartori, though far from being a leftist, was nevertheless anti-Berlusconi, which thereby gave him credit on the left.

This debate, once started, was further fuelled by the 9/11 terrorist attacks, which in Italy led, as the most noteworthy example on the cultural level, to the extraordinary and unprecedented success of Oriana Fallaci's books condemning Islam. Fallaci's trilogy became a popular and long-term bestseller, with a million copies of each volume sold (see Fallaci, 2001, 2004a, 2004b; see also my comments in Allievi, 2006a; and Bosetti, 2005). These books have since set the agenda on Islam in Italy, with surprisingly little criticism, either in the media or in politics, although there have recently been some faint signs of rethinking, which acquired a certain visibility on the occasion of Fallaci's death, in 2006.

The context of integration is obviously crucial in understanding and helping the processes of integration, including at the cultural and religious levels. The emergence of the question of Islam and of anti-Islamic sentiments has not helped address the issue of cultural and religious pluralism in a rational, unemotional, even-tempered and non-prejudicial way.

Politics and political parties have played, as we have seen, an important role in framing the issue of Islam and the West as a sort of popular clash of civilizations, in an essentialist way, ignoring the empirical reality of Muslim communities and individuals in Europe.[22]

Islam: a long way from recognition

At the institutional level there has been more caution and moderation than in the political sphere. Yet in October 2005, the minister of the interior of what could be considered a xenophobic and anti-Islamic right-wing coalition, Giuseppe Pisanu, set up a consultative body for Muslims in Italy, the Consulta per l'islam italiano. Pisanu acted despite opposition from within his coalition, in particular from the Northern League. The body is composed of nominated rather than elected members, and is of questionable representativeness, but the very creation of the body, given the period, can be considered a victory for moderate attitudes, as opposed to the pervasive radicalization that drew in the principal media, intellectuals and academics, and even religious leaders, particularly in the majority Catholic Church and the minority Jewish community.

From the legislative point of view, there is another aspect of cultural pluralism that has been more profoundly debated, always having in mind, particularly, the case of Islam: the recognition of religious specificities.

The Italian legal system, with regard to religion, is based on the privileged status in the Constitution of the Roman Catholic Church, and in a system of *intese* (agreements) with religious minorities who apply for it. It is in this specific context that the presence of Islam – a 'confession' that, even though it represents the main religious minority in the country, does not yet have an *intesa* – has been widely debated from the juridical and legislative point of view. Some Muslim associations, in fact, already started to lobby for an *intesa* in the early 1990s, although they now seem much less enthusiastic and active (Ferrari, 2005; A. Ferrari 2008). However, the political and cultural climate is far from receptive to this solution. In fact, besides the first Protestant minority recognized in 1985, the Waldensians (the day after which the president of the Council of Ministers, Bettino Craxi, signed the new *Concordato* with the Catholic Church, as a clear sign of his intention to take into account the religious plurality of Italy), and the later *intese* with the Jewish community and with other Protestant reformed churches, the system in itself has been stopped by political will. While a left-wing government was in power, immediately after the first Prodi government, President D'Alema chose to sign an *intesa* with the Buddhist representatives and with the Jehovah's Witnesses, but both await parliamentary approval and have yet to come to the vote. Among secondary objections to these *intese*, as a sort of hidden agenda, was the idea to stop any possible agreement with Muslims, by far – numerically – the largest religious minority in the country. In April 2007, six new *intese* were signed, including with religious communities that represent important parts of the immigrant population, the Christian Orthodox Church and Hinduism. Parliament is expected to debate the new and old *intese* signed but awaiting ratification.[23] This may not occur for a long time, given the political approach of the present Berlusconi-led coalition government, to the issue of religious pluralism.

Meanwhile, it is important to note that a law on the religious freedom of minorities is under discussion, designed to grant significant rights to religious communities in general. This proposal, which has been discussed for more than a decade, seems to have little chance of approval with the present centre–right government. It is patently clear that the hidden agenda of the law is to resolve most of the practical problems that Muslim communities might have while avoiding any direct and specific recognition of Islam, particularly the symbolic recognition of an *intesa*, possibly for a long time. This could be a way to escape, in practice, the 'clash of civilizations' syndrome, without criticizing it, and on the contrary continuing to deploy it as an interpretative tool whenever it is politically expedient. But it is not clear, at present, if the government intends to follow this path, or indeed if it intends to manage the problem of religious and cultural pluralism in any way at all, given its own ideology and agenda, and also given its strong affinity with the Catholic Church on several controversial topics (bioethics, religious schooling and education, economic support to recognized religious communities, and more general reciprocal support in certain cultural areas), and given the fact that the Church, at the institutional level, is obviously not particularly open to the issue of religious pluralism.

As in other European countries, political decisions concerning Islam have tended to 'exceptionalize' Islam, not treating the religion on the same grounds, including legal, as others.[24] Nonetheless, these varying ways of recognizing different religious communities have had the systemic effect of implementing self-awareness of Italy as a pluralistic country, in terms of cultures and religions, something still far from apparent in the media and in public opinion. Change has begun, but is moving very slowly.

Italian Islamic exceptionalism has also been visible in the creation – as in other European countries – of a specific representative body, the Consulta per l'islam italiano, created by the minister of the interior Pisanu, and confirmed by Minister Amato, of the opposition coalition, and now 'suspended' by Minister Roberto Maroni of the Northern League. The Consulta had a relatively short history, and its discussions have been overwhelmingly monopolized by discussions and reciprocal demonizations among Muslim representatives and self-declared representatives of Islam, and in media polemics on Islamic issues, which have affected members of the Consulta or the whole body (Allievi, 2009b). This consultative body officially had no ambition to be a representative or even umbrella organization, although it may come to constitute, at least in the public's view, an Islamic representation *in nuce*. It has since been abolished and a new Comitato per l'islam italiano appointed to include academic and journalistic experts on Islam and representatives of more mainstream Islamic organizations.

Cultural (in)comprehension: anti-multiculturalism without multiculturalism

It is probably true that Italy bears an 'original sin' concerning its internal cultural plurality, its North–South cleavage, its regional differentiation, all rooted in the history of the process of unification of the country (Pratt, 2002). This cleavage might have some consequences (not necessarily negative) now, if it is true that 'incorporation and exclusion experienced by migrants and minorities [are] shaped by the processes and cleavages internal to Italian society' (Grillo, 2002).

It is also true that Italy has some difficulty in acknowledging its internal religious plurality, even before the changes wrought by international migration. Italy is a country where journalists specializing in religious issues are still called 'Vaticanists'.[25] This problem is compounded by foreign observers, who too quickly identify Italy as simply a Catholic country: in the popular imagination, and diffused even through tourist guides, in the media (where the fact that the Vatican is in Rome sometimes leads to confusion between the two), but also among scholars and serious researchers in the sociology of religion, who usually forget to take into account the plurality of the religious dimension in this country.

It is equally true, as indicated above, that Italy does not want to reflect on its memory of emigration, which might help in understanding the present social, cultural and even legal situation of foreign migrants (well demonstrated by Stella, 2002).

Finally, it is true that Italy does not have a colonial memory of racism or of management of cultural plurality (including in legislative terms). Hence there is a tendency to underestimate the racist attitudes manifested in that period (the popular myth, still the mainstream view of the colonial role of Italy, is of *Italiani brava gente*[26]) and their possible lasting effects today, including in areas such as the sexual imagination (Sorgoni, 2002).[27] This has also prevented the reading of immigration in post-colonial terms (Grillo, 2002), as is the case in Britain and France, for instance, and central to these countries' debates.

It is also the case that the social and religious role played by the Catholic Church has had important integrative effects on foreign immigrants, just as it did during the period of internal migrations, and in general concerning the traditional North–South cleavage. Given the key role played by Catholic organizations (e.g. Caritas, Sant'Egidio and ACLI, certain missionary orders, and local parishes in general) in the institutions helping migrants at all levels, and the importance of the Catholic vote for both centre–left and the centre–right coalitions (which receives by far the larger proportion), Catholic positions have in part mitigated the effects of the differences in the legislative frameworks described in previous paragraphs. The fact that some high and media-visible figures in the Catholic hierarchy are today openly expressing critical views on immigrants in general and Muslims specifically[28] does not so much contradict this historic role as show that the Catholic Church, just like secular opinion, is deeply divided over the issue of cultural and, particularly, religious diversity, especially in the case of Islam.

The traditional leftist culture of solidarity has played an important role in helping foreign workers integrate. This is particularly true in the case of trade unions, which, in contrast to other countries in Europe, have always approved of an interpretative framework based on migrant rights and policies of integration, which has been reflected in the ministers and MPs they have supported, who have sponsored some of the important national immigration laws.

In addition, the school system has played a key role in the making of the possible future Italian multicultural citizen, devoting attention to the problem, promoting self-reflection among teachers, specific training programmes and local initiatives.

Hence the emerging discussions on Islam have helped, albeit in a peculiar and often problematic way, Italians acknowledge that theirs is becoming a plural, if not a multicultural, country. And even now, when Italy, as other European countries, is going through a phase of reactive identity and cultural conflict (Allievi, 2006b), these factors are still in play, countering the mainstream discourse on (against) migrants and Muslims. In contrast to other European countries, however, this more recent phase of cultural conflict fuelled by anti-Muslim if not truly Islamophobic attitudes is producing a diffused perspective of *anti-multiculturalism without multiculturalism*. Italy, in fact, in its discussion and criticism of certain multiculturalist policies and results, and of multiculturalism in general, has adopted the practice of other European countries of treating the subject as an easy target in terms of popular media and political discourse, even before multiculturalism even existed. That is, the debate on (against) multiculturalism has been both imported and locally produced before any multiculturalist policies had even been proposed.

Anti-multiculturalism without multiculturalism it is not, then, such a strange entity. Enemies, as is well known, can be easily constructed, and used strategically in public debate. It is enough to think of the well-known example of anti-Semitic prejudice thriving in the absence of Jews – that is, anti-Semitism is alive and well in certain countries of Eastern Europe, desite the fact that their Jewish communities were annihilated during the Second World War. A more recent Italian example is the debate over the hijab, which was promptly imported from France, even before a headscarf had appeared in Italian schools.

Pluralism, conflict and cultural change – an excursus

Becoming plural is not a neutral process. The presence of ever-increasing numbers of immigrants is not merely a quantitative fact with different consequences for many social and cultural dynamics.[29] Changes in the quantitative levels of so many different indicators (economic, social, cultural, political, religious) not only produce quantitative change, they completely alter the scenario. Overall, the indicators that are currently changing as a result of the presence of immigrant populations in Europe are themselves creating new problems, new processes of interrelation, new conflicts, and new solutions to them. In a word, they are producing *qualitative* changes – nothing less than a different type of society, one quite distinct from that imagined with the rise of the nation-state and its founding principles.[30] Many European countries, and Italy in particular, as this chapter has attempted to show, have no plans or guidelines for such a society; therefore they can only proceed by trial and error, learning through experience.

Among the changes taking place, one of the most visible is the so-called 'return' of cultures – and in particular religions – to the European public space,[31] a process of which discussions on multiculturalism are both a consequence and an acceleration, at least in terms of reflexivity and self-consciousness. Immigrant communities are the main actors in this process, which elicits surprise and even amazement in observers, including multiculturalists, who are some-times reluctant to grasp the religious specificity of these cultures. A public space which used to be described in terms of secularization is now increasingly described as a territory in which a 'return of religions' is a key factor. Even if it is not the only case in point, Islam is often considered the most problematic, and problematized, expression of this process.

The process produces, among other consequences, the emergence of reactive identities – identities that in a way 'decide' or 'declare' their existence because others exist. A typical example is the plethora of Europeans who have recently claimed[32] a Christian identity (despite the fact that many of them are or were militant atheists...), because there are Muslims in Europe. But the process is also visible in Muslim and other communities, where, afraid of mixing, they try to close themselves off in ghettoized enclaves, in terms either of urban geography or cultural/religious non-territorial specificity.

As we have seen, fear is the key concept in play here, specifi-cally fear of the other – of the Muslim by the European, of one's own annihilation by either the majority or the minority; and such reciprocal fears are, in the long term an important source of potential conflict.[33]

Conflict takes place not only, and perhaps not mainly, *between* cultures and religions or, more accurately their exponents, but is *internal* to cultures, religions and communities. Societies today seems to be divided over different questions from those that divided them in the past. With the decline of class distinctions (at least in terms of common ideological interpretations and opinions, albeit less in reality), we are increasingly divided today over factors of inclusion and exclu-sion that are often very material (interests, costs and benefits, taxes, services), but that equally are often cloaked in ethnic, racial, cultural or pseudo-cultural and religious justifications. Diversity, or alterity, is becoming a problem or even a faultline in itself. This means that other social actors (including religious ones) are also being divided increasingly not so much among as within themselves – that is, between those who engage in dialogue and those who do not, between those who are open to change and those who are not, between those ready to put themselves on the line and/or put society on the line and those for whom this is not an issue (not least in the face of the facts and of changes that have *already* taken place which they do not even wish to consider), and between those who are ready to measure up to diversity and Otherness and those who deny their very basis. These positions are, of course, complemented by all manner of conceivable intermediate attitudes.

On the other hand, given that conflict is a constitutive and inevitable factor of society (not least the significance of certain changes and the fact that Islam is today the second religion in Europe), we can hypothesize that the current manifestation of Islam – with its extensive radicalization and visibility – is but a stage in an unfolding process. In the meantime the present conflict awaits suitable forms of regulation. Once they have been found, there is a reasonable hope of emerging from the crisis. A new kind of equilibrium may then be established, leading to a new dispensation in society, for which we do not yet have clear plans or rules, but which we are trying to construct under the pressure of evolving circumstances largely beyond our control.

The evolution of the perception of immigrants in Italy also seems to support this hypothesis. It is true that we are currently going through a significant period. The most recent research on this subject published in Italy[34] clearly shows this, confirming other research data. For instance, 34.6 per cent of those questioned consider that (a) 'Immigrants are a danger for our culture, our identity and our religion' (up from 27.3 per cent in 1999); 34.3 per cent consider that (b) 'Immigrants constitute a threat to employment' (a view that is more stable: the figure was 32.2 per cent in 1999); and 43.2 per cent think that (c) 'Immigrants are a threat to public order and for people's security' (a more 'traditional' fear, which has been even stronger in the past).[35] But it is also worth noting that the highest percentages are counted among those who have no contact at all with immigrants: thus the more links and personal experiences, the less fear. So the affirmative response in the case of (a) is in fact 43.5 per cent for those who have no contact at all with immigrants, 33.4 per cent for those who have occasional contact with them, and 25.1 per cent for those in frequent contact. Similarly, the affirmative response to (b) is respectively 40.6 per cent, 34.5 per cent and 24.4 per cent, and to

(c) respectively 44.7 per cent, 46.6 per cent and 30.3 per cent – still very high, but nevertheless one-third down.

In contrast, those who have a more positive view of immigration, and consider that (d) 'Immigrants are a resource for our economy' (41.5 per cent) or even that (e) 'The presence of immigrants favours our openmindedness' (46.5 per cent) (both of which are relatively high percentages, compared to those registering political and social alarm), in terms of the no, occasional and frequent contact classification, register respectively: for (d) 35.9 per cent, 39.7 per cent and 55.2 per cent, and for (e) 34.7 per cent, 47.7 per cent and 60.2 per cent.

So, given the fact that, due to the processes of integration and the emergence of second and third generations (which means, among other things, an increasing presence in schools), contact will be more and more frequent, it is possible to hypothesize that the negative image of migrants might diminish in the not-too-distant future.

Conclusion: is no model a good model?

Given the complexity of this issue, it is not easy to draw up an account in terms of good and bad. The '*criticone* syndrome', 'an endearing feature of Italian intellectuals to be spectacularly critical about the failings of their own often complex and exasperating society' (Favell 2002), is a frequent and easy way out, but does not necessarily help to understand what is happening. A little comparison might help to produce a better understanding of Italian peculiarities.

What is clear is that Italy has not yet found its reference model on which to establish a *system* of interrelations among cultures and religions.[36] 'Multiculture', 'interculture', 'pluralism' (amy personal preference), are still, to misquote the title of a Pirandello play, words in search of a character (Kowalczyk and Popkewitz, 2005).

What is also clear is that the countries with known strong models of integration and/or relations among different cultures (typically France and Britain, but also the Netherlands, Germany and others), notwithstanding specific weaknesses, are all undergoing a process of profound change and self-reflection. The explosion of the *banlieues* in France, the 7/7 London bombings in 2005, the murder of Theo van Gogh, and the Danish cartoon affair, have made this fact abundantly clear, although the problems began much earlier. What these instances have shown, among other things, is the weakness of ideologically based models; for these can be challenged, changed completely or even annulled by the simple fact of a political election. Are these countries missing models too?

A transnational (European) model does not presently exist, and its absence is probably a positive factor, given the differences that exist among the European countries with their respective histories and traditions, a heterogeneity that must be safeguarded. The vague recommendations of the Council of Europe do not constitute a model as such: rather, every country takes only bits and pieces of the model, according to its preferences, interests and the moment, and often uses nothing at all. They remain simply suggestions. And the European Commission, fairly active in promoting equal rights, seems not to have the intention of promoting *one* model of relationships with European Islam, at least for the time being (even if there are serious pressures in this direction). So, the Italian missing model, in a way, fits quite well within the European one. In the end, a pragmatic attitude, capable of learning through trial and error, willing to experiment and observe projects, seems to work better, at present, than the ideological imposition of a model. While the lack of an inspiring model and pragmatism do not necessarily go together, at least the lack of a model does not constitute an ideological obstacle to experimenting with different practices. At the empirical level, in each country experiences of various multicultural models are much more widespread at the *local level* than at the national one, where contrasting ideologies play a bigger role. This has been the case particularly in Italy, where the multicultural experiences produced have almost always been – with the partial exception of school, which has seen a push from above – the result of municipal initiatives, where problems are not only raised but also in need of being solved.

The 'great national models', as part of the narrative of modernity, no longer signify much, or at least are less able to read and interpret reality. At the practical level it is quite easy to observe significant forms of convergence starting from different models: consider, for example, the changes in citizenship laws in Germany and France, where respectively *jus sanguinis* and *jus soli* prevailed: in both cases the current trend is towards softening the rigidity of the original models.

Even more interesting is what is happening at the local level (particularly in municipalities), where the agenda is increasingly dictated by the need to solve empirical problems of interrelation among groups of citizens rather than taking different theoretical or ideological approaches. While the political colour of an administration remains important, it is now less predictive of its policies (with the exception, in most but not all cases, of explicitly radical xenophobic parties and coalitions – as is the case, in Italy, in several cities, particularly in the north-east of the country, led by the Northern League). On the contrary, one is seeing the convergence of policies in cities of different countries despite differing prevailing 'official' models and under different laws, while cities in the same country with the same system and laws may diverge significantly.

This seems to be more an opportunity than a problem or an incoherence. In this phase, before the building of new models, it remains important to experiment with their possible consequences. This is the case even in the countries with a longer experience of immigration – that is, with so-called established models.

At the other extreme, beyond national models and their respective official narratives, reflection on new forms of transnational citizenship, as well as concrete exemplification of new forms of transnational belonging, and the empirical existence of transnational networks,[37] promises to point the way to more new solutions to the new problems of plurality in European societies.

Notes

1. Many migrated to other European countries. After the United States the most important receiving countries for Italy were in Europe: France, Switzerland, Germany, etc.

2. For an extraordinary collection of information and data, see the two very complete collection of essays dedicated to the history of Italian migration by Bevilacqua et al., 2001a, 2001b.

3. For an attempt to describe this change at his first stage, see Allievi, 1991. See also Pugliese, 2002.

4. Statistics were probably exaggerated, because, as was later discovered, important distortions were produced by an inefficient statistical system that

was initially often unable to distinguish double family names, counting them twice, but also counted repeated three-month permits as four different permits at the end of the year, etc. Allievi, 1991.

5. A term that in itself is a description of the common perception of immigrants, of *all* immigrants, as 'others', different from 'us', not sharing the same rights, by definition. The perception was similar in other countries, but, particularly in Central and Northern Europe, the immigrants were both from European sending countries and from outside Europe, and due to the developing system of European laws, protections and guarantees (freedom of circulation, etc.), an internal differentiation, in terms of rights, became consolidated, with some immigrants having progressively obtained the same rights as and equality of treatment with the native population, while others were treated differently. In Italy, even if part of the immigrant population was European (and, in the period discussed here, that is most of them; and often they were not job seekers, but established and well-integrated long-term residents), the perception of migration as a whole has been in many senses 'extracommunitarian'.

6. It is no longer so: the massacre of six innocent black African immigrants (three from Ghana, two from Liberia and one from Togo) in September 2008, organized by a Camorra faction in Castelvolturno, a small town close to Naples, as a symbolic demonstration of turf control, provoked much less shock. Not to mention the hundreds of deaths occurring annually in the Mediterranean sea, on the boats of desperate human beings crossing from Libya, Turkey or Morocco.

7. These numbers cannot be summed. Many beneficiaries have used more than one regularization, having lost their residence permit and becoming irregular, often due to bureaucratic problems connected to the issuance of permits, and then apply a second time to be regularized.

8 . In this *sanatoria* (as in 1995), which differed from the others, it was the employer, not the foreigner, who applied for regularization, or at least officially...

9. The absence of the word 'urgent', and the fact that this was a law and not a decree, signifies an attempt to exit from the logic of emergency. Some useful websites on more recent legislation (and more in general on migration in Italy): www.cestim.it, www.asgi.it, www.stranieriinitalia.com, www.ismu. org.

10. On the three faces of the Italian right, see Allievi, 2002. It must be noted that Alleanza Nazionale has more recently tried to take a more nuanced position, particularly in the personal initiatives of its leader, Fini, with declarations in favour of immigrants' right to vote, or against the mainstream Islamophobia of the right-wing coalition, which shocked even his own party. These declarations, though important as a political acts, have not led to any political initiatives.

11. Equating what for the Northern League are the two great negatives: coming from abroad and being from the South of Italy... Ironically for the League, the Neapolitan in question is currently president of the Republic of Italy.

12. On the contradictions in, particularly, the north-eastern regions of Italy, where immigration is highest and integration most succesful, yet where xenophobic reactions and Northern League support are strongest, see Diamanti and Porcellato, 2007.

13. The term 'islamophobia' is misleading: it sounds too politically correct and places all the responsibility for its emergence in public discourse on non-Muslims, in a process of rhetorical 'innocentization' of Muslims. Nevertheless, it is undeniably widely used (for Italy, see Massari, 2006; Allievi, 2005b).

14. Discussion here concerns the drafts: the final texts of the new laws on migration were supposed to be approved before spring 2008, but the collapse of the Prodi government and the subsequent elections, which saw the return to power of Silvio Berlusconi, ended discussion.

15. Even though certain unrealistic aspects, and the maintaining of much of the security frame constructed by the previous law, would probably have remained part of the legislative landscape.

16. www.governo.it/Governo/Provvedimenti/dettaglio.asp?d=28863.

17. Which is close to the European average; I thank G. Zincone, who has contributed to the Italian part of these reports, for some insights on the government's intentions regarding citizenship). But in other countries it is the result of a long period of immigration, which has now changed in terms of conditions and numbers; and, in any case, the reaction in public opinion seems to be changing significantly.

18. For a detailed analysis of these draft laws, and for a shorter comment, see respectively Pastore, 2007a, 2007b.

19. See the research analysed in Bordignon and Ceccarini, 2007, to which I refer in more detail later.

20. The campaign began with a relatively minor case: a rally against the construction of a mosque in the small Lombard city of Lodi.

21. On these two aspects, see particularly Allievi, 2003.

22. See Maréchal et al., 2003 for an analysis of these processes; and Allievi, 2007 for an interpretation in terms of construction of imagery.

23. *Intese* approved under a law based on article 8 of the Italian Constitution: *Tavola valdese*, 21 February 1984; Assemblee di Dio in Italia (ADI) 29 December 1986; Unione delle Chiese Cristiane Avventiste del 7° giorno 29 December 1986; Unione Comunità Ebraiche in Italia (UCEI) 27 February 1987, Unione Cristiana Evangelica Battista d'Italia (UCEBI), 29 March 1993; Chiesa Evangelica Luterana in Italia (CELI) 20 April 1993.

    Intese which have been signed by the government but not yet approved by parliamentary law: Chiesa Apostolica in Italia; Chiesa di Gesù Cristo dei Santi degli ultimi giorni (Mormons); Congregazione cristiana dei testimoni di Geova; Sacra Arcidiocesi d'Italia ed Esarcato per l'Europa meridionale; Unione Buddista Italiana (UBI); Unione Induista Italiana. A project of *Intesa* with the Istituto buddista italiano Soka Gakkai is also under discussion.

24. On the presence of Islam in European countries, from the juridical point of view, see Ferrari and Bradney, 2000; S. Ferrari, 2003.

25. On religious pluralism in Italy, both internal and external to the Catholic church, see Garelli et al., 2003.
26. On which see Del Boca (2005). The author, in his important historiographical production, has been able to demonstrate how this myth has been nothing more than an ideological and rhetorical construction, unacceptable on serious empirical basis, but nevertheless widespread across the entire political spectrum and in public opinion at large.
27. On racism in Europe, including Italy, see the reports of the European Monitoring Centre on Racism and Xenofobia, EUMC (2006a), accessible at http://fra.europa.eu/fra/material/pub/ar06/AR06-P2-EN.pdf. Specifically on Muslims, EUMC (2006b), also accessible at http://fra.europa.eu/fra/index.php?fuseaction=content.dsp_cat_content&catid=3fb38ad3e22bb&contentid=4582d9f4345ad.
28. Including Pope Benedict XVI while he was still Cardinal Ratzinger, together with well known 'theo-con' intellectuals, such as the former conservative president of the Senate (see Pera and Ratzinger 2004). Even though he did so for theological reasons, trying to exploit the identity argument of the Italian theo-cons in the same way they tried to politically exploit Catholic positions. This was probably true until the Regensburg accident. It seems to be much less true after the Papal trip to Turkey in November 2006.
29. The observations in this paragraph are discussed in more detail in Allievi, 2006b.
30. The elements of the modern state are: *one* people, *one* territory, *one* juridical system – and often also, implicitly, *one* religion. For reasons that cannot be considered here, the three basic elements – not to mention the fourth – are undergoing spectacular changes, that have substantially led to the implausibility of using the singular. But most European constitutions have been written on the basis of this monolithic presupposition, which no longer represents reality.
31. The reciprocal embeddedness of religions and cultures is a factor that must be taken into account – it is no coincidence that 'cult' and 'culture' share the same etymology. This fact tends to be ignored in the West (and even more acutely in the universities, which may help explain academic underestimation of the persistence, force and social effects of religion in social contexts) where processes of secularization appear to be secularizing first of all readings of reality.
32. It is interesting that in this kind of debate identity is something that people are supposed to *have* (objectifying identity as if it were a thing, obvious and easy to define, like something that one can carry in the pocket), despite the fact that in other contexts the word 'identity' is more naturally supported by the verb *to be*: we *are* this and that, in a continuously evolving process, much more than we *have* clear cultural references.
33. For an excellent example of this process, see the group discussions analysed in the Italian report of the Ethnobarometer comparative research *Europe's Muslim Communities: Security and Integration post September 11* (Allievi, 2009). For all the national reports, see the Ethnobarometer website.

34. We refer to the Demos–Coop research, April 2007. For a presentation and comment, see Bordignon and Ceccarini (2007); for the full survey see www. agcom.it.

35. The data are confirmed by a more recent comparative poll promoted by the *Financial Times* and published on the 20 August 2007 issue, www.politics. ie/viewtopic.php?t=25673). In response to the question, 'Does the presence of Muslims in your country pose a threat to national security or not?', Italians were second only to the British, with some 30 per cent of those intervieed answering 'yes', despite the fact that Italy has a relatively modest number of Muslims compared to some of the other countries examined (the UK, France, Germany, Spain and the USA), and, in contrast to other countries, has never suffered actual terrorist attacks by Muslims (even if it suffers daily alarms on the subject, which is one of the fruits of the 'Fallacism' widespread in the media). To complete the scenario, and rendering it more complex, it must be said that Italy also scores second (to France this time) in terms of affirmative responses to the question: 'Have Muslims in your country become the subject of unjustified criticism and prejudice or not?', with close to 50 per cent. This is perhaps a sign that this 'Fallacism' is beginning to be reognizaed for what as it is, and what the gap between alarm and reality is becoming more visible.

36. What has been missing here is an analysis of interreligious dialogue, particularly at the grassroots level. In reality it does not furnish a model, but it offers a set of interesting examples and situations. For some analytical considerations, see my chapter on 'Relations between Religions' in the European comparative research contained in Maréchal et al., 2003: 369–414.

37. On which Allievi and Nielsen, 2003.

References

Allievi, S. (1991) *La sfida dell'immigrazione*, Bologna: Emi.

Allievi, S. (2002) 'L'anomalie italienne: trois droites et aucune gauche', *La Revue Nouvelle* 6: 18–31.

Allievi, S. (2003) *Islam italiano. Viaggio nella seconda religione del paese*, Turin: Einaudi.

Allievi, S. (2005a) 'Sociology of a Newcomer: Muslim Migration to Italy – Religious Visibility, Cultural and Political Reactions', in A. al-Shahi and R. Lawless (eds), *Middle East and North African Immigrants in Europe*, London: Routledge, pp. 43–56.

Allievi, S. (2005b) 'How the Immigrant Has Become Muslim: Public Debates on Islam in Europe', *Revue Européenne des Migrations Internationales* 2: 135–61.

Allievi, S. (2006a) *Niente di personale, signora Fallaci. Una trilogia alternativa*, Reggio Emilia: Aliberti.

Allievi, S. (2006b) 'Conflicts, Cultures and Religions: Islam in Europe as a Sign and Symbol of Change in European Societies', *Yearbook on Sociology of Islam* 3: 18–27.

178   EUROPEAN MULTICULTURALISM REVISITED

Allievi, S. (2007) *Le trappole dell'immaginario: islam e occidente*, Udine: Forum.

Allievi, S., and J. Nielsen (eds) (2003), *Muslim Networks and Transnational Communities in and across Europe*, Leiden: Brill.

Allievi, S. (2009a) *Conflicts over Mosques in Europe: Policy Issues and Trends*, London: Network of European Foundations/Alliance Publishing Trust.

Allievi, S. (2009b) *I musulmani e la società italiana. Percezioni reciproche, conflitti culturali, trasformazioni sociali*, Milan: Franco Angeli.

Ascoli, U. (1979) *Movimenti migratori in Italia*, Bologna: Il Mulino.

Bauböck, R., E. Ersbøll, K. Groenendijk and H. Waldrauch (eds) (2006a) *Acquisition and Loss of Nationality*, Vol. I: *Comparative Analyses: Policies and Trends in 15 European Countries*, Amsterdam: IMISCOE, Amsterdam University Press.

Bauböck, R., E. Ersbøll, K. Groenendijk and H. Waldrauch (eds) (2006b) *Acquisition and Loss of Nationality*, Vol. II: *Country Analyses. Policies and Trends in 15 European Countries*, Amsterdam: IMISCOE, Amsterdam University Press.

Bevilacqua, P., A. De Clementi and E. Franzina (2001a), *Storia dell'emigrazione italiana. Partenze*, Rome: Donzelli.

Bevilacqua, P., A. De Clementi and E. Franzina (2001b) *Storia dell'emigrazione italiana. Arrivi*, Rome: Donzelli.

Birindelli, A.M. (1989) 'Le migrazioni con l'estero. Chiusura di un ciclo e avvio di una nuova fase', in E. Sonnino, *Demografia e società in Italia*, Rome: Editori Riuniti.

Bolaffi, G. (2001) *I confini del patto. Il governo dell'amministrazione in Italia*, Turin: Einaudi.

Bonini, C., and G. D'Avanzo (2006) *Il mercato della paura. La guerra al terrorismo islamico: inchiesta sull'inganno italiano*, Turin: Einaudi.

Bordignon, F., and L. Ceccarini (2007) 'Gli altri tra noi', *Limes* 4: 35–45.

Bosetti, G. (2005) *Cattiva maestra. La rabbia di Oriana Fallaci e il suo contagio*, Venice: Marsilio.

Carfagna M. (2002) 'I sommersi e i sanati. Le regolarizzazioni degli immigrati in Italia', in A. Colombo and G. Sciortino (eds), *Assimilati ed esclusi*, Bologna: Il Mulino, pp. 53–89.

Chaloff, J. (2004) *From Labour Emigration to Labour Recruitment: The Case of Italy*, in 'Migration for Employment – Bilateral Agreements at a Crossroads', Paris: OECD, pp. 55–64.

Caritas/Migrantes (2006) *Immigrazione. Dossier statistico 2006*, Rome: Nuova Anterem.

Caritas/Migrantes (2008) *Immigrazione. Dossier statistico 2008*, Rome: Idos Edizioni.

Caritas/Migrantes (2009) *Immigrazione. Dossier statistico 2009. XIX rapporto*, Rome: Idos Edizioni.

Del Boca, A. (2005) *Italiani brava gente?*, Vicenza: Neri Pozza.

Diamanti, I., and N. Porcellano (2007) 'Sorpresa: nel nordest l'integrazione funziona', *Limes* 4: 47–62.

Einaudi, L. (2007) 'La porta stretta: le politiche migratorie dal 1861 a oggi', *Limes* 4: 87–94.

EUMC (2006a) *Tha Annual Report on the Situation Regarding Racism and Xenophobia in the Member States of the EU*, Vienna: EUMC.

EUMC (2006b) *Muslims in the European Union: Discrimination and Islamophobia*, Vienna: EUMC.

Fallaci, O. (2001) *La rabbia e l'orgoglio*, Milan: Rizzoli.

Fallaci, O. (2004a) *La forza della ragione*, Milan: Rizzoli.

Fallaci, O. (2004b) *Oriana Fallaci intervista se stessa – L'Apocalisse*, Milan: Rizzoli.

Favell, A. (2002) 'Italy as a Comparative Case', in R. Grillo and J. Pratt (eds), *The Politics of Recognizing Difference: Multiculturalism Italian-style*, Aldershot: Ashgate, pp. 237–44.

Ferrari, A. (ed.) (2008) *Islam in Europa / Islam in Italia. Tra diritto e società*, Bologna: Il Mulino.

Ferrari, S. (2003) 'The Legal Dimension', in B. Maréchal, S. Allievi, F. Dassetto and J. Nielsen (eds), *Muslims in the Enlarged Europe: Religion and Society*, Leiden: Brill.

Ferrari, S. (ed.) (2005) *L'islam in Italia*, Bologna: Il Mulino.

Ferrari, S., and A. Bradney (eds) (2000) *Islam and European Legal Systems*, Dartmouth: Ashgate.

Fondazione Ismu (2007) *XII Rapporto sulle Migrazioni*, Milan: Ismu.

Garelli, F., G. Guizzardi and E. Pace (eds) (2003) *Un singolare pluralismo. Il pluralismo morale e religioso degli italiani*, Bologna: Il Mulino.

Grillo, R. (2002) 'Immigration and the Politics of Recognizing Difference in Italy', in R. Grillo and J. Pratt (eds), *The Politics of Recognizing Difference: Multiculturalism Italian-style*, Aldershot: Ashgate, pp. 1–24.

Grillo, R., and J. Pratt (eds) (2002) *The Politics of Recognizing Difference: Multiculturalism Italian-style*, Aldershot: Ashgate.

Kowalczyk, J., and T. Popkewitz (2005) 'Multiculturalism, Recognition and Abjection: (re)mapping Italian identity', *Policy Futures in Education* 4: 423–35.

Maréchal, B., S. Allievi, F. Dassetto and J. Nielsen (eds) (2003) *Muslims in the Enlarged Europe: Religion and Society*, Leiden: Brill.

Massari, M. (2006) *Islamofobia*, Bari: Laterza.

Nascimbene, B. (1988) *Lo straniero nel diritto italiano*, Milan: Giuffré.

Pastore, F. (2007a) *La politica migratoria italiana a una svolta. Ostacoli immediati e dilemmi strategici*, Milan: Cespi.

Pastore, F. (2007b) 'La paranoia dell'invasione e il futuro dell'Italia', *Limes* 4: 23–33.

Pera, M., and P. Ratzinger (2004) *Senza radici*, Milan: Mondadori.

Pratt, J. (2002) 'Italy: Political Unity and Cultural Diversity', in R. Grillo and J. Pratt (eds), *The Politics of Recognizing Difference: Multiculturalism Italian-style*, Aldershot: Ashgate, pp. 25–40.

Pugliese, E. (2002) *L'Italia tra migrazioni internazionali e migrazioni interne*, Bologna: Il Mulino.

Sartori, G. (2000) *Pluralismo, multiculturalismo e estranei. Saggi sulla società multietnica*, Milan: Rizzoli.

Sciortino, G. (2009) *Fortunes and Miseries of Italian Labour Migration Policies*, Rome: CeSPI.

Sòrgoni, B. (2002) 'Racist Discourses and Practices in the Italian Empire under Fascism', in R. Grillo and J. Pratt (eds), *The Politics of Recognizing Difference: Multiculturalism Italian-style*, Aldershot: Ashgate, pp. 41–58.

Stella, G.A. (2002) *L'orda. Quando gli albanesi eravamo noi*, Milan: Rizzoli.

Volpi, R. (1989) *Storia della popolazione italiana dall'Unità ad oggi*, Florence: La Nuova Italia.

5

'Making room':
encompassing diversity in Denmark

Tina Gudrun Jensen

We in Denmark are proud of our country, and of what Danes in the present and the past have achieved, although we seek to create an ironic distance on our self-enthusiasm. We are not the least sorry to attract attention as a nation, and gladly receive praise and attention, and we are not unfamiliar with being held out as a good example. But all of a sudden to be the object of agitation and anger is not something that we are used to, or much less expect.

Every country, every people, is marked by its culture and its history. Every human being carries this mark with him or her, whether he or she stays at home or is travelling around the world, maybe to settle in an entirely new place. There, at the new place, perhaps in a quite different continent, the recently arrived meets a new country and a new society, which is conditioned by the very same country's situation and history, its culture and its customs. And that country and that people, who receive the recently arrived, will have entirely new experiences to relate to. Here in Denmark we have also had to learn this. Because certainly we have always known that the world is big, but it is when it enters our country that we have to realize how multifarious it is, and how different customs and forms of life can be.

To settle in a new country is demanding. It requires immense effort to learn to know the new, to acquire language and to familiarize oneself with the rhythm of the year and the course of daily life. New guidelines for one's existence are framed, and maybe there are habits and customs that one has to change or even dismiss entirely. Nobody should expect that the one who arrives at a new place, a foreign country, should throw all his other inherited goods overboard straight away, as if it was superfluous. It could easily lead to one becoming truly rootless. For a tree to be transplanted, it has to have a solid root web from the start. It will then be able to draw nourishment at the new spot and grow and thrive.

Here in Denmark, we prefer everything to happen without friction, and that problems, if they arise, should solve themselves. We tend to think that what appears natural to us, should also be so for everybody else. It is just not that simple. We start to realize that we ourselves have to understand and make an effort to explain what kind of values our society builds on in such a way that those who have not yet put down deep roots in Denmark can find room and settle within the society whose citizens they have become. The past year has very likely taught us a thing or two, not least about ourselves. Now we know better what we stand for, and where we neither want to nor can give in.

> (from the Danish Queen's New Year speech,
> 31 December 2006, author's translation).

This quotation describes the relationship between a Danish 'self' and a foreign 'other'. It summarizes the Danish positions on national identity and multi-ethnicity, as a sense of national joy and pride, yet also as fear of the foreign. The speech communicates the Danish people's troubles in dealing with cultural differences, represented by immigrants, and their expectations that the process of integration occur without problems or conflicts. It subtly hints at the 'cartoon affair',[1] which forms part of the context of the speech. While the speech can be read as an argument for multiculturalism, it also reflects an insistence on cultural homogeneity, for example, by pointing to 'values our society builds on', connoting assimilation. The speech thus illustrates the Danish model for dealing with multiculturalism, immigration and integration, which is the theme of this chapter.

Social researchers often conclude that Denmark does not intend to be a multicultural society (Gundelach, 2004; Hamburger, 1990; Hedetoft, 2006b; Togeby, 1998, 2003). Multi-ethnicity in Denmark – that is, a situation characterized by the presence of people with different ethnic backgrounds – is also a recent phenomenon. Whereas Denmark is multicultural in a descriptive sense, it is not multicultural in any normative sense, for example, through policies of accommodating difference (Modood, 2007).

The concept that Danish discussions on immigrants refer to is 'integration' in the sense of the absorption (*indoptagelse*) of immigrants into Danish society. The Danish debate on integration revolves around the question of immigrants' cultural capacity to harmonize their values with Danish values. The concept of 'integration', then, is generally used in the sense of assimilation, as 'cultural sameness', as a process whereby one becomes part of Danish society. The smallness of Denmark is often used as an argument for characterizing the country as a mono-cultural society. Smallness is seen as linked with cultural and historical homogeneity, and with the successful post-war development of a specific form of universalistic welfare state (Hedetoft, 2006a: 39).

The concept of integration has been described as both imprecise and political, hence in need of being conceptualized as a socially constructed and negotiated process (Preis, 1996: 229). In Denmark, as everywhere, immigration and integration are highly politicized issues. This politicization is, among other things, expressed in people's different positions on the burning question of whether Denmark has changed from being an 'ethnically tolerant' country to being a 'racist' one (Gaasholt and Togeby, 1997; Nielsen, 2002; Togeby, 1998). Immigration, generally formulated as a challenge to Danish society, is either made an object of culture-oriented critique or treated as an economic problem (Hedetoft, 2004: 69).

This chapter contributes to the research on Danes' attitudes towards immigrants and refugees by focusing explicitly on the issues of multiculturalism and assimilation. It explores the construction of the Danish model for dealing with multiculturalism, and maintains that this model represents a peculiar tension between the contradictory notions of assimilation and multiculturalism. The chapter questions the sustainability of the model, using the case of the cartoon affair as illustrating a challenge to the model, an illustration potentially leading to implosion and transformation.

The analytical focus in this chapter draws on a variety of theoretical and methodological approaches. It explores the construction of this Danish model through a focus on the historical development of the Danish nation-state, immigration history, legislation, and the implementation of immigration and integration policies. From an anthropological perspective, the chapter focuses on identity patterns that organize the relationship between a national 'self' and a foreign 'other'. The variety of empirical data consists of analyses of national and international surveys such as the the the International Social Survey Program (ISSP) and the Eurobarometer (EUMC/SORA), material on legislation on immigration and integration, material on the implementation of integration policies, royal and political speeches, and finally participant observation in public debates on integration.

Outlines of a Danish model

This section introduces some preliminary notions regarding a Danish model of multiculturalism. This model is based on theories on identity and identity patterns that structure the relation between an 'us' and a 'them' (Baumann, 2004), and about 'civil culture' in the sense of a particular nation's consciousness and patterns of relating to foreigners (Schiffauer, 1998).

Civil culture in Denmark and other Scandinavian countries is perhaps best defined by the notion of equality in the sense of 'imagined sameness' (Gullestad, 2002: 83). Implicit in this notion is a consensus that relies on a form of sociality that is closed (Sjørslev, 2004). Denmark is thus labelled a society of associations (*forenings-samfund*), which stresses the importance of belonging to a greater consensual body. The notion of imagined sameness indicates an urge to suppress difference and disagreement and an uneasiness with and reluctance to acknowledge difference (Salamon, 1992; Knudsen, 1996). Uneasiness in relation to difference represented by 'others' is reflected in the ways that Danes generally refer to immigrants as 'strangers' and 'foreigners' – that is, as people who do not belong – or as 'guest-workers', emphasizing guest–host relations (Hervik, 2004).

The notion of equality as 'sameness', which characterizes Danish civil culture, is imperative for an understanding of the ways in which the public debate addresses the relationship between 'us', Danes, and 'them', the immigrants. In this debate, two grammars of identity

(Baumann, 2004) appear to be prevalent. First, a grammar indicating distance and opposition appears in the public discourse that provides a framework of polarization between 'us' and 'them' (Sjørslev, 2004: 93). The second prevalent grammar is that of 'encompassment', or hierarchical subjection, a concept related to the idea of assimilation: 'they' (the immigrants) should become 'like us' in order to be perceived as 'real' Danes.

Together with the notion of sameness, tolerance and secrecy, which finds expression in a reluctance to tell foreigners about social rules, are the main characteristics of Danishness (Knudsen, 1992: 215). Both are likely to result in the polite reluctance to correct ignorant outsiders' 'wrong' practices or actually to inform strangers about conforming practices. As reflected in the Danish queen's New Year speech, strangers appear to suffer from a lack of information, since they have no opportunity to learn how they are supposed to behave. This is an expression of what has been called the 'particular universalism' of Danish civic culture (Mouritsen, 2006a), which is never explicitly verbalized, and therefore is a major obstacle that hinders the inclusion of 'strangers'. Foreigners are invited into the club of Denmark, but are not told the rules of membership. This behaviour reflects a discrepancy between rhetorical form and actual practice.

According to one typology of multiculturalism (Mouritsen, 2006b: 90), Denmark takes a colour-blind liberal, tolerant position on the question of equality.[2] Nonetheless, the Danish model appears to illustrate antagonisms between multiculturalism and the need for a common identity, reflected in the notion of assimilation, that are peculiar to strong democracies (Taylor, 2002: 1). The construction of the Danish model of relating to multiculturalism thus reflects a tension between multiculturalism as an ideal and assimilation as a necessity. The model is structured around the notion of 'sameness', and thus on the notion of cultural assimilation, which in principle does not leave room for difference. Other central notions such as agreement and consensus, pointing to values such as unity and democracy, further reinforce this image, reflecting a tendency towards encompassing power relations with respect to strangers. The next section illustrates the Danish model of multiculturalism by presenting some data on Danes' attitudes towards multiculturalism and assimilation.

Positions on multiculturalism and assimilation: the Danish puzzle

Comparative surveys of European values show that Denmark differs from other European countries in terms of its orientation at local, national and international levels (Gundelach, 2004). Whereas Danes are closely attached to both local and regional levels, they are less attached to the European and global levels (Hobolt, 2004). While Danes have a basic trust in their national institutions in comparison to other Europeans, they have little trust in international institutions like the EU. Furthermore, Danes are increasingly cultivating an indentification with 'Danishness' and the Danish nation (Hobolt, 2004: 326). This has appeared since the 1990s, along with an increasing tendency to express national pride and cultural superiority, coupled with a fear of the potential ramifications of immigration (Togeby, 1998).

While immigrants and refugees used to be subjects that Danes tended to avoid, this reaction changed during the 1990s. The debate as to whether Danes have replaced their often-claimed tolerance with xenophobia has attracted a degree of international attention (Gaasholt and Togeby, 1995; Hervik, 2002; Nannestad, 1999; Nielsen, 2004b; Togeby, 1998). In comparison to other Europeans, Danes position themselves among those who are more negative towards and sceptical of immigration (Goul Andersen, 2002b; Skaksen, et al. 2006). However, to present an unequivocal view of how Danes position themselves on questions concerning immigration is difficult. Danes tend to be strongly polarized into groups that are either 'intolerant' or 'actively tolerant' in relation to immigrants (Nielsen, 2001; EUCM/SORA, 2001).

One ambiguity is reflected in questions concerning multiculturalism and assimilation, which should be seen as contrasting phenomena. The survey from EUMC/SORA shows that Denmark favours questions concerning both 'multicultural optimism' and 'assimilation' (EUMC/SORA, 2001), and appears to be above average in comparison to other European countries in its support for both dimensions.[3] This coexistence of multiculturalism and assimilation somehow constitutes a paradox. On the one hand, Denmark expresses the strongest support among European countries for the statement that a country's 'diversity in terms of race, religion and culture adds to its strengths'

(EUMC/SORA, 2001: 45). On the other hand, Denmark is among the countries that voice the greatest demand for assimilation, for example by supporting the argument that 'people belonging to these minority groups must give up those parts of their religion and culture which may be in conflict with [Danish] law' (49). Besides, Danes strongly support the statement that 'the presence of people from minority groups is a cause of insecurity' (3).

Nation, church and state

The Danish nation has historically developed from diversity to unity. The construction of a modern national consciousness started at the turn of the eighteenth century, when Denmark was about to transform from a multinational state – including Norway and parts of Germany – into a nation-state. Until the mid-1800s, Danes were not unified by a national identity, and were divided by different languages. Shared identity consisted only in serving the same monarchy. Denmark was thus at the time a typical European state with a nationally mixed population. The wars in the German states in 1848–50 and 1863–64 are generally a point of reference for an understanding of the develpoment of a Danish identity (Christiansen and Østergaard, 1992: 31).

A major part of the nationalization of the peasant masses derived from the passage to freehold after the agricultural reforms of the 1780s, in the shape of the self-organization of peasants into popular movements called 'revival movements' (*vækkelsesbevægelser*) in the eighteenth century. These movements started as pietistic unions of rural laymen emancipating themselves from landowners through the means of the official church. This has formed the basis of a certain Danish way of associating liberalism and Lutheran Christianity. The peasant farmers thus played a strong role in the process of modernization and the formation of a democracy, emphasizing values such as unity, equality, consensus, egalitarianism and economic liberalism (Knudsen, 1992).

The Danish theologian Nicolai Severin Grundtvig (1783–1872) formulated the notion of the Danish people and nationality (*folkelighed*). He encouraged the emancipatory movements of the peasant farmers through his works of general education, giving the movements a pedagogical–philosophical superstructure in the form of theological, equality-oriented and liberal thinking. Grundtvig also praised Danishness as inseparable from Lutheran Protestantism. The work initiated by Grundtvig resulted in the formation of independent schools or 'free schools' (*friskoler*), the organization of folk high schools, the foundation of local associations (*foreninger*) and the creation of voluntary alternative church congregations, which formed the basis of the particular Danish structure of associations. In 1901, the peasant liberal party Venstre ('Left')[4] took over the government, and politicians from the Grundtvigian school were subsequently recruited. Populist and agrarian values entered into Danish political culture (Østergaard, 1992).

The notion of Danish nationalism is thus closely connected to values such as liberalism, open-mindedness, tolerance, equality, unity and associationism linked with Grundtvigian theology. These values are represented as core values in the construction of the particular Danish form of democracy, dating from the period of Grundvigian enlightment, self-organizing farmers, and the Danish constitution of 1849, which marks the transition from absolute to constitutional monarchy. Danish democracy has been characterized as 'embedded in a nationalistic veil in which democracy equaled the Danish "folk"' (Kaspersen and Thorsager, 2004: 261). This has led researchers to question whether the concept of a Danish people (*folk*) can be reinterpreted to include all the people living in the country.

Lutheran Christianity in several ways plays an important role in the construction of Danishness. Like other countries, the Danish state formulated religious tolerance towards minority groups as a pragmatic device to attract foreign immigration. The constitution of 1849 proclaimed freedom of faith, with the shift from a state church to a national church, referred to as 'the People's Church' (*Folkekirken*), administered by the Ministry of Ecclesiastical Affairs. The constitution ensures full freedom of faith while simultaneously emphasizing that 'the Evangelical–Lutheran Church is the People's Church (representing some 83 per cent of the Danish population), and is as such supported by the state' (The Danish Constitution §4; author's translation), thus giving it a special status. In this sense, church and state are not separated. Denmark has freedom of faith, but not equality. Different religious communities do not have the same legal rights. They are requested to undergo a process of approval, and are distinguished as either 'acknowledged' or 'approved' communities of belief.

Acknowledged communities were until 1970 defined by royal resolution, with the rights of full civil validity with regard to rituals, the keeping of ministerial books and the issuance of certificates. The only acknowledged non-Christian community today is the Jewish 'Mosaic Faith Society' (Mosaisk Trossamfund). No other belief organization has been acknowledged since 1970, when the procedure for approval changed from Royal resolution to provisions in the Act of Matrimony. Instead, the term 'approved community ' is used, though in relation only to the individual religious leader, who is entitled to perform the ritual of marriage with civil validity.

Approved communities represent other minor Christian denominations, Hinduism and Islam. In the Danish religious field, Muslim congregations have only to a limited degree become integrated into the systems of religious privilege (Kühle, 2004: 202). They have not received public acknowledgement; thus they did not profit from the symbolic value associated with such acknowledgement. Therefore, while Denmark is developing into a society that practises religious pluralism, the meaning of this pluralism is limited, not least because of the managing role of the state (Kühle, 2004: 259).

Immigration and integration in Danish politics

Today, immigrants from non-Western countries constitute about 6 per cent of the Danish population of 5 million inhabitants. In terms of the historical development of the Danish nation-state, the last 150 years of Danish history barely included any immigrants. Greenland was colonized by Denmark until 1953, yet despite their immigration Greenlanders are a neglected ethnic minority (Togeby, 2002b).

Denmark was, together with Norway, the last European country to import foreign labour (Schwartz, 1985). The major flow of immigration started at the end of the 1960s, with the appearance of immigrants mainly from Yugoslavia, Turkey and Pakistan, who came to work on condition that they took jobs that the Danes would not do. This was partly in response to a request from Danish industry and the liberal-conservative parties Venstre and Det konservative Folkeparti (the Conservative People's Party); the trade-union movement, for its part, was highly sceptical. The Danish view of the status of immigrants is reflected in the generally used term 'guest workers'. There was a shared expectation on the part of both Danes and immigrants that the 'guest workers' would return to their countries of origin. Thus immigrants were not received with open arms (as the myth often has it); they were at best an object of passing curiosity, observed at a distance by Danes. Politicians did not see the need for a politics of integration at that time. From the outset, there was a concern about immigration. In 1973 the government formally halted immigration in response to the economic recession triggered by the oil crisis. However, immigrants have continued to arrive on account of family members' right to settle and asylum-seekers. The 1980s in particular witnessed an influx of refugees from Lebanon, Iran, Iraq, ex-Yugoslavia, Sri Lanka, Somalia and Vietnam.

Increasing unemployment in the 1970s and 1980s turned immigration into an economic problem, and framed the issue of integration in terms of 'labour market integration'. Political debates on immigration policy emphasize the high costs to the exchequer on account of the high welfare payments, which are financed by taxes, and accessible to everybody with permanent residence in Denmark (Nielsen, 2004b: 51).

Ulf Hedetoft, a professor of International Relations, maintains that the construction of the Danish welfare system can be seen as an obstacle to integration in Denmark due to its association with the historical founding principles of homogeneity and equality (Hedetoft, 2006b: 403). One obstacle is political, and relates to the fact that the welfare state rests on a history of 'vertical trust' between state and society, to the degree that the two are culturally and ideologically interconnected as a whole – a relationship arguably threatened by immigration. The welfare system generates a cultural impediment in the form of negative stereotypes of immigrants, based on the assumption that they are not 'real refugees' but rather 'social scoundrels' who have not contributed to the Danish welfare system, and hence are 'a problem' for Danish society. Finally, another economic hindrance to integration is related to the discrepancy between the skills structure of the labor market on the one hand, and refugees, on the other, who are not economic migrants per se (Hedetoft, 2006b: 404–5).

From the outset, immigration has been the responsibility of the state. 'Integration' as a principle has been the declared objective of the government since 1980. During the left-wing coalition government of the Socialdemokraterne (Social Democrats) and De radikale Venstre (Radical Left),[5] 1998–2001, the politics of immigration was the remit of the Ministry of the Interior (Indenrigsministeriet). The government appeared to be increasingly split over the question of whether to implement stricter immigration policies. Meanwhile, the right-wing parties gained in popularity, both by turning the question of immigration into an economic problem, and by framing it as a threat to national cohesion (Nielsen, 2004b). The populist Fremskridtspartiet (Progressive Party) especially opposed immigration, in particular Muslim immigrants. In 1995, the politician Pia Kjærsgaard split from Fremskridtspartiet and formed the populist Dansk Folkeparti (Danish People's Party), which has an explicitly anti-immigration platform. This party came to play a crucial role in the formation of the new right-wing government that came into power in 2001.

Doubtless in an attempt to gain votes, the divided left-wing coalition government sought to accommodate the critical voices concerning immigration and integration, but they lost the election. The election campaign in autumn 2001 thus revolved around 'the issue of foreigners' (*udlændingespørgsmålet*) together with the question of welfare benefits. The liberal-conservative right, represented by Venstre under Anders Fogh Rasmussen, later prime minister, and Det konservative Folkeparti, won the election. Dansk Folkeparti supports the government, while reserving its independence on certain questions.[6] Under the new government, immigration issues were transferred from the Home Office to a separate Ministry of Immigrants, Refugees and Integration, referred to colloquially as 'the Ministry of Integration'.

Immigration and integration policies

In Denmark, the rules for citizenship follow the principles of *jus sanguinis*, the citizenship of children following that of their parents. The new government has introduced several restrictions concerning immigration, acquisition of residence and citizenship. Since 2002, citizenship by naturalization requires that a person has stayed in Denmark for at least nine years, without interruption. Additionally, the person has to give up his or her prior citizenship; dual citizenship is not accepted in Denmark. Rules governing settlement of family members and grounds of marriage have been tightened up. This further reflects concern over both arranged marriages and so-called forced marriages.[7] In 2000, changes to the foreigners' law introduced the 'affiliation claim' (*tilknytningskrav*) in regard to settlement through marriage, which requires that affiliation to Denmark be stronger than that to country of origin. The rules for refugees have also been tightened since 2002; today residence is only granted to refugees who have the right to protection according to international conventions.[8]

Denmark differs in comparison to other European countries by granting ethnic minorities the right to participate in the political process on the same basis as the ethnic Danish population. Denmark was the third European country to give ethnic minorities with Danish citizenship the right to vote, which was granted in 1981. The notions of equality and equal opportunities are thus prevalent in the discourse on integration, emphasizing democracy as a Danish core value. In 1983, the government established, among other representative organs, the Council for Ethnic Minorities (*Rådet for etniske minoriteter*, formerly *Indvandrerrådet*), which includes representatives from diverse immigrant associations. Furthermore, in 2002 the new government created integration councils in the municipalities, which are composed equally of ethnic minorities and ethnic Danes. Their function is to supervise municipality integration policy, though without any legal sanction. In comparison to other European countries, immigrants in Denmark have greater access to the political process, and also exercise this right to a greater degree. The representation of members of ethnic minorities is relatively high, especially on the municipal committees of town councils (Togeby, 2002b: 168).[9] Immigrants, however, do not appear to have the same opportunities to participate in the political process as native Danes. Ethnic minorities tend to feel that it is not accepted that they have an equal right to participate. Whether they perceive themselves as full members of the community also remains uncertain (Togeby, 1999). This might illustrate the fact that democracy, which is pointed to as a core value in Danish society, is a way of life (Koch, 1945), and consequently a cultural form that has to be acquired and mastered. Since 1970, more than 200 organizations have been formed (Mikkelsen, 2003), serving as interest groups for separate ethnic groups. The organizations tend to have an isolated and closed character. While it can be seen as an expression of associationalism that serves the cultural interests of immigrants, some commentators see this development as a step towards fragmentation and disintegration. Furthermore, while immigrants are encouraged to participate in the Danish democratic process, there are few examples of successful relations established between ethnic-minority interest organizations and the state, leaving them on their own with limited access to influence and power (Togeby, 2002b: 268). Ethnic minority interests and influences have been marginalized in political decision-making, either because of their different culture and lack of socialization into the ways of a democratic tradition (Hammer and Bruun, 2000), or because of such institutional factors as governmental cooptation, exclusion from the labour market and stigmatization by the mass media (Hussain, 2002: 160).

As in other European countries, the multiculturalism debate in Denmark revolves around the veil (hijab), halal food, prayer and other rituals that involve the public space, Muslim cemeteries, schools, family rights, and so on. In spite of much public debate about Muslim religiosity, Denmark places no legal restrictions on the public practice of other religions. In the case of Islam, there is no prohibition on religious symbols such as the hijab, on Muslim prayer, on halal slaughtering practice, or on the founding of mosques and Muslim cemeteries.[10]

Legislation outlawing discrimination was passed in 1971, with the implementation of the Race Discrimination Convention §266b, an addition to the penal code, and the law forbidding discrimination (i.e. differential treatment) on grounds of race, and so on. In 1996 a law preventing discrimination in the labour market was also on the statute book. The Danish Institute for Human Rights, which was created in 2002, has replaced the Council for Ethnic Equality (*Nævnet for etnisk ligestilling*) and serves as a committee of complaint in matters pertaining to the convention.

Immigrants' cultural rights are in fact encouraged in Denmark according to the traditional rules of 1855 concerning so-called private free schools (*friskoler*), which are supported by public funds. There are nineteen Muslim free schools, the highest number in Europe when viewed relative to Denmark's Muslim population (Borchgrevink, 1999), which in 2006 numbered approximately 200,000 (Jacobsen, 2007). In 2002, changes to the free school law posed certain normative restrictions and duties on the schools, such as 'to prepare pupils to live in a society of freedom and democracy' (Togeby, 2002b: 53; author's translation). Among other cultural rights abolished in 2002 were the duty of municipalities to offer teaching to immigrant children in their mother tongue, and grants to establish ethnic minority organizations. However, immigrant organizations still have the same right to municipal communal financial support as others (54). Taken together, these developments reflect an assimilationist approach to dealing with integration, informed by reference to universal rights.

Denmark exemplifies the operation of polyethnic rights within a liberal democracy, as defined by Kymlicka (1995), a circumstance which has, however, been reduced by the legislation of 2002 (Togeby, 2002b: 57). The present situation fits with the image of Denmark as representing a colour-blind liberal position on the question of equality (Mouritsen, 2006b: 90). The notion of equality is strongly reflected in the policies on immigration and integration, in terms of the right to participate in the political process, and to form associations and institutions such as private free schools. These universal rights thus tend to produce rights to particular cultural practices at the private level. However, since 2002, there has been a gradual diminution of cultural rights, and the exercising of a certain control in order to guarantee that (Danish) values such as freedom and democracy are maintained. The emphasis on Danish democracy as open to everybody appears to an increasing degree to sideline questions of ethnicity, and hence denotes assimilation. As a result, ethnic minorities are increasingly unable to represent minority interests in political life. They are invited to participate in Danish democracy – but as ethnic Danes. As regards the question of citizenship, the coexistence of a formal openness with fairly strong pressures towards assimilation involves tensions (Togeby, 2002b: 58). In terms of the rejection of dual citizenship and the need for an 'affiliation claim', these might be interpreted as guaranteeing commitment and loyalty to Danish identity.

The integration law and its implementation

Since 1980, integration has been a declared objective of Danish policy towards foreigners, which in 1983 resulted in the Social Democratic government's statement on immigration policy (*indvandrerpolitiske redegørelse*). From the outset, scholars have pointed that the discourse on integration is based on assimilationist principles (Hamburger, 1990). The municipalities have the main responsibility for presenting the objectives of immigration policy. In 1999, the government passed an integration law (*Integrationsloven*) addressing the issue of reunifying immigrant and refugee families (it does not apply to people from other EU or Nordic countries). The intent of the law is to guarantee that the recently arrived foreigner can participate on equal terms with other citizens in political, economic, work, social, religious and cultural life, and that he or she becomes self-supporting. Additionally, central to the law is the idea that the foreigner obtains an understanding of Danish society's fundamental values (Integration Law §1). The law outlines a three-year 'introduction programme' that includes obligatory courses in Danish language and society (*samfundsforståelse*). The programme is monitored by local authorities, at municipal offices, where the immigrant, together with her/his social worker, makes an 'individual contract' (*individuel kontrakt*), individually tailored to her or his circumstances (Ministeriet for Flygtninge, 2004: 57).

Further changes to the integration law were announced in 2006 with the so-called 'integration contract', together with the 'declaration on integration and active citizenship', which added restrictions in relation to the introduction programme as well as strengthening the emphasis on 'Danish values'. The aim of the declaration is to 'clarify Danish society's values for the individual foreigner, and stress that the foreigner should become aware that Danish society expects him/her to make an effort to become integrated as a participating and accommodating citizen on equal terms with other citizens.... By signing the declaration, the foreigner agrees to recognize the fundamental values expressed in the declaration' (Ministeriet for Flygtninge, 2006a: 10;

author's translation). The immigrant is required to respect Danish legislation and defend Danish democratic principles; to learn Danish and acquire knowledge of Danish society; to be responsible for their own self-support; to recognize gender equality and to be aware that it is illegal to use force or violence towards one's spouse or children; to respect one's children; to be aware that both female circumcision and forced marriage are illegal in Denmark; to respect personal freedom and integrity, freedom of belief and expression as fundamental rights in Denmark; to be aware that discrimination on the grounds of gender, colour or religion is illegal; to recognize that Danish society is opposed to terrorism, which is an illegal activity in Denmark. The last points concern the regulations governing the granting of a residence permit and the right to protection as a refugee. As it stands, the declaration represents a reduction of culture and values to what is deemed 'allowable'. This serves indirectly to paint a picture in which immigrants and refugees are perceived as a 'problem' (Fog Olwig and Pærregaard, 2007); furthermore it lends itself to the creation of a stereotype of the potentially dangerous immigrant (Grillo, 2003; Silverstein, 2005). The integration contract has to be signed by both the immigrant and the municipality, which will then follow up on the contract every third month. The contract permits sanctions if the immigrant does not fulfil his or her obligations (Ministeriet for Flygtninge, 2006a).[11]

As part of the 'welcome package', the Ministry offers a Handbook for New Citizens about Danish Society (*Medborger i Danmark. En håndbog for nye borgere om det danske samfund*, 2006). The introduction to the handbook, which deals with the contribution of foreigners to Danish society, reveals a certain ambiguity:

> Like most countries, Denmark is a diverse society where many different political and religious beliefs and social and cultural attitudes are represented. To maximise the benefits of this diversity, we must all share a sense of community based on certain fundamental values. These values include democracy, welfare, freedom, equality and respect for other people, regardless of gender, age, colour and beliefs. Everyone has rights and obligations and should be able to take part freely in the daily life of society on an equal basis within the scope of the law. Denmark is governed by a representative democracy, which means that citizens can freely elect their representatives in

local and national elections. Democracy also implies other freedoms: freedom of thought, speech, and expression, freedom of association and freedom of worship.... But these democratic principles also set certain limitations on the individual's freedom of action. The purpose of these limitations is to ensure that no one suffers injustice or is harmed in any way. Thus, Danish society does not accept discrimination against anyone on grounds of gender, ethnic origin, colour, religious or political persuasion, sexual orientation or disability; nor does it accept anyone being subjected to violence or mutilating circumcision. Mutual respect and understanding between people and groups of people is a fundamental principle of Danish society ... We believe that the diversity that you bring to us from outside Denmark will infuse our community with innovation and dynamism. It is therefore our hope that you will play an active part in the society of which you are now a member. With these words we would like to welcome you to Denmark and to wish you luck and happiness in your new life in this country. (Ministeriet for Flygtninge, 2006b: 4–5).

The ambiguity is that the Danish model of multiculturalism, on the one hand, praises diversity – including in terms of Denmark's own cultural complexity – as fruitful and beneficial to Danish society, and, on the other, emphasises 'fundamental values', and the expectation of active participation and contribution to the well-being of the state. It reflects the government's new course in the politics of integration from 2003, unveiled in its *Visions and Strategies for Better Integration* (Regeringen, 2003). One of the four principles that the document sets out is: 'We must leave room for diversity and learn to benefit from it'.[12] What is revealing in this document is that the words 'diversity' and 'personal freedom' appear in the same sentence as 'community of fundamental values' (Regeringen, 2003: 6; author's translation). This relates to a normative concept of culture, in the guise of 'values', in which certain (Danish) core values are held as prevalent. Hedetoft has described what he calls the peculiarity of the modernized Danish integration policy regime as a combination of three apparently divergent elements, which he characterizes as a 'strange marriage of interest-based pragmatism and identity-based nationalism' (Hedetoft, 2006b: 420). The first element is 'assimilation', which relates particularly to the importance of maintaining 'Danish homogeneity'; the second is 'integration', emphasizing an 'equal footing' and 'equal access'; and the third is 'pluriculturalism', which employs a diversity discourse reflecting the fact of ethnic diversity, but within a pragmatic–instrumental modality (419). This model of managing multi-ethnicity sustains the argument regarding the peculiar Danish contradiction between multiculturalism and assimilation.

Cultures as obstacles to integration

On 10 October 2006 the European Commission against Racism and Intolerance (ECRI) hosted a round table in Copenhagen. The themes scheduled for discussion were ECRI's report on Denmark, racism and xenophobia in political and public discourse; the legislative and institutional framework for combating racism and racial discrimination; and immigration and integration policies and practices in Denmark. The previous year, ECRI had published its third report on Denmark (ECRI, 2005), which was critical of Danish policy.[13] The Danish government subsequently maintained that the report included several factual errors. In her opening speech Rikke Hvilshøj, then minister for refugees, immigrants and integration, stressed the importance of understanding that the aim of the government was both diversity and shared democratic values, and that individual freedom went hand in hand with mutual responsibility. She was subsequently verbally attacked by some of the representatives working for anti-racist NGOs participating in the meeting. Their criticisms and comments concerned the present government's restrictions on immigration and its integration policy, and the Ministry's discourse on integration as an assimilation based on the norms and values of the majority society, which does not reflect the multicultural reality. In a robust defence, Hvilshøj emphasized that multiculturalism was not a goal for the Danish government. She argued that freedom of expression, a community founded on the rule of law, and equality are values that 'make room' (gør plads). She then stressed what she regarded as the limit case of what is culturally acceptable: 'Some cultures discriminate – that is my limit'. By saying this, she reversed the discourse on discrimination by changing the harassing agent ('they discriminate'). This talk of limit cases is an expression of the war on culture that characterizes the present-day policy of integration (Hedetoft, 2006a).

Immigration is frequently presented as a challenge, a threat or an 'external shock' to Danish identity (Hedetoft, 2006b). This perception is not limited to the political right, but tends to permeate the overall debate on integration in Denmark. In his New Year speech of 2000, the former Social Democratic prime minister Poul Nyrup Rasmussen raised the problem of 'Danish families who in certain urban areas start to feel like strangers in their own country' and urged immigrants to accommodate to (*tilpasse sig*) Danish values. In the same speech, he called for a stricter integration policy, pointing to many of the issues, such as forced marriage, which the policies of the new right-wing government subsequently succeeded in highlighting. Later, in 2000, Karen Jespersen, former minister of the interior, became internationally notorious for arguing against Denmark as a multicultural society, on the familiar grounds that other cultures are discriminatory, stating that she would not accept female oppression (thereby hinting that Muslim culture oppresses women).[14] In November 2000, Rasmussen spoke explicitly of Islam as an impediment to participation in Danish life, citing Muslim prayer as an obstacle to a normal working life. The 2003 New Year speech of Liberal prime minister Anders Fogh Rasmussen has become emblematic of the promotion of a normative and political discourse on culture:

> There should be freedom to be dissimilar. We neither can nor will meddle in how people are dressed or what they eat, or what they believe in. Danishness is more than meatballs and brown gravy. But Danish society builds on some basic values that one has to respect if one wants to live here. In Denmark, we keep politics and religion separated. In Denmark, an unbreakable respect for human life is in force. In Denmark, it is a matter of course that women are equal to men. And we will not allow these rights of freedom to be suppressed by reference to the Koran, the Bible or other holy scriptures. For too many years now, we have been foolishly kind. We have not dared to say that one thing is better than an other. But we have to do that now. We also owe it to the thousands of immigrants who every day contribute positively to Danish society. They take care of their job, their school and their studies, and enter into daily life in Denmark without problems. Those immigrants who fled the darkness of the

mullahs shall not experience us now letting medieval forces take root in Danish society. Therefore, I have two messages tonight: We shall speak clearly against fundamentalist imams and prevent religious and political fanaticism from finding fertile soil in Denmark; but we shall also show immigrants that there is room for them in a modern society, if they want to participate. (www.stm.dk/-p-7405.html; author's translation)

Rasmussen's speech has among other things become known for its assertion of the superiority of 'our' culture, norms and values, and of immigrants' culture (in the singular) as a hindrance to integration. As formulated by the government, integration as a problem is thus related to 'the fact that many people of foreign descent for self-evident reasons have other ideas of right and wrong than those which are prevalent in Denmark' (Regeringen, 2003, cited in Hedetoft, 2006b: 417). The insistence on a common national culture found in arguments about 'the values that Danish society builds on' is not only about common national culture as a value in itself, but also one that is necessary for social cohesion. It represents a politicization of culture, whereby culture is represented as a politically necessary functional homogeneity, but also a culturalization of politics, by which political values are referred to, and thereby legitimized, as culture (Mouritsen, 2006a: 73). The frequent reference to the 'core values' constituent of Danish society, to which one must subscribe in order to become part of Danish society, reflects the fact that the dialogue between cultures is asymmetrical. While the government emphasizes the necessity of 'making room' and being 'open to other cultures', it does not maintain that all cultures are equal; 'openness' is thus on 'our' side (Mouritsen, 2006a: 83). The new discourse emphasizes universal liberal values and citizenship as tools with which to include immigrants, and expresses hostility towards multiculturalism, which is perceived as being in conflict with equal rights (72).

Ulf Hedetoft points to the ways that the integration of immigrants is debated and resolved in terms of culture, in the sense of a 'thick, condensed, and politicized notion of culture as a bundle of non-contestable values' (2006b: 407). He sees this as representing a novel consensual discourse advocating a 'cultural struggle' (*kulturkamp*). Hedetoft further points to other transformations, particularly in populist policies. One such is that from compassion-based humanitarianism to nationalism, reflected in the discourse regarding the benefit Denmark derives from immigrants. Another is that from a defensive to an offensive *kulturkamp*, caused by a global macro-political shift from cultural relativism and interethnic harmony to cultural and political absolutism. A third transformation is that in the image of immigrants: from being 'dependent' to being 'self-reliant', and from having 'rights' to having 'duties' (411–14).

This development reflects the reinforced dominance of an assimilationist discourse on integration. In this image the rhetoric of 'making room' appears to be figurative for 'our' relation to 'them'. It is a statement of our acceptance and our embracing of them. Yet our embrace is at the same time an act of encompassment that draws the limits of 'their' presence in 'our' space.

The cartoon affair

The question of how to manage multiculturalism in European countries has become focused particularly on the presence of immigrants of Muslim background (Modood et al., 2006).

The ISSP survey on religion from 1998 shows that Danes' attitudes towards religion, especially as a catalyst for conflict and intolerance, was the most negative among all the thirty countries participating in the survey (Goul Andersen, 2002: 22). This appears to relate explicitly to the question of religion itself, and suggests that religion (i.e. being religious) leads to intolerance (Goul Andersen and Tobiasen, 2002: 86). In particular, the image of Islam is constructed in opposition to ideas of secularism, individualization and the privatization of belief (98). Yet both xenophobia and disapproval of religion per se represent an antagonistic attitude towards Islam. Danes' attitudes towards Islam are related to the view that immigration is a threat to national individuality,[15] which in particular appears to relate to antagonism towards foreigners, and not to religion as such (Tobiasen, 2003: 352). Furthermore, Islam is increasingly becoming the 'point of focus for an aversion to strangers' (361; author's translation).

In Denmark, the polarization between 'us' and 'them' is often expressed as an opposition between 'Danes' and 'Muslims', whereby the category of 'Muslim' includes anyone of immigrant status. Muslims are thus perceived as 'foreigners', Muslim identity tending to be seen as incompatible with Danish identity (Jensen, 2008). Islam is perceived as being in opposition to so-called Danish core values, in this context denoting an antagonism that especially concerns Islam as a religion that is in conflict with Danishness as such. What is particularly at stake in this alleged conflict between Islam and Danishness is the polarization between the idea of secular democracy and that of sharia.

The murder of Theo van Gogh, director of the Dutch film *Submission*, in October 2004, had ramifications in Denmark, where it prompted a debate on the freedom of expression. The Muslim population reuqested stricter legislation on blasphemy. Their request was, however, interpreted as sympathy for the murderer. This accusation was accompanied by other incidents in the Danish public sphere, where the media began cross-examining people of Muslim background on the issue of sharia versus 'Danish democracy'.

It was in this climate that the so-called cartoon affair took place the following year.[16] The liberal right-wing newspaper *Jyllands-Posten* was alarmed by the fact that some Danish cartoonists, presumably out of fear of the ban on images in Islam, had refused to contribute pictures of the prophet Muhammad to a book whose writer is known for his controversial representations of Islam. On 30 September 2005, *Jyllands-Posten* published twelve satirical cartoons portraying the Prophet Muhammad. The act was a provocative display of the argument that freedom of expression grants the right to publish such images. If Muslims wish to become accepted and integrated in Denmark, they must accept this. The publication of the cartoons thus aimed at showing Muslims that in a democratic society one may be submitted to scorn, mockery and ridicule. The defence of freedom of expression was formulated in a polarized discourse, arguing for the necessity of defending this democratic value, which was perceived as threatened by Islamic communities wanting to restrain Danish culture and democracy in order to impose sharia law (Hedetoft, 2006a: 1). The editor of the newspaper thus expressed his indignition at the Muslim claim to particular religious rights, which he saw as directly incompatible with secularism, democracy and freedom of expression.

On 12 October, several ambassadors representing different Muslim countries complained about *Jyllands-Posten* to the prime minister, who responded that he was unable to do anything about it since it would go against the constitutional freedom of expression. On 29 October, eleven Muslim organizations accused *Jyllands-Posten* of blasphemy and discrimination.

The publication stirred worldwide debate. This was partly orchestrated by a team of Danish imams who travelled to the Middle East to inform Muslim leaders and governments about the Danish cartoon affair and what they experienced as a general Islamophobic climate in Denmark. For Danish Muslims there were several issues at stake. First of all the cartoons were seen as a provocation to the ban on images in Islam, particularly of the Prophet Muhammad, especially since some of the cartoons were quite obscene.[17] It was thus not so much the fact that Muhammad was pictured but the way in which he was represented that was regarded as a provocation. Additionally, it was the timing of the event, representing a culmination of the newspaper's already discriminatory line on immigrants of Muslim background (Hervik, 2002). Furthermore, the government's reluctance to engage in a dialogue about the affair was perceived negatively.

Among the Danish public, the debate revolved around the question of freedom of expression, as opposed to respect for cultural differences. The debate involved Denmark's relationships beyond its national boundaries, on the international scene. National pride also influenced the public debate in Denmark. However, for others it was a matter of shame, both in relation to the idea of Denmark as a multi-ethnic society, and because of the impact on international public opinion. Former liberal minister of foreign affairs Uffe Ellemann-Jensen positioned himself strongly against publication of the cartoons. Emphasizing that Denmark is a multi-ethnic country, he pointed to the consequences of globalization, implying the necessity to show greater respect to other cultures and dignity in the exercise of freedom of expression (Uffe Elleman-Jensen, in Bech Thomsen, 2006: 238; 272). International scholarly debate has revolved particularly around the discussion of cultural respect versus liberal values, and the question of whether the cartoon affair should or should not be interpreted as a form of racism (Modood et al., 2006).

Authentication or implosion of the Danish model?

The cartoon affair was not put on public trial, and did not produce any explicit winners or losers. In retrospect, the general conclusion seems to be that it was worth the scandal. The more positive evaluations say that it has 'cleared the air' of shrill voices in the debate, allowing more nuanced points of views (www.ugebrevet a4.dk 2007). Public polls indicate a somewhat ambiguous picture: Danes appear to have become more negative towards Islam and Muslims. At the same time, immigrants and refugees appear to feel less discriminated against, while the majority of ethnic Danes presume that discrimination has become more widespread (Catinét Research, 2006). This has been interpreted as an expression of Danish self-criticism and bad conscience (www.ugebrevet a4.dk 2007).

According to an analysis of Danish newspapers covering the cartoon affair, there appear to be three general frames of interpretation. One frame deals with the theme of freedom of expression as an explicitly Danish freedom, and is based on a discourse that is absolutist and polarized. Another frame is that of freedom of expression as a universal Western human right that is threatened by Islam. A third frame interprets the cartoons case as demonizing Muslims (Berg and Hervik, 2007).

There is, however, no clear connection between positions and position-takers. While the affair led to some self-censure among those normally cultivating polarization, such as the Danish People's Party, one party member, the theologian Søren Krarup, concluded that Danishness was lost:

> Does there still exist any cartoonist who would dare to picture Muhammad? And, furthermore, is there then a newspaper that would dare to publish them? If we are to answer in the negative – and who dares to think that that is not the case – then we simply have to realize that we have lost our culture and our rights here in the country. Islam has succeeded in conquering a part of Denmark. We Danes have by this action been turned into a people in chains in our own country. (Søren Krarup, in Bech Thomsen, 2006: 285; author's translation)

The cartoon affair might have led to increased polarization between 'Danes' and 'Muslims', in the image of the so-called 'clash of civilizations'. There are, however, many levels of such polarization. A common positive evaluation is that the affair has contributed to an awareness of 'our national heritage' (*Politiken*, 30 September 2006). This evaluation points to a tendency to demarcate the boundaries between 'our Danish values' and the Others' culture (or, more precisely, between our democracy and their Islam). A result of the affair might thus be that it has legitimated a cultural struggle expressed in a political rhetoric of cultural fundamentalism and exclusion (Stolcke, 1995). The recurrent question concerns particular cultural rights, and the recognition of multiculturalism, which is seen fundamentally to run counter to Danish notions of equality, universalism and democracy.

However, the affair also appears to have opened a dialogue between Danes and Muslims, and to have shown the face of Denmark's multiethnic reality, opening up the pressing question of multiculturalism. An attempt at dialogue, and at reconciling Danish values with Islam, is illustrated by one of the outcomes from the public debate, the foundation of the association Democratic Muslims (Demokratiske Muslimer) – a name that in itself seeks to dissolve polarization. Democratic Muslims is headed by a politician from Radikale Venstre, Naser Khader, who has attempted to distance himself from association with the 'radical' imams, and to show the diversity of Danish Muslim culture. One aim of the association is to avoid polarization by demonstrating that Muslim values are compatible with Danish values such as democracy, free speech and secularism; sharia, and the notion of religious law, was thus among the first issues that the association positioned itself against. However, the association has been seen by some as an attempt to incorporate the language of power and conform to Danishness by taking on the role of the 'good Muslim', positioning other Muslim groupings in Danish society as 'bad Muslims'. This has contributed to the distinction between so-called 'moderate' Muslims and 'radical' or 'extremist' Muslims, which justifies the exclusion of the latter as bad and dangerous for Danish society. It is thus seen as a way of including Muslim immigrants by suppressing part of their identity, reflecting the encompassing efforts of Danish hegemony.

Arguments that emphasize 'dialogue' as an outcome of the cartoon affair nonetheless point out that it has been a lesson in many ways:

that freedom of expression is a right and not a duty; that Denmark is not a 'closed' society unaffected by globalization; that Danes have learned more about Muslims and Islam, not least about their diversity; and that this has altered stereotypes (Thomsen, 2006: 234). Additionally, the affair has challenged Danes' self-perception as a homogenous, harmonious and tolerant people, and has exposed their lack of knowledge about their immigrant co-citizens, while giving them insight into their lives and self-perceptions as a minority group (274). A variety of new Muslim organizations and positions have emerged on the public scene. Furthermore, various Muslim organizations have signalled the desire for dialogue by initiating debates and conferences explicitly for non-Muslim Danes, addressing such subjects as the cartoon affair itself, sharia, political Islam, terrorism, and so on.

In March 2006, the television channel DR2 chose to contract a young veiled woman of Lebanese background, Asmaa Abdul Hamid, who was also the spokeswoman for the eleven Muslim organizations that reported *Jyllands-Posten* to the police for blasphemy and racial discrimination. She is also member of the far-left party Enhedslisten (Unity List). Abdul Hamid became the first Muslim television-host on a public service channel, in the debate show *Adam and Asmaa*, which was an attempt to 'bridge the gap' between the Western and the Islamic worlds, by opening a dialogue intended to lead to mutual understanding. Many people were, however, shocked by the way she marked Muslim religiosity in public, instigating a fear of Islamic theocracy. One feminist organization, provoked by Abdul Hamid's veil, which they saw as a sign of female oppression, tried in vain to get her fired through a collection of 500 signatures of protest. Yet other feminist organizations supported Abdul Hamid for strengthening gender equality. Others praised her for being a refreshing and powerful challenge to the usual television hosts. Abdul Hamid, defining herself as 'a Muslim feminist', founded a network for Muslim women, De grønne Slør (the Green Veils) in November 2006. The staging of Abdul Hamid has appeared to open up a debate at a certain level, featuring a variety of Danish voices concerning gender, ethnicity and equality. Abdul Hamid has appeared to challenge stereotypes about Muslims with her mix of Muslim religiosity and feminism, which in public discourses would otherwise be perceived as two domains with no relation to each other. As such, Abdul Hamid might be seen as an image of hybridity (Werbner and Modood, 1997), representing a transgressive power capable of overthrowing categorical cultural truths.

The cartoon affair can in this and in other ways be seen as a breakdown of the 'old' Danish model of relating to others, transgressing the gap between 'self' and 'other'. It has thoroughly unveiled that which has remained unsaid both among Danes and among immigrants, spelling out their respective prejudices and frustrations. In this sense, talk *about* them and us has been replaced by a talking (or rather shouting) *to*. At a certain level, it has represented a deconstruction of the 'secret' Danish universal particularism and its silent intolerance, proving that this model of coping with multi-ethnicity is failing. It also reflects a development from assuming sameness to realizing difference. In that sense, the Danish model has already changed, the cartoon affair being the culmination of the last decade's verbalizations of conflicting cultural differences.

According to British anthropologist Richard Jenkins, the drama of the cartoon affair revolves around a conflict between the two important ideological themes in Danish national identity: sameness and tolerance. Tolerance relies on the condition that people are the same, which becomes difficult to sustain in a situation characterized by diversity. Jenkins thus concludes that multiculturalism is not yet a possibility in Denmark (Kristelig Dagblad, 2006). Multicultural respect is in conflict with the Danish notion of equality as sameness, which term is associated with the notion of monocultural unity, geographical smallness and economic well-being. Another possible interpretation of the cartoon affair is that it represents an implosion of existing identity structures, which no longer work in practice, expressing itself in violence (Baumann, 2004: 42), which in the Danish case is manifested on both sides, among both Muslim immigrants and ethnic Danes. In contrast to the London bombings, which led to reflections on the failure of multiculturalism (Modood, 2005), the cartoon affair in Denmark reflects a breakdown of the Danish model for dealing with multi-ethnicity, in the sense that the notions of assimilation and 'common culture' have failed. From Muslim immigrants' point-of-view, the cartoons were seen as the straw that broke the camel's back; Danish cultural core values had been imposed (in the form of freedom of expression) to the point where the imposed culture hurt. Their reaction can be seen as a demand for recognition (Taylor, 1992, 1994). The cartoon affair thus illustrates a core issue in the debate on multiculturalism: the dilemma of conceptualizing recognition in terms of difference or in terms of equality.

Conflicts have transformative power. The current noise of the debate on immigrants might reflect a deconstruction and transformation into another model that has to consider the question of multiculturalism from scratch. In that light, the cartoon affair in an old nation-state such as Denmark reflects the current frictions that accompany the process of integrating Muslims into European society, and can be seen as part of the progress of Europe's already long history of integrating new social projects (Henkel, 2006). Culture has been defined as 'a human condition in constant transformation' (Hastrup, 2004; author's translation). Human beings, the producers of culture, are always oriented towards others, entering into major combinations and communities. This process is characterized by flexibility, since people relate to new experiences. While such transformation is definitely not an easy one for Danish society, at least fissures are appearing in the construction of the Danish 'room' that may indicate new understandings and negotiations of culture, diversity and national identity.

Notes

1. The cartoon affair was instigated by the newspaper *Jyllands-Posten's* publication of twelve satirical cartoons picturing the prophet Muhammad. This triggered a long debate revolving around cultural respect versus universal liberal values.
2. This typology of multicultural measures includes three different attitudes: (1) colour-blind liberal tolerance that includes measures against discrimination in the strong sense; (2) a liberal neutral culture that includes measures against discrimination in the weak sense, or against the bias of the majority; and (3) liberal multicultural compensation through complex equal treatment (Mouritsen, 2006b: 90). The Danish position is based on the safeguarding of rights to participate in society's social, economic and political programmes and activities, guaranteed by anti-discrimination laws. It furthermore ensures the right to the free exercise of one's own cultural practices, and the right to practise collective symbols.
3. The dimension of 'multicultural optimism' is defined as consisting 'of attitudes towards the enrichment of a society's cultural and social life by minority groups'; the dimension of 'cultural assimilation' concerns the pro-

motion of 'cultural assimilation of minority groups' (EUCM/SORA, 2001: 16–17).

4. The name 'Left' is misleading for this is a liberal right-wing party.

5. 'The Radical Left' is a misleading name for this party, which positions itself to the left, but not in any radical sense.

6. Danish politics is not based on the division of government and opposition, but on a division into three parts, where so-called supporting parties in principle are interested in keeping the government in power, but do not guarantee full support on all issues. Since the existence of the government relies on a supporting party, that party also occupies a powerful position, and plays an important role in decision-making.

7. In 2002 the so-called '24-year rule' was issued, raising the age from 18 to 24 years for both parties involved in marriage reunion. In addition, this rule imposes certain demands that ensures that the person who applies can guarantee their economic independence and affiliation to Denmark (Schmidt and Jakobsen, 2004). One consequence of this rule is that Danish citizens who want to marry foreigners have moved to Sweden. The city of Malmø in southern Sweden, in particular – about a half-hour drive from Copenhagen, across the Øresund bridge – is a locus of immigration for family-reunited Danes.

8. Before 2002, there were three categories of refugee: conventional refugees, quota refugees, and de facto refugees (Togeby, 2002b).

9. In 2001, 51 out of 4,647 members of the *kommunalbestyrelser* were people from so-called 'third countries' (Togeby, 2002b: 171).

10. There is, however, only one official mosque. Additionally, the one Muslim cemetery was established in 2006.

11. For instance, lack of participation in the introduction program can have consequences such as reducing the economic benefits, or even the possibility of obtaining unlimited citizenship.

12. The publication outlines four principles. The other three are: (1) We must leave room for diversity and learn to benefit from it; (2) We must put an end to 'clientelization' and show respect by making demands; (3) We must not use 'culture' to excuse oppressive family forms. The enabling strategies involve: (i) Efforts to safeguard a cohesive and open democratic society; (ii) efforts to ensure that persons with a different ethnic background than Danish fare better in the education system; (iii) efforts to ensure that more foreigners are able to acquire jobs (Regeringen, 2003, cited in Hedetoft, 2006b: 416).

13. Among other things, the authors of the report pointed to restrictions concerning citizenship and a discriminatory attitude to immigrants, particularly of Muslim background. It was maintained that the anti-racism clause was only rarely involved, and that certain media and politicians should be more responsible in the ways they represent Muslims, which are often directly or indirectly discriminatory (ECRI, 2005: 26).

14. In August 2000, Jespersen, in speaking about what to do with criminal asylum-seekers, suggested that they should be sent to a desert island. This

utterance came to reflect a very hard Danish attitude towards immigrants (Nielsen, 2004b: 91).

15. This has become apparent in the responses to two additional questions in the ISSP survey, addressed exclusively to Danes, aimed at assessing sympathy for Islam and gauging if immigration was perceived as a threat (Goul Andersen and Tobiasen, 2002: 22).

16. In Denmark, this affair is generally referred to as the 'Muhammad conflict' (*Muhammed konflikten*), which some Muslims interpret as further insulting them.

17. Especially one cartoon picturing Muhammad with a bomb in his turban.

References

Andersen, J., and H.J. Nielsen (2003) '"Indvandrere og indvandrerpolitik"', in J. Goul Andersen and O. Borre (eds), *Politisk forandring. Værdipolitik og nye skillelinjer ved folketingsvalget 2001*, Aarhus:.Systime Academic, pp. 327–46.

Baumann, G. (2004) 'Grammars of Identity/Alterrity: A Structural Approach', in G. Baumann and A. Gingrich (eds), *Grammars of Identity/Alterity: A Structural Approach*, New York: Berghahn Books, pp. 17–50.

Bech Thomsen, P. (2006) *Muhammedkrisen*, Copenhagen: People's Press..

Berg, C., and P. Hervik (2007) '"Muhammedkrisen". En politisk magtkamp i dansk journalistik', *Amid Working Paper Series* 62.

Borchgrevink, T. (1999) *Multikulturalisme: tribalisme – bløff – kompromis?* Oslo: Institutt for Samfundsforskning 99(3).

Bræmer, M. (2007) *Muhammed-krisen har renset luften*. Ugebrevet A4.

Catinét Research (2006) *Integrationsstatus*, Copenhagen: Catinét.

Christansen, P., and U. Østergaard (1992) 'Folket, landet og nationen', in *Dansk identitet?* Aarhus: Aarhus Universitetsforlag, pp. 13–56.

ECRI (2005) *Tredje rapport om Danmark*, Strasbourg: ECRI.

Ejrnæs, M. (2001) 'Integrationsloven – en case, der illustrerer etniske minoriteters usikre medborgerstatus', *Amid Working Paper Series*, 1.

EUMC/SORA (2001) *Attitudes towards Minority Groups in the European Union: A Special Analysis of the Eurobarometer 2000 Survey*, Vienna: EUMC/SORA.

Fog Olwig, K., and K. Pærregaard (2007) *Integrationsbegrebet: Antropologiske Perspektiver*, working paper.

Gaasholt, Øystein, and Lise Togeby (1995) *I syv sind. Danskernes holdninger til flygtninge og indvandrere*, Århus: Forlaget Politica.

Goul Andersen, J. (2002) 'Danskernes holdninger til indvandrere. En oversigt', *Amid Working Paper Series* 12.

Goul Andersen, J., and M. Tobiasen (2002) 'Forhold mellem religioner og mellem etnisk og religiøs tolerance', in C. Albrekt Larsen et al. (eds), *Danskernes forhold til religionen – en afrapportering af ISSP 98*, Aalborg: Aalborg Universitet, pp. 80–100.

Grillo, R. (2003) 'Cultural Essentialism and Cultural Anxiety', *Anthropological Theory* 3(2).

Gullestad, M. (2002) *Det norske sett med nye øyne*, Oslo: Universitetsforlaget.

Gundelach, P. (2002) *Det er dansk*, Copenhagen: Hans Reitzels Forlag.

Gundelach, P. (2004) 'Det særlige danske?', in P. Gundelach (ed.), *Danskernes særpræg*, Copenhagen:.Hans Reitzels Forlag, pp. 11–26.

Hamburger, C. (1990) 'Assimilation som et grundtræk i dansk indvandrerpolitik', *Politica* 22(3).

Hammer, O., and I. Bruun (2000) *Etniske minoriteters indflydelseskanaler*, Aarhus: Aarhus Universitetsforlag.

Hastrup, K. (2004) *Kultur. Det flexible fællesskab*, Aarhus: Univers.

Hedetoft, U. (2003) '"Cultural Transformation": How Denmark Faces Immigration', www.openDemocracy.net.

Hedetoft, U. (2004) 'Magten, de etniske minoriteter, og det moderniserede assimilationsregime i Danmark', *GRUS* 71.

Hedetoft, U. (2006a) 'Denmark's Cartoon Blowback', www.openDemocracy.net.

Hedetoft, U. (2006b) 'More than Kin and Less than Kind. The Danish Politics of Ethnic Consensus and the Pluricultural Challenge', in J.L. Campbell and H.J.A Pedersen (eds), O K. *National Identity and the Varieties of Capitalism: The Danish Experience* Quebec and Copenhagen: McGill-Queen's University Press, pp. 398–430.

Henderson, A. (2006) 'Tolerance på prøve', *Kristeligt Dagblad* 3 June.

Henkel, H. (2006) '"The Journalists of *Jyllands-Posten* are a Bunch of Reactionary Provocateurs" The Danish Cartoon Controversy and the Self-Image of Europe', *Radical Philosophy* 143.

Hervik, P. (2002) *Mediernes muslimer. En antropologisk undersøgelse af mediernes dækning af religioner i Danmark*, Copenhagen: Nævnet for Etnisk Ligestilling.

Hervik, P. (2004) 'The Danish Cultural World of Unbridgeable Differences', *Ethnos* 69(2).

Hobolt, S.B. (2004) 'Lokal orientering', in P. Gundelach (ed.), *Danskernes særpræg* Copenhagen: Hans Reitzels Forlag, pp. 338–63.

Hussain, M. (2002) 'Etniske minoriteters politiske organisering i Danmark', in *Bevægelser i demokrati*, Århus: Åarhus Universitetsforlag, pp. 160–76.

Jacobsen, B. (2007) 'Muslimer i Danmark – en kritisk vurdering af antalsopgørelser', in *Tørre tal om troen. religionsdemografi i Danmark i det 21. århundrede*, Copenhagen: Forlaget Univers.

Jensen, T.G. (2008) 'To Be "Danish", Becoming "Muslim": Contestations of National Identity?', *Journal of Ethnic and Migration Studies*.

Kaspersen, L.B., and L. Thorsager (2004) 'Associationalism and Democracy: Some Reflections on the Danish State and Civil Society', in L. Dhundale and Erik André Andersen (eds), *Revisiting the Role of Civil Society in the Promotion of Human Rights*, Copenhagen: Danish Institute for Human Rights, pp. 235–66.

Knudsen, A. (1992) 'De hemmelighedsfulde indfødte', in U. Østergaard (ed.), *Dansk identitet?* Aarhus: Aarhus Univerversitetsforlag, pp. 211–3.

Knudsen, A. (1996) *Her går det godt, send flere penge*, Copenhagen: Gyldendal.

Kristeligt Dagblad (2006) 'Tolerance på prøve', 6 March, Copenhagen: Kristeligt Dagblad. Mikkelsen, F. (2003) 'Indvandrerorganisationer i Danmark', in F.

Mikkelsen (ed.), *Indvandrerorganisationer i Norden*, Copenhagen: Akademiet for Migrationsstudier i Danmark, pp. 95–170.

Kühle, L.M.V. d. A. (2004) *Out of Many, One: Atheoretical and Empirical Study of Religious Pluralism in Denmark from a Perspective of Power*, Århus: Det Teologiske Fakultet.

Kymlicka, Will (1995) *Multicultural Citizenship*, Oxford: Oxford University Press.

Ministeriet for Flygtninge, Indvandrere og Integration (2003) *Bekendtgørelse af lov om integration af udlændinge i Danmark (integrationsloven)*, Copenhagen.

Ministeriet for Flygtninge, Indvandrere og Integration (2004) *Introduktionsprogrammet m.v. efter integrationsloven. Vejledning.* Copenhagen.

Ministeriet for Flygtninge, Indvandrere og Integration (2006a) *Integrationskontrakten og erklæringen om integration og aktivt medborgerskab i det danske samfund. Informationsmateriale til kommunerne.* Copenhagen.

Ministeriet for Flygtninge, Indvandrere og Integration (2006b) *Medborger i Danmark. En håndbog for nye borgere om det danske samfund*, Copenhagen.

Modood, T. (2005) 'Remaking Multiculturalism after 7/7', www.openDemocracy.net.

Modood, T. (2007) *Multiculturalism*, Cambridge: Polity Press.

Modood, T., et al. (2006) 'The Danish Cartoon Affair: Free Speech, Racism, Islamism, and Integration', *International Migration* 44(5): 3–62.

Mouritsen, P. (2006a) 'The Particular Universalism of a Nordic Civic Nation: Common Values, State Religion and Islam in Danish Political Culture', in T. Modood et al. (eds), *Multiculturalism, Muslims and Citizenship: A European Approach*, London: Routledge, pp. 70–93.

Mouritsen, P. (2006b) 'Kulturbegreber og kulturproblemer i liberal multikulturalisme', in S.L. Jørgensen and M. Sandberg (eds), *Kulturlighed – temaer om kulturel identitet*, Aarhus: Philosophia, pp. 85–122.

Nannestad, P. (1999) *Solidaritetens pris. Holdninger til indvandrere og flygtninge i Danmark 1987–1993*, Århus: Århus Universitetsforlag.

Nielsen, H.J. (2001) 'Er vi mere negative mod fremmede og andre folk?', *Nyt fra Rockwool Fondens Forskningsenhed*, 20 January.

Nielsen, H.J. (2004a) 'De etniske minoriteter', in P. Gundelach (ed.), *Danskernes særpræg*, Copenhagen: Hans Reitzels Forlag, pp. 293–312.

Nielsen, H.J. (2004b) *Er danskerne fremmedfjendske? Udlandets syn på debatten om indvadrere 2000–2002*, Aarhus: Aarhus Universitetsforlag.

Preis, Ann-Belinda (1996) *Kan vi leve sammen? Integration mellem politik og praksis*, Copenhagen: Munksgaard.

Regeringen (2003) *Regeringens vision og strategier for bedre integration*, Copenhagen.

Regeringen (2005) *En ny chance til alle*, Copenhagen.

Salamon, K.L.G. (1992) 'I grunden er vi enige. En ekskurs i skandinavisk foreningsliv', *Tidsskriftet Antropologi* 25.

Schiffauer, W. (1998) 'The Civil Society and the Outsider. Drawing the Boundaries in Four Political Cultures', working paper.

Schmidt, G., and V. Jakobsen (2004) *Pardannelse blabndt etniske minoriteter i Danmark*. Copenhagen: Socialforskningsinstituttet.

Schwartz, J.M. (1985) *Reluctant Hosts: Denmark's Reception of Guest Workers*, Copenhagen: Akademisk Forlag.

Silverstein, P. (2005) 'Immigrant Racialization and the New Savage Slot', *Annual Review of Anthropology*, 34.

Sjørslev, I. (2004) 'Alterity as Celebration, Alterity as Threat: A Comparison of Grammars between Brazil and Denmark', in G. Baumann and A. Gingrich (eds), *Grammars of Identity/Alterity: A Structural Approach*, New York: Berghahn Books, pp. 79–98.

Skaksen, J.R., et al. (2006) *Holdninger til immigration. Er danskere specielle?* Centre for Economic and Business Research.

Stolcke, V. (1995) 'Talking Culture', *Current Anthropology* 36(1).

Taylor, C. (2002) 'Democratic Exclusion (And Its Remedies?)', www.Eurozine. com.

Tayob, A. (2006) 'Caricatures of the Prophet. European Integration', *ISIM Review* 17.

Thalhammar, E., et al. (2001) *Attitudes towards Minority Groups in the European Union. A Special Analysis of the Eurobarometer 2000 Survey on behalf of the European Monitoring Centre on Racism and Xenophobia*, Vienna: SORA.

Thomsen, P.B. (2006) *Muhammedkrisen - hvad skete der, hvad har vi lært?* Copenhagen: People's Press.

Tobiasen, M. (2003) 'Danskernes verden var den samme efter 11.september: terror, islam og global solidaritet', in J. Goul Andersen and O. Borre (eds), *Politisk forandring. Værdipolitik og nye skillelinjer ved folketingsvalget 2001*, Aarhus: Systime Academic, pp. 347–62.

Togeby, L. (1998) 'Danskerne og det multikulturelle', *Politica* 30(2): 184–203.

Togeby, L. (1999) 'Et demokrati, som omfatter alle, der bor i Danmark?', in Jørgen Goul Andersen, Peter Munk Christiansen, Torben Beck Jørgensen, Lise Togeby and Signild Vallgårda (eds), *Den demokratiske udfordring*, Copehagen: Hans Reitzels Forlag.

Togeby, L. (2002a) 'Etniske minoriteters deltagelse i demokratiske processer, herunder politiske partier, valg og offentlig debat', *Amid Working Paper Series* 20.

Togeby, L. (2002b) *Grønlændere i Danmark*. Aarhus: Aarhus Universitetsforlag.

Togeby, L. (2003) *Fra fremmedarbejder til etniske minoriteter*. Aarhus: Aarhus Universitetsforlag.

Werbner, P., and T. Modood (1997) *Debating Cultural Hybridity: Multi-cultural Identities and the Politics of Anti-racism*, London: Zed Books.

6

Assimilation by conviction or by coercion? Integration policies in the Netherlands

Thijl Sunier

The foreign press has been puzzled lately by an apparent reversal in the political climate in the Netherlands towards Islam following 9/11, and the murder of the filmmaker Theo van Gogh, in November 2004, by a radical Muslim. A country previously often perceived as multi-cultural, libertarian, open, tolerant towards 'other cultures', seems to some commentators to be turning into a country that offers almost zero tolerance towards cultural diversity, with one of Europe's strictest immigration policies and an uncompromisingly assimilationist policy. This, according to many in and outside the country, is the necessary price to pay for years of benign neglect, laissez-faire, unproductive cultural relativism, multicultural illusion, political correctness and conflict-avoidance. Foreign journalists observe, even feel, the total failure of Dutch multiculturalism in day-to-day encounters in the street. For example, Jane Kramer writes of the 'un-Dutch' attitude in the *New Yorker* (April 2006) remarking that 'after fifty years of insistent official harmony, the hatreds on both sides of the cultural divide have surfaced [and] that peculiarly Dutch myth of a democracy integrated but not assimilated might be not only a contradiction in terms but a dangerous fiction'. Multiculturalism Dutch style has, in the eyes of many, become shorthand for turning a blind eye towards evident cultural derailments. Kramer's grotesque caricature meticulously replicates the discourse of neoliberal and neoconservative opinion formers in the Netherlands: multiculturalism has turned the country into a disaster, but we still cannot say it for fear of offending 'the Other'. Others (see Silverstein, 2005), however, see 9/11 and subsequent events as a pretext for harsh and oppressive policies towards Muslims and a farewell to at least some notion of cultural equality. Both sides consider the recent events as a turning point in the political climate.

It is certainly true that the backlash from 9/11 has caused a tremendous shift in attitude towards Muslims. They are addressed and expected to account for acts committed in the name of their religion. But which intepretation is right? Does 9/11 and even the murder of Theo van Gogh, explain the shift? Is the Netherlands indeed a quagmire of Muslim violence, where 'multicultural neglect' has placed the country in danger? Was the country indeed ever a multicultural laboratory, a paradise of mutual tolerance, understanding and interethnic socializing?

The image of the Netherlands as an erstwhile laboratory of multiculturalism is as big a myth as the idea that today the country is torn by violence and has come adrift. The Netherlands' experience with Muslim violence is certainly not exceptional, let alone unique. In the USA almost 3,000 people were killed in a massive attack on the Twin Towers; in Spain over 100 people were killed in a bombing at a railway station in Madrid; London suffered a deadly attack on the Underground in 2005. In 2006 Belgium experienced several senseless and gruesome murders, of which the alleged perpetrators were 'of North African descent', while riots in the impoverished suburbs of Paris demonstrated the limits of French assimilationist policies. To that extent the Netherlands remains an island of peace and boring quietness. The murder of filmmaker Theo van Gogh, a professional provocateur, was committed by somebody who hated him because of his constant insulting of Islam. His abject but rationalized act did not harm innocent people but was directed towards a 'combatant'. Other potential targets, such as the former populist minister Verdonk, the racist politician Geert Wilders, or Ayaan Hirsi Ali with her well-known crusade against Islam are, not very surprisingly, hated by many Muslims. An alleged network of terrorists, the so-called

Hofstadgroep, was arrested before committing any serious crime, and the prosecutor has struggled to make a case during the ongoing trials against the members of the network. We will probably never know whether they would have actually done something. While Pim Fortuyn, an avowed adversary of Islamic morality, was murdered by a Dutch animal rights activist, his assassination fits well within the above narrative of political chaos. So much for the recent facts. I do not argue that nothing has happened in the Netherlands, but while the countries listed above had reasonable grounds for alarmist comments, nowhere in the Western world have more words been written and spoken on the 'Muslim issue' than in the Netherlands. Costa-Lascoux, a member of the laicist Stasi Commission in France that prepared the law to ban visible religious symbols in public schools, 'was shocked to see that integration in the Netherlands had failed totally'. She even went so far as to assert that the real motive behind the creation of the Commission was the 'disastrous' situation in the Netherlands as the prime bad example of integration (*NRC*, 2 February 2004).

The call for a 'new politics' and the eradication of 'past failures' was probably also nowhere as ubiquitous and outspoken as in the Netherlands. Nonetheless, in the general election campaign of 22 November 2006, the 'integration issue' was much less prominent than in 2003. Wilders's xenophobic Party for Freedom gained nine seats in parliament with a very explicit anti-Islam programme, and in general nationalist political voices gained some ground; however, other extreme right-wing alarmist politicians were wiped out and in general parties on the left of the political spectrum gained seats.

Is the Netherlands, a country that 'invented' pillarization, indeed a laboratory of multiculturalism that now has been woken up from a delusion? I would question this image. First I will show that there has been much more continuity in Dutch integrationist policies than the heated debate seems to suggest. These policies have always been focused on three areas which have constituted the basis of the integration fabric: housing, labour and education (Ministry of the Interior, 1983) The aim has always been to achieve equality and full participation in all three areas. Over the years there have been shifts and ruptures as regards the best particular policies to achieve these aims, but the Dutch government has never adopted any policy based on the equality of cultures. It is true that in the 1970s and 1980s immigrants were primarily categorized as members of religious and ethnic groups, and from the 1990s through to today as 'allochthonous'. These terms should be understood as discursive attributes of the integration fabric. It is true that the government had a lenient attitude towards cultural diversity and has stated in policy reports that cultural and religious identities are important human prerequisites. Such statements, however, were always related to these three areas. And it is also true that the government subsidized cultural and even religious activities, but this has always been a temporal matter. It should be understood as technical and pragmatic rather than a measure of principle. The final goal has always been total absorption (assimilation) of immigrants into the Dutch moral community. Although, as I will show, there are many fields, particularly in local politics, where 'the management of cultural diversity' is part and parcel of the political agenda, cultural diversity as a goal in itself is and has always been subservient to economic equality. To put it differently, even in the 'lenient 1980s' the crucial fields of housing, labour and education were always firmly kept out of the cultural realm.

In the 1980s and the early 1990s there was a widely held belief that this process of assimilation would evolve gradually and naturally, when immigrants would integrate socially and economically and realize that Dutch society is morally superior to theirs. It was the Dutch version of the modernist thesis that societies can be constructed and immigrants would soon be absorbed by society. In the Netherlands this social engineering always had a strong pedagogical foundation. In France, assimilation is good for the Republic; in the Netherlands, it is good for the immigrant. This is what I would call 'assimilation by conviction'. It is based on the idea that immigrants have to be made socio-economically equal, but that their cultures are not equal. Through a successful integration programme that enhances economic equality, immigrants will 'in the end' understand that it is in their best interest to subscribe to the Dutch moral community (Schiffauer et al., 2004). It differs from the French 'republican' philosophy that cultural and religious differences are irrelevant for the building up of nationhood and citizenship, but it also differs from any multiculturalist creed that considers cultures as being equal.

The relation between economic and social integration, on the one hand, and the 'politics of diversity', on the other, has thus always been unidirectional, but the prevailing political agenda produced a shifting discourse on cultural difference. From the publication of the first policy document on integration in 1983, there are, roughly speaking, three distinctive periods in which the integration policy took a particular shape.

The 1980s: cultural diversity as a transitory status quo

In the 1960s and 1970s thousands of labour migrants arrived in the Netherlands, initially from Italy, Spain and Portugal, but later on from Turkey and Morocco. Until the late 1970s there was a political consensus about the temporariness of labour migration: migrants would return to their countries of origin after some years. Their social position was that of a group of outsiders who lived on the margins of society. They worked in those sectors of the labour market where they hardly met Dutch people. They were housed in boarding houses, often located close to the workplace. They were in no way part of society and the idea was that they should not become so. That is why the government adopted measures to prevent alienation from their countries of origins and rooting in the Netherlands. This was called 'preservation of culture', but it bore no relation to Dutch society in any way. In fact it was a very pragmatic policy aimed at preventing migrants becoming rooted in society. The government wanted to stimulate return migration. Educational activities, such as Dutch language courses, were left to private initiative.

In the late 1970s the government recognized that many of the temporary migrants would stay permanently. One of the main reasons for this shift in perspective was that the government acknowledged that the Dutch industry could no longer do without foreign labourers (Tinnemans, 1994: 100). In 1983 this resulted in an official 'change of policy', namely from deliberate isolation to economic integration. The Netherlands adopted what was probably one of the most explicit integration policies in Europe in the early 1980s. It was designed to absorb immigrants eventually into the host society. The means to accomplish this were not the existing legislative principles of citizenship such as in France, but a trajectory from 'immigrant' to 'citizen', in which the 'target groups' were defined very explicitly on the basis of ethnic markers. Here we find the origins of the ethnicized discourse on social status and integration, which is not unique to the Dutch but certainly unique in its consequences (see Penninx, 1988; Rath, 1991).[1] It is based on the idea that ethnic origin influences the immigrant's career in the host country. Ethnic and cultural background influences the person's attitude (see, e.g., Lindo, 1996). Immigrants almost pass through different stages of the integration trajectory and at each stage one is able to evaluate the situation and to determine where the immigrant stands. Integration is measured by the migrant's position in the labour market, housing, and schooling. The pace at which this takes place depends on ethnic background. In these so-called social fields a complete equality should be reached. Immigrants who had not (yet) achieved this level of equality were considered to be in a state of social backwardness (*achterstand*). The basis for this policy was laid down in the *Minderhedennota* (Minority Document) issued by the government in 1983. The policies to be developed were based on the assumption that 'persons of non-Dutch origin would be permanently part of society' (Ministry of the Interior, 1983: 11). This would imply that the integration policies should be directed towards eliminating deficiencies in the social position of immigrants. The new policies were clear: the Netherlands would now accept that most immigrants would stay permanently.

With respect to culture, two aspects are noteworthy. Although the policy document referred to the 'multicultural character of society and the growing cultural diversity due to immigration' and the 'equality of cultures', as stipulated in the Constitution, it was clear from the outset that this equality of cultures must in no way infringe upon the 'established norms and values which are to be considered as fundamental to Dutch society' (Ministry of the Interior, 1983: 107). 'The culture of the majority is rooted in Dutch society' (12). Thus economic equality would imply cultural absorption. Economic and social equality would eventually lead to an erosion of the migrants' cultural baggage, or at least relegate this to the non-political, private realm. Multiculturalism or cultural diversity was an actual state of affairs and not a choice

220 EUROPEAN MULTICULTURALISM REVISITED

based on principle. Cultural diversity was a challenge that implicated a particular pedagogical programme to overcome this diversity. In those days there was a genuine conviction by policymakers that with such an integration policy, oriented towards social and economic equality, immigrants would not only socially but also culturally become part of mainstream society. They would eventually 'lose' their cultural background and become Dutch. This, however, was an implicit goal, never explicitly mentioned in policy documents.

A consequence of those early Dutch integration policies was that culture was a matter of fact, but hardly a topic for debate. Immigrants were called 'ethnic minorities'. This was their starting position. This was partly the heritage of the 1970s in which, as we saw, the 'preservation of culture' was aimed at keeping migrants oriented towards their countries of origin to which they would return eventually. But in the new integration policies the collective connotation attached to the term 'ethnic minority' had a very pragmatic origin. Immigrants bring with them their culture. For that reason society has to face a 'multicultural reality' (11) and the government should take into account that cultural background is a 'safe haven' in a strange environment. Multicultural thus had a very specific meaning, denoting 'people's origin'. The general assumption was that origin 'sticks on you' for some time, even some generations, and it cannot be ignored. Only step by step should the immigrant become part of the new society. Immigrant associations and networks could play a decisive role in this process. All kinds of associations were thus incorporated into the integration politics. They could function as a bridge between the individual immigrant and the new society. 'Multiculturalism Dutch style' had thus a very pragmatic character, in which cultural *in*equality was the guiding principal, framed in a hierarchical discourse.

The year 1983 was in all respects a true turning point. Not only did the 'Minority Document' constitute the official farewell to the idea that most immigrants would return to their home countries, but the constitutional changes that took place in the same year marked the end of the still existing ties between church and state. Some have argued that these constitutional changes can be considered as the actual end of the pillarization era. In fact it is precisely the combination of a more explicit stipulation of constitutional equality and the legal remnants of pillarization that have made some observers conclude that this is multiculturalism, Dutch style.

The Dutch constitution of 1983 stipulates that all religious denominations are valued equally.[2] Although this principle actually dates back to the liberal constitution of 1848, the idea was reinforced and reformulated in 1983 by severing all financial and other ties between church and the state. An important aspect is that the Dutch system does not grant formal religious recognition and registration as in Belgium or Germany. Thus, generally speaking, there are no religious denominations in the Netherlands that formally have more privileges than others.

The era of pillarization shaped Dutch society and its political landscape from the 1920s until the 1960s. The Dutch pillar system is one of the more complicated aspects of Dutch political history, although pillarization is certainly not uniquely Dutch. Most European countries have had some sort of pillarization. The politico-ideological pillars determined to a large extent political culture in the Netherlands, and produced the country's characteristic political (according to some critiques, rigid) stability. This stability gave the system its seemingly 'natural' character. In the mid-1960s the system virtually ceased to function and in most sections of civil society a process of decategorization and breakdown of the pillar structure took place. Nevertheless, pillarization has survived until today in certin legal principles, such as in the educational system. Thus it is on the basis of this combination of legal principles that Muslims are able to set up their own schools. Collective actors have a crucial instrument with which to gain access to resources (Sunier, 2004). It would, however, be a fundamental misapprehension to consider the existence of legal opportunities for Muslims to set up schools as a continuation of pre-war pillarization. For the constitutional changes of the 1910s, the *de jure* beginning of the pillarization era, were the result of a political struggle in which Protestant and Catholic political actors and their constituencies were a very powerful political force. The political power of Muslims today in no way compares to that of their Protestant and Catholic counterparts of the early twentieth century.

The history of pillarization has, however, produced a discourse that 'understands' religious institutionalization, especially in Christian circles. Demands for cultural autonomy fit within the pillarization ideology. This has been mistakenly branded as multiculturalism. In the 1980s the social and economic backwardness of minorities, wedded to the idea of cultural backwardness, produced a relatively optimistic discourse on integration: immigrants would eventually understand that assimilation and absorption into Dutch society would be in their best interest.

The 1990s: assimilation in jeopardy?

The late 1980s again marked a turning point in the status of cultural diversity, for two main reasons. The first was that the socio-economic integration of immigrants did not meet expectations. To begin with, unemployment remained high – the rate among 'ethnic minorities' was above the Dutch average. Turks and Moroccans were in a relatively weak position (WRR, 1989). School results and outputs remained relatively poor (ISEO, 2001). But one of the most alarming developments in the eyes of many politicians was increasing segregation in the neighbourhoods where most migrants resided. Most of these areas were of cheap, poor-quality housing with few services. Tensions between different categories of residents often erupted. Although several community studies showed that the ethnic factor in these conflicts was somewhat complicated (see, e.g., Niekerk et al., 1989), for many politicians cultural diversity was a source of problems rather than enrichment.

In 1989 the WRR, an influential government advisory board issued a report in which they concluded that integration policies should be more oriented towards the individual social mobility of migrants. It considered the government's policy to be based excessively on migrants as ethnic communities. Community-based policy diverts attention from the individual characteristics and individual trajectories of migrants, and endangers the constitutional principle of equality. The government had, for example, subsidized all kinds of activities by migrant organizations that could contribute to the integration process. But, according to several reports issued in the 1980s, most of these organizations were using the money for their own benefit to improve their organizational networks and to strengthen their communities, instead of promoting the integration process. In other words, the WRR concluded, government policies were having the opposite effect from that intended. In fact, the board proposed the reconfirmation of state neutrality, as was originally formulated in the famous liberal constitution of 1848, and reformulated in the revised constitution of 1983.

It was also in this period that migrants became increasingly referred to as 'allochthonous'. The WRR introduced the term, a central trope in the Dutch integration discourse, in reference to national origin and culture of migrants and their descendants, irrespective of their legal status, but without any substantial qualifications, and without any official policy status (WRR, 1989). The term used by the government, 'ethnic minorities', was excessively reliant on the complex relationship between background and social status. All inhabitants of non-Dutch descent are allochthonous, even when they were born in the Netherlands to parents with a Dutch passport who were not born in the Netherlands, and regardless of their social status.

In fact the WRR proposed a gradual decoupling of culture from socio-economic status and the adotion of a more neutral position by the state on cultural diversity. To a large extent the proposal was to follow the French assimilation path. Where the relation between culture and social status had been formulated in terms of mutual reinforcement, they now should become separate and independent fields. A neutral government should facilitate cultural expression without interfering materially and ideologically. Policies would only be directed towards social, political and economic assimilation. Culture would play a role in policies to the extent that inherent in the concept of 'allochthonous' was the notion of 'having a different cultural background' and a 'different cultural make-up', a qualification that may or may not influence someone's attitude, *but not government policies.*

Although the WRR gave a very precise definition of 'allochthonous', in practice the term referred only to non-Western inhabitants; a German industrial manager would never be called allochthonous. Many people, born and raised in the Netherlands, having a Dutch passport but with foreign parents, are still referred to as allochthonous. Allochtonous has acquired a degrading and exclusionary meaning. Due to its absolute vagueness and plasticity, the term is applied in a wide variety of situations. It gradually made its way into the dominant discourse and in practical political matters in the early 1990s. The intrinsic contradictory connotations in the term, however, can produce paradoxical situations. In the recent debate over the alleged genocide of Armenians by the Ottoman rulers in the 1910s, Dutch citizens of Turkish descent, born and raised in the Netherlands, were almost required to take a position on the issue, even when they claimed to be Dutch. Even when they fully satisfy the requirements of assimilation, their background haunts them.

Although the government was initially critical of the advice given by the WRR, the policy document issued by the government in 1999, ten years later, largely espouses the 1989 WRR positions. In the 1990s a much more individualized integration trajectory was already being applied. In the late 1990s the government formulated an official new integration policy (Ministry of the Interior, 1999). The three areas of integration – work, housing and education – remained central and although the government had long abandoned its policy of investing in the cultural infrastructure of migrants, the idea that culture (that is, cultural attitudes) influence migrants' relation towards society remained intact. The 'ethnic-groups paradigm' also continued to characterize the political agenda. However, the government remained vague regarding the evaluation of cultural difference and multicultural principles. On the one hand cultural diversity was an actual state of affairs; on the other hand it was not something that the state should in any way monitor. The following quotation expresses the position of the state: 'Each of these groups carries its own cultural heritage, history and world vision. As such, one can indeed speak of a multicultural society.... The extent to which existing cultures develop in relation to each other, is primarily dependent on the choices of the respec-tive cultural actors' (Ministry of the Interior, 1999: 7). The policy document also reflected the political landscape of the 1990s. Although the Rushdie affair was a shock to those political circles that were in favour of a certain degree of multiculturalism and cultural equality, the emphasis on cultural hierarchy, assimilation and nationalist assertion was typically a right-wing creed. A majority of the Social Democrats, Christian Democrats and the left remained in favour of some sort of multiculturalism. This was the time when the Dutch government con-sisted of the so-called purple parties (liberal, social liberal and social democrat). Although a majority of these parties strongly supported the idea of a neutral state, there was also some support for a certain cultural autonomy. The above quotation reflects this ambiguity. For all parties, however, cultural diversity remained firmly subservient to integration into the three societal fields indicated earlier. The numerous 'diversity programmes' that flourish in many municipalities have an explicitly non-political character and are confined to folklore.

Already in the 1980s there was a gradual 'Islamization' of the policy discourse on cultural diversity. The proverbial cultural other, the socially backward, increasingly became equated with 'Muslim', not least because people with an Islamic background continued to perform poorly (SCP, 1996). This resulted in the intensification of the 'civilizing' mission of the government. Cultural differences were increasingly equated with 'non-conformist', ill-bred behaviour (Rath, 1991). Migrants have to be re-socialized in order to be able to become decent citizens. The Rushdie affair in 1989 was catalytic in emphasizing assimilationist political thinking, particularly with respect to Muslims. It was claimed that the affair, particularly the public burning of books, showed that Muslims still did not know how a democratic society functions.

But the Rushdie affair also marked a turning point. Since the majority of Muslims were 'here to stay', it invigorated a debate about the place of Islam in Dutch ('secular') society. Integration is not just a matter of civilization; it is also an issue that goes to the very roots of the Dutch nation, it was claimed. The first opinion leader refer explicitly to Islam in relation to immigration was liberal leader Frits Bolkestein in a speech in 1991 at the International Liberal Conference in Lausanne. In his speech he called on European societies to be aware of the presence of Muslims and to think about how 'we' should relate to Islam and to 'our' own liberal roots (Bolkestein, 1991). Bolkestein referred not so much to the assumed effects of Islam on the individual migrant's attitude, but more to the place of Islam as a religious denomination in Western societies. In hindsight, the Bolkestein address appears moderate compared to those of many later opinion leaders. In a more recent publication he predicted, with typical liberal optimism, that Muslims will eventually be absorbed by modern liberal society (Bolkestein, 1997: 175). He thus rearticulated the assumptions of the

Dutch government formulated in the first minority report in 1983. But Bolkestein explicitly referred to Islam as being culturally complex, and asserted that it cannot be accepted on a par with 'our' Western civilization. In other words, it was not only a matter of cultural accommodation of a group of religious newcomers; the very character of the Dutch nation was at stake. This, like other Western European nations, according to Bolkestein, has gone further down the road to modernity than Islamic societies. Bolkestein urged European liberal politicians not to give in to some sort of multicultural idea of cultural equality. By relating religion to citizenship, civilization and nation-building he opened up a new field in the debate, one soon taken up by others.

Towards the end of the 1990s, the relation between culture and social status became more complicated. Whereas the majority of Muslims still occupied the lowest social stratum of society, an increasing number of young Muslims were performing relatively well; their school results were close to the average. The assumption that Muslims occupied the lowest ranks of society was increasingly being refuted. The image that dominated much of the 1980s and 1990s, namely that Muslims are predominantly 'pre-modern' and stick to habits that prevent them from taking part in modern society, gradually eroded but did not disappear altogether. Instead, an awareness grew that especially young Muslims will demand their place in society more articulately. These young Muslims cannot simply be discarded as 'not-yet-integrated' individuals. Many were born in the Netherlands and consider it to be their society (Sunier, 1996). Their ability to articulate their demands not *towards* but *within* society brought about new challenges. This threw into relief the fundamental question as to how society relates to these 'new citizens'.[3] Some welcomed these developments as a sign of genuine integration; others feared the gradual 'Islamization' of Dutch society.

In the late 1990s the debate assumed a more alarming undertone. Worried by the increasing articulacy of young Muslims, the demands addressed towards Dutch society, and not least their increasing visibility in the public sphere, a reconsideration of 'Dutchness' took shape. A growing number of intellectuals argued for a deepening and dissemination of national awareness and protection of Dutch cultural identity, in relation to both the presence of ethnic minorities and

European unification. Their plea for more attention to be paid to national roots fitted in with a general change in the political climate that took place in the course of the 1990s. The main idea is that the Dutch seem to be at a loss when they have to define precisely what the Dutch nation is. What is Dutch about Dutch national culture? What does it consist of? Why is the nation (still) an important frame of reference? The answers are equivocal (van Ginkel, 1999). The cultural feeling of national belonging has become so 'natural' in the Netherlands that for a long time many thought it hardly needed contemplating. Some have mistaken this self-evidence for a lack of national consciousness, and even a denial of 'Dutchness'. This poses a dilemma for ethnic minorities: if they are willing to integrate into the nation, what is required of them? Exclusion may be a consequence of not knowing how to be included in a concept that is deeply hidden. How can they become fully fledged citizens when it is hard to know how to play by cultural rules that are unclear and changing all the time? How can you become a member of Dutch society when it is unclear what this membership implies?

In short, the 1990s brought important issues to the surface. To many the Rushdie affair had demonstrated that with Islam, the West had brought in a truly alien religion. Many considered the 'cultural distance' between Islam and the central tenets of Western civilization big enough to become worried about the future. The civilizing mission of the 1980s was increasingly replaced by a quest for loyalty. Young migrants may integrate socially and economically, but are they to be trusted? Lest we urge Muslims with more convincing means to assimilate into Dutch modern society, we must simply force them. In short, towards the end of the 1990s already much of the trust of the 1980s was gone. The time of noncommitted conviction must be replaced by committal coercion.

The 2000s: the turning tide

Thus already prior to 9/11 a shift had occurred in the thinking about the relation between culture and integration. In 1999 and 2000, two influential opinion leaders wrote essays on multiculturalism in the Netherlands. The first, written by Amsterdam sociologist Paul

Scheffer in 2000, is the key text marking a turning point in the discourse on integration in the country. The other, by Paul Schnabel, director of the government 'think-tank' the Social Cultural Planning Office (SCP), was probably less well known to the general public, but no less influential. Both authors, who frequently appear in the media, strongly criticize 'multiculturalism' and advocate assimilationist policies. Both, in their own way, comment on the present situation and analyse how it arrived, and both conclude that multiculturalism is a dangerous myth capable of further culturally segregating society. In doing so they also evaluate governmental policies over the last two decades and trace the outlines of future policy.

Paul Scheffer, a member of the liberal wing of the Social Democratic Party, and a well-known opinion leader, published his long article 'The Multicultural Drama' in one of the big Dutch newspapers in January 2000 (Scheffer, 2000). In the article Scheffer warns the government and policymakers to be very serious about integrating Turkish and Moroccan immigrants. He refers to the successful integration of poor Dutch people in the mid-twentieth century, which was accomplished through a very active struggle against poverty, an effective schooling programme, and numerous other measures meant to improve their position. Although we know, Scheffer continues, that this civilizing mission for the poor Dutch was successful, and although we can immediately see that present-day ethnic groups live under similar conditions, we do nothing to change this for fear of interfering in the private sphere.

Scheffer blames a slack government attitude for this situation. Such warnings could be heard across the political left for years, but Scheffer takes his argument further. He argues that the cultural diversity we observe in the public sphere, such as Islamic schools, all kinds of language programmes, along with strong ethnic cohesion among many migrants and their children, and not least an increasing cultural assertion and visibility, is the direct result of this laissez-faire attitude. This, Scheffer argues, is multicultural policy in practice. There is, he says, significant ethnic tension in society just below the surface. But instead of trying to address these problems, we have believed in the problem-solving capacity of multicultural equality. Scheffer then invites all those protagonists of multiculturalism to look

at what happens in the poor neighbourhoods of the big cities. He also
refers to the fundamental differences between Islam and Christianity,
and accuses all who argue that a hundred years ago Catholics and
Protestants were no less each other's adversaries than Muslims and
Christians today of naivety.

Scheffer not only suggests a direct link between culture and
backwardness, he also predicts that the problems will be even more
difficult than those with 'our own underclass'. The cultural distance
between 'us' and 'them' is much bigger than we seem to believe.
Although Scheffer does not openly evaluate cultures, he implicitly
assumes that it is in the best interest of migrants to assimilate into
Dutch society. In other words, a lasting cultural diversity is the
direct proof of a failed integration project and an open invitation for
even bigger future problems. Such a multicultural neglect endangers
the very foundation on which our society rests. Increasing cultural
diversity implies diminishing national cohesion. Multiculturalism,
a term which Scheffer neglects to explain, is a typical example of
an ideology born out of the lack of capacity to define what binds
together a nation. 'We boast of a national identity having no national
identity', Scheffer argues, but says that this will certainly not invite
immigrants to participate in that society. He then concludes by stating
that cultural reciprocity in an 'open society' sets a limit to the extent
of cultural diversity, and hence the only way to prevent a second
Rushdie affair is to make clear what Dutch national identity implies
and, above all, to establish a strictly neutral public sphere.

Although Scheffer was comparatively moderate in his use of nationalist discourse, right-wing populists have subsequently used his
argument to defend a pessimistic, exclusionary kind of nationalism.

The article by Paul Schnabel put the emphasis on slightly different issues, but arrived at roughly the same conclusion as Scheffer
(Schnabel, 1999). He also starts with a gloomy picture of the weak
social position of many migrants. But, unlike Scheffer, he then
elaborates the concept of multiculturalism meticulously, by making
the distinction between a 'multi-ethnic' and a 'multicultural' society.
The Netherlands is multi-ethnic in the sense that there are people
from many different backgrounds, but it is highly undesirable that it
becomes a multicultural society. This, according to Schnabel, would

imply that cultures of whatever sort are principally equal to each other. This is an illusion, he argues. He then poses the reader with the rhetorical challenge of defining exactly what 'other cultures' have actually contributed to Dutch culture, besides some restaurants, music and festivals. More than three decades of immigration, he claims, have not produced any serious cultural hybridization. The immigrant cultures are typical 'lower class cultures', and no serious match for the Dutch general culture based on the principles of the Enlightenment. This is a well-known argument, but Schnabel proposes a distinction between what he calls 'A, B and C cultures'. Level A concerns the 'general public culture that is normative to everybody in society', which constitutes the constitutional and democratic foundation of society. B culture refers to daily collective practices, ways of behaviour; people do have a certain freedom here to act as they wish, but there are limits to that freedom. C culture refers to individual lifestyle, which is a personal pursuit. Evidently, according to Schnabel, A culture is hegemonic and always overrules the other levels. Thus the wearing of the headscarf resorts to level B or C, so long as it does not interfere with level A.

It is clear that what kinds of cultural traits belong to what level it is a question of power. Schnabel admits that, but he rejects the tacit covering up of power inequality. This, he argues, is the typical hypocrisy of multiculturalists. Under the banner of 'anything goes' multiculturalists advocate cultural equality while knowing very well that multiculturalism as a political ideal only exists within the framework of an enlightened A culture. This leaves, according to Schnabel, no option for immigrants but to assimilate completely into Dutch society. Even if they resist assimilation, they will in the end 'lose the battle'. Schnabel seems to be confident that his B and C cultural traits will also eventually wane. He therefore proposes applying assimilationist pressure where it concerns the central values (A culture) and being attentive, though understanding, towards B and C cultural traits.

We must bear in mind that both Scheffer and Schnabel belong to the centre-left of the political spectrum, which speaks for a majority of the Dutch population. Their texts and subsequent reactions constituted a new turn in the political debate. It resulted in a breakthrough in the traditional dividing line between left and right on issues of integration and multiculturalism. These opinion leaders made a socially acceptable intervention (*salonfähig*) on mono-cultural assimilation, which therefore became something that was no longer taboo and could be part of public discussions. It was now possible even for those on the left openly to question any multiculturalist creed purportedly in the best interests of immigrants.

The post-Gogh events:
the politics of assimilation by coercion

The apparent shift in the Dutch discourse has to do with 'a loss of trust' based on perceptions of an eroding effect witnin 'our own culture', and certainly not with a re-evaluation of cultural differences. Today the belief that cultural diversity is tearing the country apart and that social equality cannot be achieved without strict and coercive assimilationist policies has become widely held. Today's adage, 'if they are not convinced themselves, we have to force them', is in other words a shift from 'assimilation by conviction' to 'assimilation by coercion'. In short, 9/11 has intensified certain political trends. It did not, however, turn the tide from a multiculturalist to an anti-multiculturalist discourse; for there is much more continuity in Dutch integration policies over the last two decades than is often assumed.

The attacks on 11 September 2001 made the ideological shift easier. Already in 1999 the populist opinion leader Pim Fortuyn had published a book entitled *Tegen de islamisering van onze cultuur. Nederlandse identiteit als fundament* (Against the Islamization of Our Culture: Dutch Identity as Foundation). Fortuyn focused on Islam, but his main point of concern was Dutch national identity, hence the subtitle of the book. Although the ideas put forward by Schnabel and Scheffer were in no way a direct consequence of Fortuyn's attack on Islam, 9/11 provided the necessary link between deeply felt worries about the effects of the 'multicultural neglect' of the 1980s and the negative image of Islam among a considerable proportion of the population. The ideas written in the book constituted the basis of the political movement Fortuyn founded in early 2001, the Pim Fortutn List (LPF). After he was murdered in May 2002, the LPF won 26 seats in the 150-seat parliament, becoming the second largest party. In the new right-wing government the LPF acquired considerable influence. But a shift occurred also in the Liberal Party. The traditional progressive wing, with its emphasis on the neutrality of the state and freedom of religion lost influence to the populist right wing with its emphasis on forced assimilation and recurring critique of Islam. Rita Verdonk, the self-appointed leader of this wing, became the new unofficial spokesperson. Under these new circumstances even the Christian Democratic Party, traditional defender of pillarized legislation, expressed open doubts about whether or not this legislation should also be applied to Islam. It is a climate in which the aforementioned racist politician Wilders can openly speak of a 'tsunami of Islam', or where another extreme right-wing politician can compare the attitude of the present government towards Islam to the indecisiveness of the Dutch government towards the Nazi occupation in 1940.

This new, post-9/11 assimilationist thinking found its ultimate expression in the new integration laws introduced by the government in January 2007. It comprised at first extremely restrictive immigration legislation, a de facto closing of the borders. Second, it implied a zero-tolerance policy on cultural diversity and a very strict and coercive programme of citizenship trajectories. Although the constitutional freedom of religious expression prevents any ban on particular cultural manifestations, there is a majority in parliament in favour of the total prohibition of face-covering devices. In short, the post-9/11 political climate has produced a situation in which there is a broad political consensus that non-Dutch, non-Western cultural expressions should always be subordinate to Western culture.

To conclude, a few remarks should are necessary in order to put the discussion into perspective. Although in the Netherlands, as stated, there has never been any official form of political multiculturalism, the notion that cultural background and cultural heritage are crucial prerequisites has always been an implicit guiding principle. In a variety of professional fields there is an abundance of multicultural practices such as in medical therapies, teaching methodology, housing and lifestyle projects. This sometimes leads to outrageous proposals. Thus, in order to 'lure allochthonous people to nature in order to acquire an environmental consciousness', an environmental organization proposed to develop a 'gourmet wood' with all kinds of fruits, nuts and mushrooms to pick. 'That is what they are used to in their own culture', it added. There is a rich variety of projects in popular culture that very explicitly refer to the 'multicultural character of our society'. But with respect to attitudes, political affiliation, organizational activities, leisure time patterns, there is a general consensus that 'culture matters'. Furthermore, events post-9/11 have served to produce a big increase in occasionally dubious studies on the relation between cultural background and, for example, criminal behaviour. But there is also a growing concern for the fact that a 'tough on cultural diversity' policy has put the constitutional freedom of cultural expression in jeopardy. An unintended consequence of the continual attacks by right-wing opinion leaders, journalists and politicians is that around the November 2006 elections there was a growing concern about the persistent discrimination with which many Moroccan and Turkish people are confronted. This has certainly not stemmed the anti-multiculturalist tide, but it has at least addded nuance to the tone of the debate.

The new government that took office in March 2007 has certainly been more temperate in its statements, and has criticized the heated rhetoric that characterized the debate over the previous five years. But it is very doubtful whether it will change the basic assumption that guides integration policy: integration in the social and political sphere will eventually erode cultural and religious difference.

Notes

1. The Dutch foundation for scientific research, NWO, even developed a special research programme to investigate the relation between ethnicity and culture.
2. The first article of the constitution, the so-called anti-discrimination article, stipulates that all who find themselves within the boundaries of the Netherlands must be treated equally in equal situations. Discrimination on the basis of race, religion, gender or conviction is forbidden. This article forms the basis of a series of laws on equal treatment.
3. Talal Asad addressed this issue for Britain in the early 1990s (Asad, 1993).

234   EUROPEAN MULTICULTURALISM REVISITED

References

Asad, T. (1993) *Genealogies of Religion. Discipline and Reasons of Power in Christianity and Islam.* Baltimore: Johns Hopkins University Press.
Bolkenstein, F. (1991) *Address to the Liberal International Conference at Luzern* The Hague: VVD.
Bolkenstein, F. (1997) *Moslims in de Polder*, Amsterdam: Contact.
Fortuyn, P., (1997) *Tegen de islamisering van onze cultuur*, Utrecht: Bruna.
ISEO (2001) *Minderhedenmonitor 2001*, The Hague: ISEO.
Lindo, F. (1996) *Maakt cultuur verschil?* Amsterdam: Het Spinhuis.
Ministry of the Interior (1983) *Minderhedennota*, The Hague: Ministerie van Binnenlandse Zaken.
Ministry of the Interior (1999) *Kansen Krijgen, Kansen Pakken*, The Hague: Ministerie van Binnenlandse Zaken.
Penninx, R. (1988) *Minderheidsvorming en emancipatie. Balans van kennisverwerving ten aanzien van immigranten en woonwagenbewoners.* Alphen aan den Rhijn: Samson.
Rath, J. (1991) *Minorisering. De sociale constructie van 'etnische minderheden'*, Amsterdam: SUA.
Schiffauer, W., G. Baumann, R. Kastoryano and S. Vertovec (eds) (2004) *Civil Enculturation*, Oxford: Berghahn.
Scheffer, P. (2000) 'Het multiculturele drama', *NRC*, 29 January
Schnabel, P., (1999) *De multiculturele illusie- Een pleidooi voor aanpassing en assimilatie*, Utrecht: Forum.
SCP (1996) *Sociaal Cultureel Rapport*, The Hague: SCP.
Silverstein, P.A. (2005) 'Immigrant Racialization and the New Savage Slot: Race, Migration, and Immigration in the New Europe', *Annual Review of Anthropology* 34: 363–84.
Sunier, T. (1996) *Islam in beweging*, Amsterdam: Het Spinhuis.
Sunier, T. (2004) 'Naar een nieuwe schoolstrijd? (Towards a New School Struggle?)' *BMGN* 119(4): 610–35.
Tinnemans, W. (1994) *Een gouden armband. Een geschiedenis van Mediterrane migranten in Nederland 1945–1994*, Utrecht: NCB.
Van Ginkel, R., (1999) *Op zoek naar eigenheid. Denkbeelden en discussies over cultuur en identiteit in Nederland*, The Hague: Sdu.
Van Niekerk, M., T. Sunier and H. Vermeulen (1989) *Bekende Vreemden. Surinamers, Turken en Nederlanders in een naoorlogse wijk.* Amsterdam: Het Spinhuis.
WRR (1989) *Allochtonenbeleid*, The Hague: Staatsuitgeverij.

CONCLUSION

Mistaken models of integration?
A critical perspective on the crisis
of multiculturalism in Europe

Christophe Bertossi

The essays assembled in this book seem to me to raise fundamental questions. They address issues of ethno-cultural and religious diversity in a particular political and historical moment: all concern member states of the European Union in the year 2010. In doing so, they also testify to the universal importance of the interplay between ethnic and racial diversity, inclusion and equality in immigration societies, far beyond the borders of Europe.

The contradictions one finds in the European framings of multiculturalism are immediately striking, particularly when compared to countries like the United States, Canada or Australia: if Europe has become international migration's first choice of world destination, member states of the European Union have not yet developed a self-reflexive definition of their 'identity' that is able to integrate immigration and diversity into collective national narratives of common belonging. Not only do immigration and diversity appear outside these self-reflexive narratives in Europe, but the EU appears under particular stress when it comes to these questions. Ten to fifteen years ago, this book would have discussed the EU as a laboratory for the invention of a post-national and multicultural form of common belonging and citizenship (see inter alia Soysal, 1994; Bauböck, 1994). Today, the scenario of the EU as an alternative to national-focused thinking of equality and diversity seems unlikely: the EU finds no more room in the new politics of a crisis of migrants' integration. Nation-states have indisputably 'won' (temporarily) this battle: nationalism and national identity are the key frames in which multiculturalism is being discussed, disputed and challenged today.

In their search for a 'European multicultural model', the authors in this book share one conclusion: such a model does not exist – and has never existed, even in countries such as Britain or the Netherlands which reputedly implemented 'multiculturalism' as a model of integration for minority groups. Normative multiculturalism seems out of reach in Western European countries, which are going through a multicultural crisis without having actually experienced any multicultural model. It is not conceived of as a 'desirable' objective but increasingly takes the form of an 'anti-role model', irrespective of the normative, political or historical differences between the various national perspectives on integration and citizenship one finds in countries such as France, Britain, Germany, the Netherlands, Denmark or Italy. Multiculturalism stands everywhere as a symptomatic challenge to national integration policies – it has become the synonym of a would-be 'crisis' of migrant integration and citizenship. To put it simply: normative multiculturalism appears to be an outcome of the recent politics of migrant integration and citizenship in Europe in recent years, without any of the Western European countries studied in this volume having really implemented something that Canadians or Australians would call 'multiculturalism'. Instead of a (normative) 'multicultural model in Europe', one finds complex and contradictory perceptions that situate the future of citizenship in Europe under the sign of normative national homogeneity.

For those who cherish the normative project of multiculturalism, this will be a cause of great concern. However, this concern can also be shared by those who do not conceive of themselves as 'multiculturalists' but who still endorse the project of social justice among equal citizens in increasingly diverse and 'global' societies.

This issue concerns the second argument made consistently by the authors of this book: there is a critical disjuncture between empirical ethnic and racial diversity in Europe, on the one hand, and the political framings of this actual diversity through conservative and homogeneous views on national identity, on the other. This is not merely an issue of a conflict between multiculturalism and homogenous conceptions of national identity. It concerns a more profound problem that directly impacts the effectiveness of policies – and even the ability of policies to be effective at any point: namely, the incommensurability between empirical *reality* (the 'problems' that must be solved) and public and political *narratives* (the solutions proposed, irrespective of the actual problems). In constructing an apparent conflict between 'multiculturalism' and national identities, which stands as a fantasy in most cases, European policymakers and other opinion leaders find these narratives very useful in current political competition. However, such narratives have a side effect. Key questions of, let us say, intergenerational social mobility, socio-economic integration, and the issue of racial, ethnic or religious discriminations no longer sound politically or socially relevant. As a result, one conception of integration dominates in the public and political discussions in Europe: a socio-cultural definition that emphasizes essentialized and culturalized notions of identities. The social dynamic at stake is lost in the process. This is probably the most puzzling argument made by the book. It must be taken very seriously by scholars and policymakers as well as by citizens who are convinced that the future of citizenship in Europe depends upon our capacity to *understand* how our societies really work and, at the same time, to *clarify* the fundamentals of the equality project which European societies claim to be founded on. This is one of the most demanding tasks we are facing today: how can one conceive of societies based on justice and equality if we are not realistic about the issues at stake that must be addressed in order to progress towards justice and equality? How can we make such progress if the solutions that are proposed are based on unrealistic, mistaken and ambiguous conceptions of what the problems are? While 'multiculturalism' is depicted by the new politics of migrant integration in Europe as the main problem that nations must solve, it seems that the answer to this problem converge towards a no less problematic homogenous conception of national identities in Europe. This raises serious questions about how European immigration nation-states will be able to address properly the concrete issues of discrimination, racism and xenophobia. I think this may be the most pressing finding of this book and it must be addressed urgently.

I had the great honour of being asked by Alessandro Silj and his co-authors to contribute to some general reflections on these issues. I shall partly rely on their work to indicate why I believe the authors have produced a valuable work of clarification, and why I am certain they have raised the central questions. In doing so, I shall try to highlight how a comparative perspective of the issues they raise can help us better understand today's politics of migrant integration and citizenship in Europe, and what stands behind the apparently obvious 'crisis of integration of migrants' in the European context.

Questioning models of integration

As the different chapters of this book clearly show, the questions about (anti-)multiculturalism in Europe are intrinsically connected to the strong idea that existing traditions of national integration of migrants are going through a crisis. That is, the respective national thick and path-dependent approaches of French republicanism, Dutch or British multiculturalism are perceived as failing and, what is more, as being at the same time the very roots of such a failure. If France, Britain or the Netherlands are going through a critical moment in integrating their immigrants, that is – so is it claimed – because the policies of the past have failed and because they have been misleading in their addressing of ethnic and racial diversity. This rather tautological assumption that French republicanism explains the crisis of French republicanism, as much as Dutch multiculturalism explains the failure of Dutch multiculturalism, plays a huge role in the domestic politics in these countries but also in the discussions among policymakers who meet at the EU level. The crisis of French republicanism and the failure of Dutch multiculturalism have become a 'received wisdom' for most of the policymakers in Europe. Observing the recent political, media and, to some extent, scholarly debates about integration and citizenship in Europe, it seems obvious that this crisis of multi-culturalism is believed to be rooted in the perception that European immigration countries have problems with their traditional models of integration: multiculturalism would be the root of the murder of Theo van Gogh in 2004 in the Netherlands; republicanism would explain the riots in the French suburbs in November and December

2005; British race relations would have paved the way for the London 7 July 2005 bombings.

My claim – and I think this book helps make a striking case – is that it is impossible to accept this dual narrative of 'failing models' according to which models are deemed to have failed and are at once held responsible for that failure. I would argue that such a diagnosis cannot stand as an explanation of the current politics of integration in European immigration countries, for a very simple reason: that these so-called models – that we label 'French republicanism', 'Dutch multiculturalism', 'British race relations' – simply do not exist, or at least they do not exist in the way most of the scholarship on integration and the politics of integration has claimed since the 1980s.

Most of the time, we have wrongly held up these respective models as an independent variable for explaining the integration pathways of migrants and minority groups in different (paradigmatic) national situations: France was conceived of as an non-multicultural country because of its so-called assimilationist approach to diversity (see Amiraux in this volume); the Netherlands and Britain have been sketched as un-French inasmuch as they were apparently multiculturalist (see Malik and Sunier in this volume); and Germany has for a long time been conceived of as un-French in its definition of national identity (see Koopmans et al., 2005; Brubaker, 1992) and as un-Dutch and un-British in its approach to diversity (see Lanz in this volume).

In this scholarly approach to the existence of mutually contradictory national models of integration, we have also taken very seriously the idea of culturally and historically thick path-dependent models. Instead of really investigating the complex interplay between these big and thick 'models' and the respective institutional settings, political competition, collective mobilization, or even the everyday social life of ordinary individuals in each country, we have been using a simplistic definition of models – what I shall call 'mistaken models'; that is, we have been taking for granted the existence of one univocal model of French republicanism, Dutch multiculturalism or British race relations. Once these oversimplifying models themselves begin to shape our understanding of policies and social processes, they can take the place of empirical research rather than provide an instrument to enable it. Political stereotypes are not far from these alleged scholarly ideal-types. This is what has been happening in most of the scholarship on integration and citizenship in Europe: under the pretence of normative coherence and consistency in policymaking regarding migrant integration in European countries, scholars as much as policymakers have reduced the complexity of reality to the caricature of national public philosophies (cf. Favell 1998).

The costs are huge. First, there is an evident cost for the scholarship of citizenship: how can we work with 'models' – a notion that is omnipresent in any comparative research on issues of race, ethnicity, migrants' integration, citizenship – if the very foundation on which such comparative work is based misleads us? This is, of course, one of the most difficult questions scholars face, as it implies that we must think *what* (i.e. models) we have been used to think *with*. Second, there is a detrimental cost for the evaluation of policies: how can we assess the 'successes' or 'failures' of integration and citizenship policies if this assessment is based on highly ambiguous and, I would say, incorrect narratives? I think the answer to this question is simply obvious: it is impossible. This is the aspect of the costs of our discussion about a would-be 'crisis of integration' that I address in the following sections.

Revisiting European traditional models

What do I mean by this notion of 'mistaken models'? Most of the time, we assume that national models – for example, 'French republicanism', 'Dutch' or 'British multiculturalism', 'German ethnonationalism' – are ideologically thick, culturally defined, historically path-dependent, and institutionally performed patterns that have modelled the social, institutional and political processes of the construction of national identity *and* a corresponding way to define, institutionalize and perform migrant integration.

France would be a colour-blind – though much ambiguous – model, so alien to multiculturalism, while, to the contrary, the Netherlands and Britain would have modelled these questions in such an 'un-French' way that anyone writing about multiculturalism would be tempted to consider France as a strikingly good illustration of what multiculturalism is not. History, as much as politics and institutional structures, is mentioned as ultimately proving the coherence and the consistency of each national 'model', and establishing the mutual contradictions between these different 'models'. French republicanism would find its roots in the 1789 Revolution; Dutch multiculturalism would be a legacy of pillarization; and we could discuss extensively how far the British approach to minority group relations is a direct outcome of British imperialism. As a result, it seems possible to understand the issues at stake with ethnic, racial or religious diversity in a country like France, Britain or the Netherlands without making any effort, but to think in terms of 'French republicanism', 'British race relations' and 'Dutch multiculturalism'. I think that such views considerably compromise our ability to explain anything at all, for we simply remain at the surface of these widely accepted grand narratives.

If we compare the countries which have a long tradition of integration in Europe, we find nothing like these thick, clearly defined, and path-dependent models. The argument by Thilj Sunier in this book echoes what Jan Willem Duyvendak and Peter Scholten have already argued (Duyvendak and Scholten, 2009): they demonstrate how the politics of the failure of Dutch multiculturalism hides the fact that multiculturalism never was a model for the Netherlands. If one wishes to consider the 'minority policy' of the end of the 1970s as a form of multiculturalism (see Koopmans et al., 2005; Joppke, 2007), it is necessary to observe that this policy has shifted from a focus on minority groups to an individualist, liberal form of migrant integration in the 1990s, and to assimilation in the 2000s. How is it then possible to explain the 'tragedy' of integration in the Netherlands by reference to a form of integration policy taken for a model that was implemented only for a decade more than twenty years ago? The question in itself tells much about the organization of today's politics of identity in the Netherlands. Multiculturalism stands as the outcome of a debate about multiculturalism as a model that never existed as such in the Dutch society.

We can replicate very similar arguments about the 'republican model' in the French case. Valérie Amiraux's chapter highlights the 'reflexive turn' of the French approach to integration in recent years

– from a strict republican colour-blind and abstract conception of
equality to what she calls the beginning of the possible retreat from
this traditional reading through principles. I would go even further:
the non-thickness of the French 'model' goes way beyond this
conflict between a formal, abstract form of equality (i.e. the classical
republican conception of France as a non-multiculturalist country),
on the one hand, and a more substantial conception of equality
(i.e. the emergence of anti-discrimination, for example, pursuant to
the Amsterdam Treaty), on the other. Over the past thirty years
of French politics and policies of integration, I see at least four
ways in which the 'republican paradigm of integration' has been
shaped, focusing each time on one particular 'integration problem'
to be solved, and leading each time to a deep reconfiguration of the
very normative definition of what ought to be understood as the
'republican tradition' (Bertossi, 2009). Interestingly enough, in each
case, the call to the 'republican tradition' has introduced a breach
in this tradition. In the 1980s, the issue was about the incorporation
of post-colonial migrants into French nationality law and this paved
the way for the 1993 reform of the nationality law which abandoned
the 'republican conception' of automatic birthright to citizenship for
children born to foreign parents. In the 1990s, the problem became
discrimination, and the new anti-discrimination agenda profoundly
challenged the previous nationality-based definition of the project
of republican integration of migrants. In the 2000s, in turn, this
anti-discrimination definition of republican integration shifted to
laïcité, the problem being framed as the irreconcilable relationship
between Islam and the principles of French citizenship, and the
anti-discrimination standpoint was challenged as being naive and
wilfully idealistic. In doing so, the 1905 law's principles of state
neutrality vis-à-vis religious affairs and of equal treatment between
religions shifted to a conception of laïcité as a cultural principle of
national identity. I would say that the 2010s will probably witness the
emergence of a new framework of republican integration conceived
of as a 'civilizing project', and the replacement of 'integration' by
'assimilation' – a notion that had disappeared at the moment the
republican model was reinvented in the 1980s (Feldblum 1998).
Consequently, when we address the would-be 'crisis of republican

French citizenship', to which definition of French republicanism exactly do we refer? Is it a crisis of the nationality-based conception of integration, or of the anti-discrimination framework, or the failure of the principle of *laïcité*?

The British situation can also be looked at through a similar critical lens. When politicians, opinion leaders and scholars dispute the 'failure' or the 'successes' of the British policies of integration in terms of 'multiculturalism' being (or not) a 'solution of the past' and implying (or not) 'separation', the normative battle around 'multiculturalism' hides the rapid transformations these policies have gone through over the past thirty years, with a shift of their focus respectively from 'race' to 'ethnicity' and now to 'religion', including Islam.

To state clearly, one crucial aspect of our discussion about 'models' through which this book reads the future of 'multiculturalism in Europe' is thus that 'models' are not an empirical, stable, comprehensive cultural matrix that both describes and realizes the incorporation of migrants and minority group members into European national citizenships. To speak of a crisis of traditional models is therefore a highly ambiguous and politically overloaded notion since it is difficult to conclude in any crisis of this type that the models of which the crisis is being discussed today in fact exist.

The performative effect of models

However, challenging this 'mistaken' conception of models as thick, consistent, coherent, cultural, path-dependent, institutionalized – in a word, total – definitions of one 'nation's self-understanding' (cf. Koopmans et al., 2005: 4) is not in itself sufficient to understand what we are dealing with now in Europe where race, ethnicity, citizenship, immigration and national identity are concerned. It is as important (if not more so) to insist on the fact that, despite being puzzling, 'models' are not *entirely* a fantasy or a fallacy.

This is, I believe, another key aspect of our discussion about the crisis of integration models in Europe. When we deal with issues of integration and citizenship, we are always confronted with a vast array of social actors (including scholars) who *believe* in the thick existence of models, and who use models to *justify* their choices and the course of their own actions or strategies. This argument is not an abstract or theoretical reflection that belongs merely in the sociology of knowledge, but a much more concrete and empirical question: it is not adequate to say that models do not exist, because the reality scholars study *is* de facto fulfilled with 'model thinking' and 'modelling practices'. People believe in the existence of one French model since the French Revolution or of one Dutch multiculturalist model embedded in Dutch pillarization. They discuss these models in popular cafés, in the corridors of hospitals and other welfare organizations; among policemen, militaries or schoolteachers; in meetings of trade unionists and NGO representatives; in their comments posted in response to newpaper articles published on the Internet; or in official gatherings of European ministers of the interior.

In other words, it is not sufficient to say that models are not to be taken seriously, because we deal with actors who themselves take models very seriously. There is no way *not* to speak of French republicanism, Dutch or British multiculturalism because these are notions used, imagined, negotiated, disputed – and, I would add, misunderstood – by very different types of actors, including those who appear as the object of the politics of integration: minority group members themselves who mobilize around equality, identities and their membership of European countries. And yet it is not possible to take models as comprehensive and reliable means for making sense of this reality scholars try to understand. How can we resolve this contradiction?

Relying directly on research Jan Willem Duyvendak and I have been carrying out together recently (Bertossi and Duyvendak, 2009), I would like to offer five propositions on how it is possible to go beyond both the too absolute and non reflexive use of models (i.e. how French republicanism or Dutch and British multiculturalism would shape and explain institutional, political, and social practices) and the excessively relativist conception of models (i.e. models do and explain nothing at all). These empirical hypotheses are, we believe, very useful for the comparative study of integration and citizenship politics in Europe today.

Our first hypothesis is that 'models' are highly *contradictory.* The comprehensiveness and coherence of 'national models' are far from evident. 'Models' are constantly contradicted by policy and social practices at different levels (national, regional, local) as well as in different spheres of policies and public institutions (schools, urban policy, etc.). A 'national model' is a fiction that faces severe contradictions in the implementation and orientation of integration policies, either directly or indirectly.

Second, in turn, this shows how much 'national models' are not stable but *vary* through different periods in one national society, according to the way debates on integration (and the different perceived 'problems' of integration) are developing. Speaking of a French or Dutch 'model' says little about the evolution of the dominant ideological and policy frameworks that are being used for framing the issue of 'integration'. Hence my statement earlier that the different frameworks that have been used in France, the Netherlands and Britain cannot be read as a single, thick, cultural definition of one 'total' model. Here, the contradictory feature of models reappears: these successive frameworks are not only a succession of problem-solving frames; they are also mutually contradictory.

Third, a 'model' is more often justified *ex-post* than *ex-ante*. French universal citizenship or Dutch liberal tolerance to diversity is not the start but the outcome of the discussion. They are produced by and in the very same process that creates a temporary consensus around one legitimate and acceptable 'model' for integrating migrants or minority groups in the dominant society. This echoes the discussions in the different chapters of this book. Clarification of the recent politics of (anti-)multiculturalism involves a sociology of enunciation (who justifies what?) and a careful study of the process of politicization of the issue of race and ethnicity in the different countries.

Fourth, models are not absolute notions, expressing always the same ideas and being understood by social and political actors in the same way. Models are *polysemic* – what Harold Garfinkel calls 'indexical' expressions – that is, the replication of a word does not necessarily name the same thing. 'Their denotation is relative to the speaker' (2008: 5), as much as it is relative to the time and the place when and where the word is used. If scholars claim that 'French republicanism', 'Dutch multiculturalism' or 'British race relations' exist, so do politicians, journalists and ordinary citizens. But the

t they all give to 'republicanism' and 'multiculturalism', as
is to 'pillarization', '*laïcité*', 'state neutrality', and so on, is very
rent. They all apparently discuss the same issues, but behind the
icated words social actors intend very different meanings without
ays being aware they do so. This has very practical consequences.
France, in the name of the defence of women's equality, one can
t the same time want to enfranchise individuals (let's say a woman
with a Muslim headscarf whom some consider as being dominated
by a very macho husband or brother) and yet exclude these women
from citizenship (as was recently the case when the Council of State
refused in 2008 to naturalize a Moroccan woman, wife to a French
citizen and mother of two French children, because she was wearing
a burqa). In the Netherlands, notions of pillarization, citizenship,
tolerance, or national identity can also be viewed as 'indexical
expressions'. In the name of tolerance (let's say tolerance towards
the sexuality of same-sex people) one can endorse a very intolerant
attitude (let's say against Muslims). In Britain, multiculturalism is
also much disputed, along very different lines, without always being
very clear what definition is at stake in the dispute.

Consequently, models are contradictory, unstable, constructed
ex-post, polysemic; and yet these non-thick models have a thick
impact – *they do exist*. This is what Jan Willem and I have called
the *performative* effect of models (cf. Austin, 1962). Models are not
comprehensive tool kits that are used to make policies and to analyse
these policies' results – but one cannot conclude that 'national models'
are not real and would not exist because of these contradictions,
ex-post construction and variations in time. On the contrary, they
have a concrete existence in social life, which must be analysed per
se. Analysing this existence suggests we must be modest with models
and favour empirical research rather than deductive reduction of institutional, social, political life, whether it be to French republicanism,
Dutch multiculturalism, British race relations, Danish integration or
the Italian lack of model. Models impact in a performative way on
routine social relationships among people who share beliefs about the
normative consistence and coherence of social and political life, but
who provide this normative existence of models with very different
significations.

A crisis of integration, really?

How can we revisit the crisis of national models of integration and citizenship in Europe on the grounds of my claim about models being non-thick – that is, contradictory, variable, defined *ex-post*, polysemic, but still having a 'thick' performative effect on social and political life? I would argue that the 'crisis of integration' in the European immigration countries that are studied in this book can be understood as a further development of existing but contradictory and unstable national discursive and political framings of integration.

We are witnessing a new stage of the discourse on citizenship, and certainly not the critical 'rupture' that is often depicted. Instead of a vanishing of – or a convergence among – models (Joppke 2007), the new politics of integration in Europe is a moment of re-politicization of ethnicity, race and immigration, which leads to the reframing of traditional discourses on integration-cum-national identity. The crisis here does not concern migrant integration per se. The fact that scholarly claims about integration being a rather successful process (if we do not consider the level of discrimination against migrants and minority-group members in Europe) are not heard in the national debates about these issues (see Malik in this volume) is symptomatic. The theme of 'integration crisis' is a strategic and discursive idiom of European politics today, and it results in the ultrapoliticization of immigration, race, and ethnicity.

This ultrapoliticization certainly takes apparently similar forms from one country to another: the shift to Islam as the main policy problem; the emphasis on 'coercive integration' solutions, as illustrated for example by the generalization of citizenship tests and the conditioning of the access to formal citizenship by the demand made to migrants to explicitly endorse the values and principles of the dominant society (see Joppke, 2007); the consensus that socio-cultural integration must outweigh definitions of integration in socio-economic terms and the subsequent relative erosion of the anti-discrimination agenda; strong negative framings of the post-colonial legacy; and the moralization of values, including the 'governance of private manners and modesty' (Amiraux in this volume), sexuality (homosexuality in the Netherlands), gender (the fast transnational circulation of the 'headscarf issue' in France, the Netherlands, Switzerland, Belgium, the UK, Italy, Spain, etc.).

However, behind this apparent convergence along similar lines, the ultrapoliticization of migrant and minority group integration takes very different forms in France, the Netherlands and Britain and in the different countries addressed in this book. The 'politics of a crisis of integration models' is a proxy for the politicization and the culturalization of integration issues. But this is far from blurring the distinctions between the different national discursive singularities in so far as we take these singularities in terms not of a 'thick' but of a highly contradictory definition of 'models'. Another probably central dimension in this process of ultrapoliticization of ethnicity and race in the different countries concerns the reshaping of the ideological cleavages in post-Cold War Europe (including between mainstream conservative and progressive parties, and their relationship with far-right opinion leaders). If we understand the 'crisis of integration' as a proxy of such a politicization moment in European immigration countries since the 2000s, we also find that such a politics of an 'integration crisis' has very different effects on how 'models' are reformulated in each case.

In the Netherlands, the 'mistaken model' (i.e. the idea of a Dutch traditional multiculturalism) works as an 'anti-model' that structures public, political and academic debates. The main questions concern the very *existence* of multiculturalism, its costs and the virtue of reformulating a national identity as a firm ground on which the 'successful' integration of Muslims could be based. The Dutch politics of a crisis of integration has led to the construction of a negative model. In France, the 'mistaken model' (i.e. the idea of a consistent French republican tradition since 1789) results in a re-emphasis on so-called 'republican values' that must be defended against the challenge of Islam, and in a return to policy narratives that had been abandoned in the mid-1980s when 'integration' replaced the notion of 'assimilation' (Bertossi, 2001). It also takes the form of contradictory debates among scholars about how empirical reality in institutional and political life, which is fulfilled by racist frames, challenge the would-be colour-blind 'republican credo' (Bertossi, 2009; see Fassin and Fassin 2006; Streiff-Fénart 2009). The very existence of the 'republican model' is not discussed. The focus is put on the 'corruption' or the 'deviance' of republican values, and their hidden racist effects beyond universalistic values (Laborde, 2010). The French politics of a crisis of integration has led to the reinforcement of the political relevance of the republican approach. In the UK, the apparent multicultural backlash has only been a matrix for reformulating the focus of what can produce 'good relations' among different groups (a shift from ethnic to religious categories) in order to pursue a collective negotiation about how substantial equality should be achieved in contemporary Britain. This apparent multicultural backlash has not paved the way for a new implementable approach of integration policies (Vertovec and Wessendorf, 2009). Beyond the apparent trial of multiculturalism, the debate focuses on the *evolution* of existing policies towards a normative and consistent form of multiculturalism.

Finally, one striking feature of these different reformulations is the absence of any substantial reference to the supranational European dimension. When we seek a model of European multiculturalism – the title of this book – we find strikingly few references to the project of a European new model of citizenship. As mentioned earlier, fifteen years ago, these references to a very European project of citizenship would have been the main focus of this book. Today, the focus has dramatically shifted: Europe no longer presents an alternative to homogenous conceptions of national identity. In other words, the issues of 'models', 'crisis of integration', 'future of citizenship' and 'national identity' in Europe become the field of a political and moral crusade towards the consecration of homogenous conceptions of liberal common belonging.

Under the pretence that multiculturalism is the problem, national politics in Europe have converted to the idea of homogeneity, which stands as an impossible political narrative on which de facto multicultural societies will achieve the project of equality and inclusion they claim to be grounded on. The European dilemma, in the way Gunnar Myrdal spoke of an American dilemma (Myrdal, 1944), is far from being solved. It is my concern that such a dilemma will only grow bigger in the next decade, because of the political strategic framing of ethnic and racial diversity that dominates today's European national politics of citizenship and immigration, and further strengthens the incommensurability between empirical *reality* and public and political *narratives* on race, ethnicity and identity.

Will an inclusive conception of citizenship survive this disjuncture? The arguments made by this book on the situation of Britain, France, Germany, Italy, Denmark and the Netherlands are certainly a call to all of us – policymakers, journalists, scholars, NGO activists and 'ordinary' citizens – to address, each of us in our way, this most pressing question. There is probably little time left for us to do so, if we do not want this politics of a crisis to transform into the ultimate crisis of citizenship, way beyond the mere issue of integrating migrants in Europe. After the 'crisis of multiculturalism' Europeans must prepare for the eventuality of a new crisis: a backlash against nationalistic homogeneous conceptions of common belonging, the cost of which will probably be extremely high.

References

Austin, J. (1962) *How to Do Things With Words?*, Oxford: Clarendon.

Bauböck, R. (1994) *Transnational Citizenship: Membership and Rights in International Migration*, Aldershot: Elgar.

Bertossi, C. (2001) *Les frontières de la citoyenneté en Europe: nationalité, residence, appartenance*, Paris: L'Harmattan.

Bertossi, C. (2009), 'La République modèle et ses discours modélisants: l'intégration performative à la française', *Migrations Société* 21(122), March–April.

Bertossi, C., and J.W. Duyvendak (2009), 'Penser le modèle, changer de question', *Migrations Société* 21(122), March–April.

Brubaker, R. (1992) *Citizenship and Nationhood in France and Germany*, Cambridge MA: Harvard University Press.

Duyvendak, J.W., and P. Scholten (2009) 'Le modèle multiculturel néerlandais en question', *Migrations Société* 21(122), March–April.

Fassin, D., and E. Fassin (2006) (eds) *De la question sociale à la question raciale. Représenter la société française*, Paris: La Découverte.

Favell, A. (1998) *Philosophies of Integration: Immigration and the Idea of Citizenship in France and Britain*, Basingstoke: Palgrave-Macmillan.

Garfinkel, H. (2008) *Studies in Ethnomethodology*, Cambridge: Polity

Joppke, C. (2007) 'Transformation of Immigrant Integration in Western Europe: Civic Integration and Anti-discrimination in the Netherlands, France, and Germany', *World Politics* 59(2), January: 243–73.

Koopmans, R., P. Statham, M. Guigni and F. Passy (2005) *Contested Citizenship: Immigration and Cultural Diversity in Europe*, Minneapolis: Minnesota University Press.

Laborde, C. (2010) *Français encore un effort pour être républicains!*, Paris: Seuil.

Myrdal, G. (1944) *American Dilemma: The Negro Problem and Modern Democracy*, New York: Harper & Row.

Soysal, Y. (1994) *Limits of Citizenship: Migrants and Postnational Membership in Europe*, Chicago: Chicago University Press.

Streiff-Fénart, J. (2009), 'Le modèle républicain et ses "autres": construction et évolution des différentes catégories de l'altérité en France', *Migrations Société* 21(122), March–April.

Vertovec, S., and S. Wessendorf (eds) (2009) *The Multicultural Backlash*, London: Routledge.

About the contributors

Alessandro Silj studied at Trinity College Dublin and the University of Rome, where he graduated in political economy. He is founder and director of Ethnobarometer, a European research network on migration and inter-ethnic relations, and secretary general of the Italian Social Science Council (CSS). He has previously worked for Euratom, Brussels; the Center for International Affairs, Harvard University; the European Community Office, Washington DC; the Ford Foundation, New York; and was a founder and coordinator of Il Politecnico, a multisisciplinary cultural and social centre based in Rome. He is the author of several books and essays on European affairs and Italian politics.

Stefano Allievi is Professor of Sociology at University of Padua. He specializes in migration issues and the sociology of religion and cultural change, with a particular focus on the presence of Islam in Italy and Europe, the subject of many of his publications. His research on Islam in Europe has been financed by, among others: European Science Foundation, EEC, Fondazione Agnelli, Ministero dell'Interno, Ministero dei Beni Culturali, Ministero dell'Università e della Ricerca Scientifica, Forward Studies Unit of the European Commission. He is the Secretery of the Italian Association of Sociologists of Religion (AIS, sezione Religione).

Valérie Amiraux is Professor of Sociology at the University of Montreal. She holds a Canada Research Chair for the study of religious pluralism and ethnicity. Her research interests focus on the interaction between national regimes of secularism and the implementation of pluralist religious governance (including empirical research on Sikhs, Muslims, Jews and Jehovah's Witnesses), and on the statistical measurement of religion in the European context. She has worked extensively on Muslims in Europe and is the co-director of the MUSMINE project, a joint initiative of the Ethnobarometer project (CSS) and the Robert Schuman Centre for Advanced Studies (EUI).

Christophe Bertossi is Research Program Director in the Migration, Identity and Citizenship program at the Institut français des relations internationales (IFRI, Paris). Before joining IFRI in 2003, Bertossi completed his Ph.D. in Political Science at the Institut d'Études Politiques in Aix-en-Provence (2000). Now an Associate Research Fellow, he was a Marie Curie Research Fellow at the Centre for Research in Ethnic Relations at the University of Warwick (UK) between 2001 and 2003. He has supervised numerous international collaborative projects, notably with the Amsterdam University, the Washington University in St Louis, the Social Science Research Council (New York) and the American Sociological Association. He has been a visiting fellow at the New York University and the Institute for Advanced Studies–Collegium in Lyon. He also lectures on political science at Sciences Po (Paris).

Tina Gudrun Jensen holds a Ph.D. in Anthropology from the University of Copenhagen. She is a researcher at SFI, the Danish National Centre for Social Research, where she is part of the research unit on Children, Integration and Equality. Her main areas of interest are ethnic minorities, social integration and inter-ethnic relations. She has conducted research on ethnicity and religion in Brazil and Denmark. In a major recent research project she studied Muslim movements in Denmark, focusing on the construction of Danish-Muslim identities and relations between Muslims and Danes. Another area of research interest is the intersection of gender, culture and violence. She has published several articles, co-authored a book on Muslim identities in Denmark, and written reports on policies against honour-related violence in Europe, and on the construction of masculinities among ethnic minorities.

Stephan Lanz is an urbanist and a lecturer in Social Geography and Cultural Studies at the Europa-Universität Viadrina Frankfurt (Oder), Germany. His main research interests are urban governance, migration and urban development, urban cultures and urban movements. In recent years he has conducted research in Berlin, Istanbul and Rio de Janeiro.

Maleiha Malik is a Reader in Law at King's College London. Her principal areas of research are British and European anti-discrimination law; jurisprudence and legal theory; European Union law (with special reference to minorities and gender).

Thijl Sunier, an anthropologist, holds the VISOR chair of Islam in European Societies at the VU University Amsterdam. He has conducted research on inter-ethnic relations, Turkish youth and Turkish Islamic organizations in the Netherlands; comparative research among Turkish youth in France, Germany, Great Britain and the Netherlands; and international comparative research on nation building and multiculturalism in France and the Netherlands. He is currently working on styles of popular religiosity among young Muslims in Europe, religious leadership, and nation-building and Islam in Europe. He is a member of the Amsterdam School for Social Science Research (ASSR) and chairman of the board of the Inter-academic School for Islam Studies in the Netherlands (ISIS). He is editor of the anthropological journal *Etnofoor*, and chairman of the board of the Dutch Anthropological Association (ABV).

Index

race relations, immigration link, 41–4,
   49; UK legislation, 37, 51
Race Relations Amendment Act UK
   2000, 51
Race Relations Board, UK, 48
racial disadvantage, investment to
   overcome, 50
racism, 24–5, 237; anti-Muslim, 88, 95;
   criminal law use, 47; cultural, 26,
   32, 37, 116; German education, 128;
   Italy, 153; 'with a distance', 120,
   136; 'without races', 114
Rasmussen, Anders Fogh, 191, 199–200
Rasmussen, Poul Nyrup, 199
'rationalist universalism', as European
   ethnocentric, 80
Rawls, John, 14
recognition, collective mobilization, 94
refugees, 183; Denmark, 192, 196
religion: accommodation claims, 26;
   colonial practices, 89; intolerance
   link perception, 201; Muslim rights
   claims, 202
religious minorities, Italy, *intese*, 163–4
Republicanism, France, 68, 73, 78, 90,
   93–4; ideology, 8, 67, 72; historical
   myth/legacy of, 69, 80, 87;
   integration model, 81, 248; national
   identity role, 65; tradition
   reconfigurations, 242
'respect', 21
return migration, Dutch policy, 218
Revival movements, Denmark, 187
Rex, John, 2
Richard, Jean Luc, 84
right-wing populism, Netherlands,
   Islam obsession, 232
Roma people, 13; Britain historical
   presence, 36
Roman Catholic Church, Italy, 6, 152,
   165; Islam contradictory positions,
   162, 167; integrative effects, 166;
   privileged status, 163; migrant
   solidarist approach, 156
Romania, Italy immigrants, 161
Rome airport, Palestinian attack 1985,
   152
Rushdie, Salman, affair, 9, 224–5, 227,
   229

Sant'Egido, Catholic organization, 166

Sarkozy, Nicolas, 79
Sartori, Giovanni, 162
Schäuble, Wolfgang, 116
Scheffer, Paul, 228–31
Schily, Otto, 126
Schmid, Thomas, 118, 135
Schnabel, Paul, 228–31
Scholten, Peter, 241
schools: Danish free, 194; equality
   rhetoric, 93; France integration role,
   72, 74–5; France religious symbols
   law, 73; integration in, 3; Italy, 167;
   Muslim, 221, 228
Schröder, Gerhard, 125–6
Scotland, Scottish National Party, 35
'secularism': critique, 24; 'moderate', 27
self-segregation, talk of, 54–5
Sen, Amartya, 2
Separation Law, France 1905, 73
sharia, 205; secular polarization, 202
Silj, Alessandro, 238
Simon, Patrick, 85
Simpson, Ludi, 55–6
skin colour, 86
Skinner, Quentin, 59
slavery: abolition commemoration, 32,
   87; colonial law legitimized, 36;
   controversy over, 11, 32, debate, 32
Smyth, Marie Breen, 56
Social Cultural Planning Office, Dutch
   government, 228
Social Democratic Party, Germany, 119,
   122, 125–6
Social Democratic Party, Netherlands,
   228
social exclusion, real phenomenon, 55–6
social housing, access to, 83
social mobility, upward, France, 75
social sciences, black people
   rediscovered, 86
Socialdemokraterne, Denmark, 191
socio-economic redistribution,
   minorities, 25
Soskice, Frank, 46
'Southerner', immigrant stereotyping,
   West Germany, 108
Spain: emigrant labour, 147, 218; West
   Germany migrant labour treaty, 106
'spiritual and mental inheritance',
   identity as, 115
Stavo-Debauge, J., 86